SPIRIT VISIONS

This book will change your way of looking at the universe, forever.

"How I loved this book! Amongst all the other books in this field, what makes this one stand out to me is its utter simplicity and childlike innocence. I can personally attest to this quality in the authors. I have known Dennison and Teddi since long before this book was put together. These folks just don't have it in them to embellish. In fact, they tend to understate things, due to their unassuming ways." —Rocky Notnes, Hinton, AB, Canada

"Dennison Tsosie's book, *Spirit Visions,* has allowed me to be able to pull together in a cohesive manner all of the other works of prophecy that I had already read. It let me understand the things that were going on in my life and make sense about why they were happening or had happened. When later I was privileged to meet Dennison, I felt that being in his presence was the personification of the Greek work 'agape,' unconditional love for all mankind.

"He is giving these teachings not to frighten us, but to let us understand love and how to survive in the times ahead." —Carol Lindsey, Benton, KY

"It was quite by accident that I picked up a piece of Dennison's jewelry one day. Because of the energy I felt from his artwork, I went on to meet him and attend his gatherings.

"His quiet nature and gentle humor have enriched my life.

"I thank the Creator for that blessing, so long ago, that has filled my spirit with love, smiles, and tears, and the knowledge that all things are possible." —Marilyn Cooper, Showlow, AZ

"This is a book of wonder. It was never planned, but has come to be through its own force—a force that has touched me at a very deep level."
—Marit Fjelldal, Tonsberg, Norway

"Spirit Vision: The Old Ones Speak has a life of its own. You feel the power going through you when you read it. It is the most amazing and best book I've ever read. I know it's the Truth in it that makes me tingle all over as I read the messages over and over again." —Juanita Montague, spiritual healer

"Spirit Visions is such a wonderful book, you don't want to put it aside until you have read it all—which is hard to do in one sitting. The information given to Dennison by the Grandfathers is mind-provoking. I personally feel it should be 'required' reading for going into the new century."
—Beth DeVillez, Paducah, KY

SPIRIT VISIONS

THE OLD ONES SPEAK

DENNISON & TEDDI TSOSIE

BLUE DOLPHIN PUBLISHING
1996

Published by
Blue Dolphin Publishing, Inc.
P.O. Box 8, Nevada City, CA 95959
Orders: 1-800-643-0765

ISBN: 1-57733-002-1

First printing, January 1997

Library of Congress Cataloging-in-Publication Data

Tsosie, Dennison, 1949–
    Spirit visions : the old ones speak / Dennison & Teddi Tsosie.
        p.   cm.
    ISBN 1-57733-002-1 (pbk.)
    1. Visions.   2. Prophecies (Occultism).   3. Tsosie, Dennison, 1949   .
    4. Tsosie, Teddi, 1946–   . I. Tsosie, Teddi, 1946–   . II. Title.
    BF1101.T76 1996
    133.9—dc20   96-30477
                                                                CIP

Cover Art: Dennison Tsosie

Please Note: The artwork in the book are quick sketches, done by Dennison shortly after his experiences, to help me visualize what he was seeing. They in no way reflect his true talent as an artist. —*Teddi Tsosie*

Printed in the United States of America by
Blue Dolphin Press, Inc., Grass Valley, California

10   9   8   7   6   5   4   3   2   1

DEDICATED
TO ELAINE

Contents

~1991~

~ Table of Contents ~

~1992~

~1993~

~ Table of Contents ~

~1994~

~1995~

~ Table of Contents ~

Foreword

WE ARE LIVING IN A TIME OF INCREDIBLE UNCERTAINTY the world over, a time when special people are needed to help to put things right in the world. There are many people who are doing God's work through the healing of self, families, communities, and Mother Earth. There are "healers" in the world today, some self-proclaimed, some lost in their own struggle for power through money and recognition, and some wanna-be healers who have no idea about the power they're messing with. Fortunately, there are also healers who oftentimes go unnoticed until such time as Creator and the grandfather and grandmother spirits see fit to push them to the forefront. Dennison Tsosie is that kind of healer. While it is up to each of us to work toward the healing of Mother Earth by addressing our own human weaknesses and exercising the power of will gifted to us by Creator, we naturally seek those healers who can help shine a flashlight on the path ahead. Dennison has been such a person for me.

In 1990, my then thirteen-year-old son, Caleb, was diagnosed with acute myogenous leukemia and underwent seven months of chemotherapy while we searched for a healer to help him. We connected with a healer from Wyoming who put Caleb through six days of intensive healing bouts in the sweatlodge. Caleb pronounced the cancer gone, but I still had lingering doubts. About that time I began hearing "Arizona" in my mind, so much so that it was beginning to annoy me. I began paying attention to people I met who were connected to Arizona in some way.

In February, 1991, I conducted a workshop on "Healing Ourselves, Healing Mother Earth" with my brother, Rod, and an Elder friend, Eva Cardinal. After the workshop an elderly man came and hugged me and then told me that he really hoped I could meet his daughter from Phoenix, Arizona, since she was very interested in the types of things I was teaching. I gave him a few items from the Mother Earth Healing Society to give to her. She wrote a few weeks later and sent a pendant made by Dennison Tsosie, whom she called her teacher and friend. When I picked up the pendant and saw his name, I knew he was the reason I had to go to Arizona.

I had little money and an old van not fit for cross-country travelling, but still I knew I had to get there. I prayed for help and picked a day, July 27, to leave for Arizona. In May, I awoke one morning with the words "Rainbow Society" in my mind. I phoned them and discovered they granted wishes to children with cancer. I submitted a proposal and told them our desire to go and meet Dennison, a healer, who I knew would put my mind at rest about my son's cancer.

In late July, we received a cheque to cover travel expenses, and the Rainbow Society rented us a Winnebago. Seven of us set out for Arizona. Three days before our arrival, I dreamed of Dennison: he walked by me, stopped, turned around, and held my face in his hands while looking into my eyes and said, "Yes, you're the one."

When we drove up to Teddi and Dennison's driveway, it felt like we were reconnecting with long-lost family. I knew, then, Dennison would be my lifelong teacher and friend. I must also say that Teddi, with her gifts, complements Dennison and his work through her love and dedication to the healing work.

I asked Dennison to see if my son was truly healed. Dennison put Caleb on his massage table and began working on him. Caleb promptly fell asleep. Dennison later told me that their spirits travelled together and Caleb informed Dennison that the cancer was all gone.

That was five years ago, countless telephone calls, and several visits together since. With the assistance of our friend, Rocky Notnes, we brought Dennison to Canada on several occasions for healing work and to share his knowledge with our circles of friends and family. Without exception, everyone who meets Dennison is taken with his gentle nature and his wisdom. Always there are more people who are asking us when he's coming to Canada again. Dennison is a special teacher who is gifted with prophecy to help guide us towards an old way of knowing in this new age we are living in. His gifts are needed in the world now more than ever before.

I feel truly blessed to have been a part of bringing Dennison to Canada and seeing and hearing about the lives that he has touched here. Working with people on their spiritual healing journeys is time-consuming, tiring, yet at the same time fulfilling in a quiet way. I say this because in working with spiritual healing, one doesn't see immediate results of their work, therefore one must work with others in a truly selfless way. Dennison has overcome his own humanness by having the faith in Creator and the gifts that he's been given to do Creator's work.

For some of us who work in various healing disciplines, though, there are times when the aloneness is profound, the questioning of the Universe endless, and the desire for human support immense. Those were the times when I have phoned Dennison—times when the betrayal of a friend cut to the core of my being, when I didn't know if I believed anything anymore . . . times when my heart was wounded so deeply that I didn't think I could ever feel joy again . . . times of feeling completely and utterly alone. Without exception, Dennison and Teddi were able to offer me the bigger picture and remind me of faith, or gently admonish me for forgetting that it's Creator's plan we're living and Creator's work we're doing. And always, always, Dennison and Teddi have been there to share my joy when I would manage to struggle through a necessary teaching to give me the strength, discernment, and wisdom required for this healing of human hearts work that we do.

Dennison is kind, unassuming, humble, wise, and truly gifted. A part of me rejoices in being a small part of sharing him with others, and another part of me cries silently. The sadness comes from knowing how wise and gifted men have been treated throughout history by the multitudes. The sadness, though, is tempered with the knowing that all things happen as they must, because we are spiritual beings having the experience of being human. It is with faith and hope that I send my blessings to Dennison and Teddi in the work that lies ahead of us all.

—Lorraine Sinclair
(Asanee Watchew Iskwiw)
Founder of Mother Earth Healing Society
Edmonton, Alberta, Canada

Acknowledgments

THIS BOOK IS OUR PERSONAL SPIRITUAL JOURNEY. Throughout we have never walked the path alone. We want to thank our families who stand behind us every step of the way, even though they don't always understand where we are going, and our friends, Rocky, El, Irene, Marilyn, Katharine, Scott, Henry, and Beth, who have been there for us without question, when we needed them most. To everyone who has encouraged us, believed in us, and offered a helping hand, there are no words to convey our deep love and appreciation.

Introduction

LET ME FIRST BEGIN BY TELLING YOU a little about Dennison himself. Dennison is a Navajo. He was born on the reservation, where he lived a simple life, in balance with Mother Earth, for that was the Navajo way.

His family had a long tradition of medicine men and women. It was realized at an early age that he too was gifted, and as he grew, he was taught small things to prepare him to follow in their footsteps. Both his Grandfather and Grandmother were Hand Tremblers, his Grandmother's brother, a Crystal Gazer. It was hoped he would one day feel the call of Spirit and follow in one of these traditions. Sadly, by the time he answered his calling, his teachers had passed away.

Shortly before he turned five years old, he was taken from his home and forced by law to attend a government boarding school. He wasn't to see his family again until the end of the school year, because parents were forbidden to visit—an eternity to a small child who doesn't understand why. Our wise government wanted to assimilate Native people as quickly as possible, and it was believed losing their culture would help accomplish this.

Like many others there, he spoke no English at first. Even so, these children were not allowed to speak Navajo to each other and were promptly punished if they did. Most of the food was strange and unappetizing. The rules were strict and incomprehensible; punishment for infringements was severe. When he became ill with the chicken pox shortly after arriving, he was locked in a room, alone and without comfort of someone who cared. This was a terrifying and confusing place.

Nighttime would find many of the children, including himself, silently crying in their cots, some quietly chanting the songs of their elders in order to find comfort in the familiar. A few even tried to run away and return home, only to become lost and cold and hungry. Some died of exposure. These things deeply affected him, and he quickly learned to hate school.

Summers became a precious time, when he was able to return to the life he loved so much, with his family. To rise at dawn and pray, and take the sheep up the canyon to graze. Or ride free on horseback after working with his Grandfather in the corn fields. Sometimes he would help his Grandmother gather herbs, or help his Mother card and spin wool. He would attend Squaw Dances, sit in on healings, shear sheep, help haul water, and simply become Navajo once again.

As he grew older, the school situation changed. A school was built within bussing distance, and he was allowed to return home each night. Now he stayed home periodically for long periods of time, because he was needed. His father was away working for the railroad, building track for the logging trains; his beloved Grandfather was bedridden with a stroke. He was the oldest boy and was relied upon heavily.

Adding to this, the family periodically left the reservation to live in the logging camps with his Dad, and he would be put into the nearest school for awhile. Not surprisingly, he fell behind. The schools were mainly interested in getting him through the system, so he was passed on from grade to grade. These things all resulted in his reading comprehension and writing skills being below normal. It is important to understand this. He does very little reading, and his knowledge of such things as history, geography, global affairs, etc., is minimal. The world has not required otherwise of him until recently.

Dennison left the reservation when he was in his early teens, returning only to visit and help his Grandmother. Life on the reservation was changing, as was his desire to live in the traditional ways. By the age of seventeen, his Grandparents were both dead, and his parents had moved off the reservation permanently, in order to follow his Dad's job. There was nothing to return to but empty cornfields and old hogans filled with memories. He turned his back on the old ways and tried to integrate into the society of the White middle class.

His next several years were unremarkable: he married, had a family, worked many jobs, and focused his spare time on art and silversmithing.

January of 1988 found him working at a paper mill near Snowflake, Arizona. We were newly married, a second marriage for both of us. We were also both artists, and it was our goal to make our living with our art, allowing Dennison to quit his job at the mill.

We were both represented by a gallery in the artist community of Sedona, Arizona, a town which also supports a flourishing community of New Age shops and bookstores. We were not particularly interested in the New Age movement, demonstrated by the fact that we had not yet visited any of these places of business. In late January of 1988, we made a trip to Sedona to deliver some art work to the gallery. While we were there, I made the suggestion we visit one of the crystal shops to look at some of the new crystal jewelry that was becoming popular. My thought was perhaps Dennison could try making some crystal pieces of his own design, thereby exploring the possibility of a new market. His mind was pretty well locked in his traditional Native designs, and I met with some resistance, but in the end we did go into one of the shops.

As I zeroed in on the jewelry counter, he went in the opposite direction, to a case containing a large display of crystals. To say he was transfixed would be an understatement. I could not pull him away. Before we left, he had purchased a beautiful crystal which we could not afford.

In the days that followed, he became obsessed with wanting to learn more about crystals. He said that he had seen them used in Native medicine work and believed them to be very powerful, if used properly. Something seemed to be calling him back to his beginnings.

Dennison's next day off found us going back to Sedona and buying a couple of books on crystals, the idea being that I would read them to him. This project was to become very trying for me, as Dennison did not understand a lot of what I was reading. Time and time again it would be necessary to reword what I had just read to him, in order for him to fully understand what they were saying. Next, I tried reading the books to myself, then summarizing them for him. He had so many questions that I would have to go back through the material to seek the answers, and for many questions, I could find no answers.

To be perfectly honest, I was skeptical of all the claims being made about the wonders of crystals and felt it was pretty much a bunch of hogwash to sell stones. But he was so excited and curious to learn how to use them for medicine work, and so I humored him. Besides, the idea was nice, and I wanted to keep an open mind, as much as I could.

During this time, I read about some crystals having raised triangular markings on their faces. The book said these triangular markings contained data much like a computer disk. Such crystals were said to be encoded by the beings who had created the vibrational energies that allowed human life to evolve on earth. These special marks contained information about past civilizations, such as Atlantis, Lemuria, or teachings by cosmic beings, etc. The crystals were called *Record Keeper* crystals. Information contained in these crystals could only be accessed by individuals with compatible energies.

I tried to tell Dennison about these crystals; however, his interest at this point was limited to their alleged healing powers. Such information as Atlantis or cosmic teachings meant nothing to him.

Oddly enough, the idea of the Record Keeper crystals intrigued me, and the next time we went to Sedona, I made a point of looking for one. I found a small one in a $3.00 bargain box, and without saying anything to him, I purchased it and placed it under my pillow that night, as suggested in the book. I didn't really expect to experience anything; I was just toying with the idea of "what if," and wondering what this crystal craze was all about. I don't know if what follows has anything to do with the crystal or not, but the experience was a turning point in our lives.

—Teddie Tsosie

The Crystal

APRIL 1988

IT WAS THE NIGHT OF APRIL 12, 1988, and we had just gone to bed. My new Record Keeper crystal lay secretly under my pillow. I felt a little foolish for even considering the possibility of information encoded in a stone, but I was intrigued nonetheless.

I sat up reading, while Dennison turned over to go to sleep. After a few minutes, I turned out the light and was beginning to relax, when Dennison turned over and softly said to me, "Babe, are you awake?" I replied, "Yes." He said, "I saw the most beautiful city; it's like a glass or crystal city, so beautiful and bright, with this light coming from the buildings." I asked, "Just now? Were you asleep already?" He replied, "I don't know. I don't think so." He was silent after that, and I thought maybe he had gone to sleep. A couple of minutes passed, and he spoke again, "I'm still there. I can see it when I close my eyes, and I'm not asleep!" His voice was full of wonder as he continued to describe what he was seeing. "I'm walking up a street, or more like a path or a walkway of some sort. . . . There is a low wall on the side and a drop off. I can't see what's down there; it's too dark. . . . I can see a large, circular building, across the way. It's like a courthouse. Something tells me it's like a courthouse. . . .

"It's big, really big. There's bright light coming out of the windows, but it isn't harsh light; it doesn't hurt your eyes." I asked, "Can you see inside the building?" He replied, "No, but I don't need to see inside. It's like I've been here before; I already know what's in there. Somehow, the walls seem to reflect the light. . . . The light comes from a big crystal, and it, like, reflects energy to the walls. There are lots of buildings. They seem to be made of glass or crystal. There's light, and it shines up and out like this. (He motioned his hand in the dark; I could just see it by the light of the digital clock.) There's huge crystals all around the city, and they sit at an angle, like this and this." I tried to ask more questions, but he said, "I have to be still now, 'they' are telling me to be still; there's more. . . ."

~ 3 ~

He was quiet for what seemed a long time. Many things rushed through my mind as I tried to comprehend what was happening. I felt sure he wasn't dreaming, and the wonder and fear in his voice left no doubt he was actually experiencing something. I fleetingly wondered who "they" were. It also began to occur to me that I had placed the Record Keeper crystal under my pillow, only it was too fantastic to believe he could be getting this from it. His breathing was shallow and regular, and I was again wondering if he had fallen asleep, when he began to speak.

"Babe, I see a valley, a hidden valley. It's the most beautiful place I've ever seen. *Sooo beautiful.* . . . I don't know where it is, but I think it exists now, somewhere. . . . There is a lake down there, and it's so blue. I really wish you could see it, it's so perfect. . . .

"I'm coming up on the edge now . . . uhhh! I'm going over the edge, and I'm like flying . . . hold me. Babe, I'm scared! I'm shaking and I can't stop. Please hold me tight, and don't turn me loose. I need to feel you! . . . Now someone is telling me, *'Don't be afraid; we'll only show you a little and see how you do.'*" Dennison seemed to grow calmer after this, and he continued, "The valley exists now; I'm sure of it. I'd really like to go there. There is a city by the lake, but you can't see it. Some of it is under the lake. People who see it think there is just a lake. . . . I have to be still again; there's more."

By this time I was really feeling overwhelmed. Something extraordinary was happening, and I had no idea how to handle it. In my helplessness, I felt tears stinging my eyes. Another part of me said I had to remain calm for Dennison; I needed only to go along.

Quietly, he began speaking again. "I see a gray building. . . . It looks like a castle, surrounded by a wall and towers with pointed tops at each corner. . . . There's a huge, faceted crystal in the middle of the roof. There's buildings inside the walls. The crystal is turning around slowly, and there's a beam of light . . . of energy going up. It's like a generator. . . . I think it's another time."

He fell silent for awhile, then continued. "Now I see a volcano; a crater. The landscape is bare and burned looking, black all around. No life at all. There's a red glow coming from the crater; like lights coming from within it. . . . Oh, there's a city under it! People live inside the earth! . . . I see beings, but I'm afraid to look at them. . . . 'They' are saying not to be afraid.

"The people look kind of like ants. Really big ants, but they have two arms and two legs and large eyes. I think they are workers. They move sort of funny, kind of a bobbing motion. It scares me to go in there. I don't want to see any more."

After another pause, he said, "I'm seeing symbols, like numbers or something. They are coming at me and going into my forehead. I think it's like a history maybe. . . . Time passing. Lots of time. . . . I'm asking what the symbols mean, but 'they're' telling me it's not important right now, just experience it, let it happen. . . .They're so strange—little triangles and lines and circles. . . . Nothing I've ever seen before.

"There's buildings in the distance. . . . It's gray all around, and the buildings are gray. I think maybe it's underground. . . . Now I'm moving really fast. Everything is speeding by me. Hold me! I'm afraid I'll fly off and won't be able to come back; I need to feel you. . . . Now I'm coming up on the city; it's still about thirty miles away. There's mountains in the background, and trees, and there's a bright glow coming from the city, beaming up into the sky. . . ."

Another long pause, and I began to wonder if it was over. I was just about to speak to him when he said, "I see a dark brown planet with these rectangular shapes. . . . Maybe it is a circle of houses in some sort of a pattern. Oh. Something tells me it's a calendar of some sort, an ancient calendar. . . . It's beginning to fade now."

Dennison was silent for awhile, then he sighed deeply and said, "Man, that was really weird! What's happening!!?" I confessed I had no real idea, then told him about placing the Record Keeper crystal under my pillow earlier and wondered if it could have caused the "visions." He seemed to dismiss the idea; then, believe it or not, he fell right to sleep. I wanted to discuss what had just happened and ask lots more questions, but he was sleeping so soundly. I couldn't wake him when I spoke to him, so I let him sleep and got up. I went into the kitchen, made some tea, and wrote down as much as I could remember. I noticed the whole episode had taken nearly two hours.

The next morning, Dennison awoke full of wonder. "Man, that was really weird last night! What happened to me?" I replied I didn't really

Courthouse, Crystal City

Crystal City

Hidden Valley

Gray Castle — Generator?

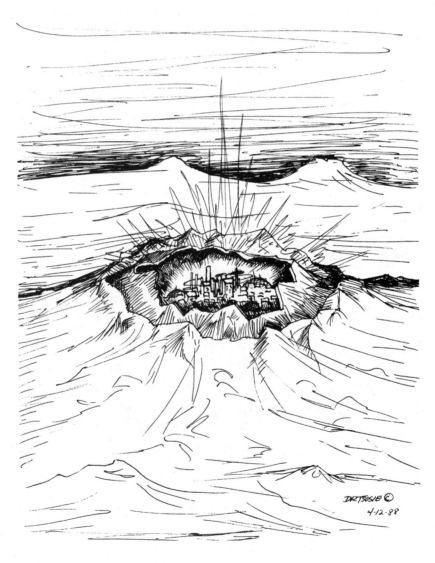

City Inside a Crater

Beings Inside of Crater — "Ant People"

Distant City—Underground?

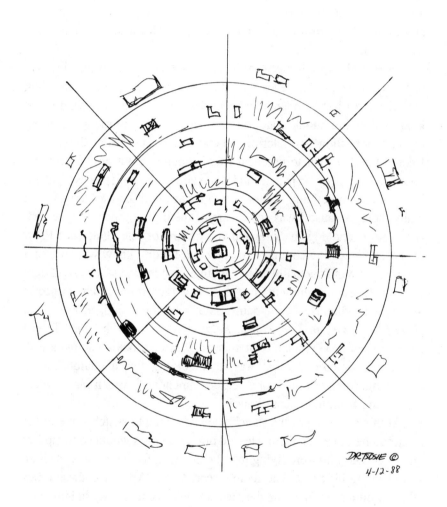

Dark Brown Circle—a Planet or a Circle of Houses?
An Ancient Calendar?

know, and again mentioned the Record Keeper crystal and what it was supposed to do. Showing him the stone, I said, "See these little triangles on the face? They are supposed to be sort of like information recorded on a computer disk. Maybe somehow you were able to extract the information stored in them." He looked at the small places I indicated, but remained unconvinced, though he was willing to concede the possibility. To me the thought was almost inconceivable that a stone could be programmed with information, but what if? . . . How else to explain what had happened?

I asked him to tell me what he could remember of everything that happened. He closed his eyes and sat quietly for a few minutes, recalling the scenes. At last he opened his eyes and said, "I was just lying there, kind of thinking about what you had been reading to me about using crystals for healing—wondering if it could really mean something and if I could put any of it to practical use. I thought about how everything seems like it's part of a puzzle, and when you get enough pieces together, it will mean something. By that time, I was about half asleep, but not really there, because I was still aware of the night sounds. I could hear cars passing and dogs barking and you turning off the light. Then I saw or sensed something coming into view, but I didn't know what it was. I was aware I wasn't actually asleep, though. Suddenly, I saw a bright light coming close and shining in my eyes, like a light from a movie projector or bright headlights. At the same time, something said, in my mind, *'Don't be afraid; just go with it. Relax and go with the light.'* Then I found myself in a crystal city on this pathway and looking across a wall at a house or building that was lit up bright, like a guardhouse or something. Someone said, or I sensed somehow, it was a place where records are kept, like a courthouse."

At this point he got his sketch pad and began to sketch some of the scenes as he described them. He said often the cenes would come up fast and he felt as if he were flying into them—even feeling at times as if he were leaving his body. The feeling scared him. Always at these times "they" would calm him, and the scenes would continue. My holding him seemed to help keep him grounded in this reality. During the pauses, when he would fall silent for awhile, he was seeing and hearing things, but he felt so much a part of it that he would forget to describe them to me. He had a feeling of soaking information into every part of himself, in blocks of knowledge, but couldn't remember what it was later.

A couple of days later, he confessed he had been hearing voices in his head periodically since the experience, and it frightened him very, very much. Distressed, he confessed he was afraid he was losing his mind or maybe even was possessed. I tried to reassure him that neither was the case. He also complained that he felt like he was being watched and even being tested in some way. Sometimes he felt like someone was beside him and even inside him, looking out through his eyes. He half jokingly worried he was becoming an alien, saying, "Lovey, do you think I'm weird? Sometimes I expect to find antenna growing out my head. I feel like I'm an alien. Something's happening to me, and I don't know what it is." He expressed a fear of being taken away by some unknown source. Afraid "they" might come and get him, and he would never return. He would dream strange dreams of similar scenes and get "teachings" daily.

He was given much regarding the use of crystals. He was also given different ways of thinking, different outlooks. I'm sorry to say I didn't record much of this. The whole thing was very confusing to me, and I guess I only half believed this was valid information. I couldn't sort it all out.

Dennison was also very upset and feared ridicule or worse if anyone found out he was having these experiences. I wanted so much to talk to someone else about what was happening and to get some outside input, but I didn't know who to talk to or how to approach the subject. It seemed too unbelievable. When I mentioned I'd like to get an outside opinion, he would beg me not to tell anyone, so I just let it go.

What was most disturbing was that my husband was normally quite unflappable. His nature is calm, quiet, and deliberate. To see him like this was very upsetting. Definitely, something strange was going on.

Ant People
APRIL 1988

I DID WRITE DOWN ONE VIVID DREAM of Dennison's. He was in a tunnel or underground cavern. There were several beings inside, similar to the "Ant People" he had seen in his earlier "visions." These, however, were somehow different, more bug-like and less clean and streamlined. They had holes or vents along their backs, which he described as looking sort of like those old cars from a long time ago that had vents in their hoods.

He focused in on two of the beings; they seemed somewhat different from each other, and he sensed one was male and one was female. They were moving some black things, which looked like large eggs. He sensed they were babies, not yet hatched. He also had a sense that these were like slaves or workers who took care of the young; a nursery. He felt they were connected in some way to the other beings he had seen. He could hear them breathe through their vents, and it sounded similar to a bellows or a valve opening and closing, swishhh click, swishhh click. Suddenly, he was on top of the earth again, and there was a woman going into a trap door in the ground. She paused and looked at him and said, "Forty comes forth." He awoke, feeling the phrase was very significant, and it has haunted him since. He also had a strong impression that there are beings who live inside the earth, and that they are in a way connected to us.

I have since learned that the number forty is symbolic of a period of cleansing or testing, as in the Biblical raining for forty days and forty nights, and Moses' forty years in the desert.

Our lives began to return to a more normal state, though changed somehow. As he became more comfortable with his experience, we began to search for answers. Where to go was the question. Shirley MacLaine was popular, and I read her book, *Out on A Limb,* but it didn't really address what seemed to be happening to us. I ended up buying some of the various books available in the metaphysical bookstores in Sedona.

I read a book about channeling, and though it didn't really seem to cover what he was experiencing, perhaps it was a part of it. To be honest, I had some trouble with the idea of channeling, and just couldn't (really still can't) accept most of the claims about it. I admit this is a bit hypocritical, and I know others may feel the same about Dennison's experiences.

Strangely, as the weeks went by, Dennison seemed to be growing very psychic, knowing things or sensing things he couldn't have had any way of knowing. Once I came home with a book I had just purchased and laid it down on the kitchen table, still in the paper sack. He came over and asked, "What did you get, another book?" I said, "Yeah, it looked pretty interesting." He picked up the sack as if to open it and asked, "What's it

Ant People

about?" Before I could answer and before he opened the sack, he went on to tell me what it was about. After I read the book, I found he was very right.

He continued having many odd experiences, and I finally began to write some of them down. The next significant occurrence happened two months later.

Leprechauns and Triangles
JUNE 1988

In June of 1988, I was called for jury duty. When I arrived at the courthouse, I saw a couple of familiar faces, those of Travis Walton and his wife Dana. Travis was allegedly abducted by a UFO back in the mid-1970s; his experience received world attention. Travis and Dana were from the nearby town of Snowflake. Having once lived there myself, I knew who he was, and I had taken some college classes with Dana. The story had always intrigued me, but she didn't seem receptive to inquiries about it, and I never had the nerve to push the subject.

This day, as we sat there waiting to see if we would be selected, I looked for an opening where I could comfortably ask him about his abduction experience. I never had the courage to ask.

Later that evening, when Dennison returned home from working swing shift, I told him of my day and asked if he knew Travis Walton. He thought for a bit, then said, "Yeah, I think I went to high school with him, why?" I explained, "I saw him at the courthouse today, and I just wondered if you knew him." He replied, " I knew who he was, but I was a couple or three years ahead of him, so I didn't talk to him much." I asked him what he thought of Travis' abduction experience, and much to my surprise, he said he knew nothing about it. It seems he wasn't living in Snowflake at that time and simply hadn't heard about it, or maybe hadn't paid any attention to it. I briefly told him what I knew and asked if he believed it could be true. He replied, "I guess it could have happened; I don't have any problem with the idea, at least. The Navajo have stories of the Star People who came down and taught our People to make tools and weapons, how to plant, and weave, etc."

I found this pretty interesting, so I asked, "Do you think the Star People could be the same beings who are supposedly abducting humans, and if they are, why?" He just shrugged and really didn't seem to know or care much about Star People, UFOs, or Aliens. If anything, he seemed a little uncomfortable with the subject. I tried to involve him in a discussion of what or who they might be and where they might come from, but he said he was tired and wanted only to shower and go to bed.

We had been in bed a few minutes, and I was nearly asleep, when Dennison asked, "What's a dish?" I was startled and somewhat confused by the question. I gathered my wits and thought maybe he was setting me up for a joke. Carefully I replied, "A container to put food in?" He went on to ask, "What's a cup?" By now, I was sure it was a joke, so I obliged with another definition. Again he asked, "What's a saucer?" This was beginning to get a little silly, and I was feeling uncomfortable with the whole turn of events. I defined "saucer" with a bit of sarcasm in my voice, but still playing along. Again he asked, "What's two saucers put together and thrown in the air?" This was just too absurd, and I could see no point in answering. The whole conversation was very out of character for him and more than a little confusing to me. Insistently, he again asked his question. I replied, "Okay, what's the point?" At this he began to giggle and exclaimed, "A flying saucer!" I couldn't believe he was acting so childishly, and it occurred to me he might be making fun of my interest in UFOs. My feelings were a little hurt, thinking he could be doing that, when he went on to say, "Want to have some fun?" Again he began to giggle like a small child. He was beginning to scare me, and I said, "Dennison, why are you acting so weird? You're scaring me, so please stop!" He took a deep breath, like a sigh, and fell into rhythmic breathing, as if he had fallen asleep. After several seconds, he began to speak again, but his voice had a different quality to it, sort of wispy and far away.

"What is it you wish to know about UFOs?" I was completely taken aback and sensed right away this wasn't Dennison talking. I thought to myself that if indeed Dennison were channeling, then this must be a spirit guide or some such entity speaking through him. I decided to go along with whatever was happening and see what would come next. After I was

able to organize my thoughts to some degree, I replied, "I guess I want to know who they are and what they want."

"They are like cosmic farmers, and mankind is an experiment."

"I read somewhere that we were sort of seeded here; is that what you are saying?"

"In a sense. They used available genetic material."

"Where do they come from?"

"They come from the Source."

"What is the Source?"

"The All Knowing, The One."

"Is that what we call God?"

"God is love. God is in all things. God is energy, like light."

I was not too clear on who or what the entities were that people channeled, or really where they were. I asked, "Who am I speaking to?"

"Why must you have a name? I simply am."

"Are you from the Source, the All Knowing?"

"Yes. I am from the Source."

"Are you a Guide or Master?"

"No, I am a Watcher."

I wanted to ask what is a Watcher, but I felt I was straying away from my original questions and was not sure how long this would last, so instead I asked, "Who and what are Aliens?"

"Some of them are Watchers."

A chill went through me as the implications of this soaked into my mind. "Watchers? What do they do, watch us?"

"Yes, they have watched over Mankind from the beginning. They observe Mankind, like a scientist observes a laboratory experiment."

"Then why do they abduct some people, and do probes, implants, and other bizarre things? It seems they would have enough knowledge about us by now."

"They randomly check on Mankind, again as a scientist would check on an experiment. They implant genetic changes in people; they implant information to manipulate social changes; they monitor pollution levels in the atmosphere; they check the soil, animals, plants, etc., in order to be able to test for toxins, to see where Man is in his evolution."

"Are the Aliens actually from other planets?"

"Some are. Some are from earth; they live inside the earth. They vibrate at a different frequency and thus pass through seemingly solid material."

"What is their ultimate purpose? Why do they manipulate our genetic material and implant information?"

"Ultimately they want to bring mankind to a higher level of consciousness. To bring the realization that we are all One. Unconditional love. No more prejudice, no more war, no more governmental systems, no more monetary systems, no more hunger."

When will this take place?"

"That depends on Mankind. He is being guided, and in a sense genetically manipulated toward these aims, but the realization must come from within him. Some will be lost. Do not weep for the lost ones. All are part of the whole."

"What if that never happens?"

"Then Mankind will destroy himself, and they will begin again, either on earth or somewhere else."

"Are we just an experiment then? Do they have no feelings for us?"

"No, not in the sense you mean. They do not have your human emotions, but they love Mankind in an unconditional sense. Souls are forever and a part of The Source. The human body is a vehicle for the soul to navigate the three-dimensional plane. If a blade of grass fails, the farmer replants a new one; so it is with Mankind. The soul is not lost. The Watchers oversee this process, and Mankind as a whole. They interact with many individuals who are able to interact with them on various levels. Many cannot. . . . That is your information for now."

Dennison's voice was very faint by this time, and he sounded tired. He sighed and stretched. I waited a few moments to see if there was any more to come, then I softly said, "Babe, did you get all that?" He acted like he had just awakened and said, "What?" I asked, "Were you aware of what was going on?" He seemed confused and brushed my questions aside and started telling me of a dream he had been having. He began to giggle again, as he had earlier, saying, "I was dreaming of a little old man with a long white beard, a funny old codger. He was a riot, and we had a ball, just throwing this triangle-like thing up in the air and catching it."

Leprechaun on a Triangle

As he talked of his dream, he would chuckle and giggle like a child. I had never seen him act like that, and it still scared me a little. Dennison continued, "He was a funny little guy, jumping all around, so happy. We played like a couple of kids; I never had so much fun."

I asked, "You were just now dreaming this? Do you remember talking to me at all?" He replied, "No, I was asleep. I dreamed about this little guy, and he said to me, *'What's a dish? What's a cup? What's a saucer?'* and as he said it, he started throwing this Frisbee thing up in the air. I could see it was shaped like a triangle. No matter how far he threw it, it would always come back to him. It looked like lots of fun. Then he said to me, *'So you want to try it?'* I told him I did. He said to me, *'Go on ahead, throw it, and keep your eye on it. Keep playing with it, and we're going to play with your mind a little and see how it goes.'* Then we just started having a ball. He had another triangle, like a little trampoline. He would jump on it and turn somersaults, and that's quite a trick for an old codger. He was so funny! He had a triangle, dragging along on a chain, hanging from his waist, and sometimes he would throw it up and catch it. He told me triangles were the key to the universe, and he was going to teach me some things that would help me in my jewelry designs. He told me a lot of other things, but I didn't really understand, and then he showed me a bunch of symbols, and he told me not to worry with understanding them for now. There was a lot more, but mostly we just played. Then he said he had to go, but we could do it again any time I wanted. I loved that little guy; it was like he was my best friend."

After this, Dennison said he was very, very thirsty and got up and drank some water straight out of the bathroom faucet. I got up too and tried once again to tell him about what I had gotten, but he was still enthralled with his "dream" and couldn't seem to listen. In a way it was almost like he still wasn't himself. He seemed very childlike as he went back to bed, still chuckling.

This was confusing and still a little scary. I stayed up and made notes on both experiences.

The next morning, he was still chuckling over "that old codger." I had him draw a picture and was surprised to see it looked like a leprechaun! The whole episode seemed more and more bizarre. I was finally able to get him to listen to what else had happened, and it upset him a lot. He felt "used" and out of control, as well as resentful, as if he had been pacified while it happened.

A Long Short Cut
MARCH 1988

THESE EXPERIENCES AND THE INFORMATION coming from them was so far from Dennison's normal self that I searched my mind repeatedly for an explanation. After the above experience, I began to wonder if this was some sort of alien contact. The fact that I was there when it happened didn't necessarily mean "they" weren't somehow doing this from a distance; controlling his mind. Maybe it was implanted information? Could he or we have been abducted at some earlier time and had no memory of the experience? I had read how missing time could be an indication of an abduction experience. I also recalled an odd happening about a month before Dennison's first visions, where there seemed to be some time missing.

We were returning from Sedona after taking some art work to the gallery and visiting with the owners at their home in Oak Creek Canyon. We headed back home through Flagstaff, stopping in town for a burger. Right before we left, I called my son to tell him we'd be home by 10:00 p.m. at the latest. It was a little past 6:00 p.m. when I made the call.

We took I-40 to Winslow, fighting the large eighteen-wheelers all the way. As we approached the town, Dennison suggested the possibility of taking a short cut through the National Forest, which began a few miles southeast of the town. It made sense, as it was a more direct route to Heber, as the crow flies. I got out our bundle of maps and found one for the Sitgraves National Forest. I soon discovered the road he was thinking of. It was a dirt road, but fairly well maintained, and it would cut twenty-five or thirty miles off our trip. We were in our Jeep; even if we had to drive slower, we could still make good time. It was better than dealing with the trucks and their crazy antics.

When we reached the road, we found we were at a fork, the other road leading to a ranger station and on to a popular lake, not too far from our home. We calculated the miles each way and decided to take our original choice, as it ended up on the edge of Heber and was a little shorter. After traveling a couple of miles, we were surprised to find the road becoming very muddy and getting worse the farther we drove. It hadn't snowed for weeks and such road conditions were totally unexpected. Knowing we would be driving down into and up out of a canyon along the way, we decided to turn around and take the other fork, past the ranger station. At least that way there were no canyons to cross. This road was paved for a few miles, and we were just congratulating ourselves for our good fortune, when it gave way to dirt road, also muddy. By this time, the mud was freezing up, so after discussing our option of returning some thirty miles or more back to Winslow to catch the Interstate and noticing we didn't have a lot of gas left, we decided to risk the mud. Within minutes, the mud puddles had turned to ice spots, then to stretches of ice and snow. We passed the ranger station and farther on a sign, which said it was still some twenty miles to the lake. We knew home was still another fifteen or more miles beyond that. Our gas was really low at this point and would never have made it back to Winslow.

As we drove on, the road became a solid stretch of plowed snow. We traveled like this for a few miles, when suddenly the plowed snow stopped in a wall, as if the snow plow had just quit and backed up. There was no turning back now, so with the Jeep in four-wheel drive, we went around the wall of snow. From here on, the road wasn't plowed at all, and we drove up on top of the frozen snow. I remarked over and over in my mind how impossible this seemed. We were driving on *top* of two feet of snow!

Later, we came to a barrier across the road, a metal pipe gate with a sign proclaiming that the road was closed. Again, we drove off the road and made our way around the gate and continued smoothly on our journey. It seemed like a dream, so quiet driving along, with only a slight hiss of the tires on the snow. We came to another barrier, and we knew we were nearing the end of the road. We could see headlights of a passing car on the highway far in the distance. This barrier was not so easy to go around; an embankment where the road cut into a hill was on one side and a deep ravine on the other. All was covered in snow. At last, Dennison got out of the jeep and scouted a way down the side of the ravine with a flashlight. When he returned, he said he had found a possible route through the boulders and the trees. We would only have to go a little way down the side, then climb the jeep back up. He had me walk down with him to show me what he had in mind. My legs sank deep into the snow as I followed. Again, I wondered how we could be driving on top of the snow.

I was totally unconvinced we could negotiate the path he was suggesting and feared we would go plunging down the side, maybe rolling over in the process. I protested, but he insisted it would work and suggested I wait on top while he drove the jeep. I couldn't let him do this alone, so together we climbed in the jeep. I closed my eyes and ridiculously covered my ears as we plunged into the unknown over the side of the ravine. Slowly, we bumped our way along and up the other side.

Within a few minutes we were on the highway and heading home. It was with great relief and an empty gas tank that we pulled up into our yard. When we got inside and settled a little, I glanced at the clock and realized it was after 3:00 a.m.! Surely it didn't take nine hours to get home! The whole trip was taking on the feeling of a crazy dream.

Several weeks later, we had some extra time, and we decided to take the same route again, this time during the day. The road from the ranger station on seemed totally different than we remembered, and the last barrier, where there was an embankment on one side and a ravine on the other, was nonexistent. Farther up the road, nearer the highway, was a gate that was closed during bad weather, but it was not near an embankment or a ravine. So where in the heck were we, and why did it take so long to get home? In light of the strange happenings of the past two months, I now wondered if there could have been a forgotten encounter during our journey.

A Dream of Digging in Peru
JUNE 1988

AT THE END OF JUNE, Dennison had a dream, and even though it was a dream, it was particularly vivid and unusual, so I wrote it down in case it proved to relate to something later.

"I dreamed of some people digging a large hole somewhere. The area was heavily forested. There was a castle-looking thing, or maybe some

Excavation in Peru

ruins in a background. The name Peru comes to my mind. Several people were gathered around the hole and looking inside. These people were wearing, like, turbans on their heads, with cloth hanging down on one side. Someone is telling me something will be discovered in a hole dug in the side of a hill, which will be of *great* significance, possibly relating to the Egyptians or to Atlantis.

Vision of a Comet
SEPTEMBER 1988

THERE WERE NO MORE EXPERIENCES throughout July and August, and at times I wondered if they had stopped completely. It was so upsetting to Dennison when they happened, I thought maybe he somehow had found a way to shut them off. I was soon to find this wasn't the case.

Dennison was once again working swing shift. It was about 1:30 a.m. on September 10, 1988, and we had just gone to bed. I was just getting relaxed, when he asked me, "What does a comet mean?" I searched my memory, "I think they were once considered to be bad omens or something; why do you want to know?" He was quiet for a few moments, then said, "I just closed my eyes and was relaxing to go to sleep, when all of a sudden I saw a comet with a long tail. I'm wondering what it could mean?" After a moment he continued, "The tail is slowly fading now . . . getting shorter and shorter. It's turning into a dragon, and its head is moving from side to side. There is fire coming from its mouth like light rays. . . .

"The rays are coming from the sun. They're hot . . . like a hot wind blowing. *Dry . . . hot*. It's a strange kind of heat; strange kind of wind.

"Now the sky is yellow-brown. I can't see the sun any more. It's so dry and hot. There's piles of sand, wrecked boats, pieces of trees, dead birds and animals laying everywhere. . . .

"Now I see some people gathered on a hill just above the beach area. All different kinds of people. They're all holding lighted candles and wearing blankets and singing spiritual songs. They're looking toward the East, and there's a bright light coming from there . . . *very* bright.

"The sky is dark now; only the light in the East. It is like a beacon or a search light beam, sweeping back and forth. There's other beams of light joining it, sweeping back and forth along the coast. I see a flying saucer-like thing, and someone is saying, *'You've been warned before time. Move to higher ground; go up in the mountains; you'll be safe there. Stay in the mountains!'"*

I lay there waiting to see if there was more, when Dennison said, "Why on earth would I see something like that?" I too was at a loss what it might mean, other than a possible warning of some upcoming disaster. I asked, "Did you get any verbal messages with it?" "No, I was just relaxing, trying to go to sleep, when I started seeing that comet. It just stayed there awhile, until I asked you what it meant; then the rest of the scenes started happening. Man, I don't like the feeling it left inside me, like I'm really sad."

The Mayan Connection
DECEMBER 1988

A FEW UNUSUAL THINGS were received over the next several months, but I didn't keep notes on them, until a series of further unusual events began taking place in December of 1988.

Dennison was working swing shift on December 2. He had just gotten home, and after finishing a bowl of soup, we sat relaxing with a cup of tea. The TV was on, but turned down low. Out of the clear blue he said, "I see a man in a white robe, kind of real fancy." When I looked over at him, I noticed his eyes were closed. He continued, "I feel he's a priest or holy man of some sort. He's trying to hide something from someone. . . . I sense it's sacred knowledge . . . something sacred. . . . He's hiding it in the back of a cave. . . . Uh-oh, there's someone coming into the cave, some Indians. . . . They have bows and arrows . . . unnnh. They're shooting me!" He flinched and opened his eyes, startled. We both took a deep breath and he said, "For a minute there, I felt like that was me!"

He was quiet for a few minutes, then with anguish in his voice he said, "Lovey, what's happening to me? Why is all this stuff happening? I don't even understand what I'm seeing and hearing. I don't know what I'm supposed to do. Why don't 'they' leave me alone and find someone else who knows something?"

I, too, was at a loss to understand what was going on or what these things were supposed to mean. I did know something very unusual was happening, and in a way it was quite exciting to me.

The following night, he got home from work about 2:00 a.m., after putting in a little overtime. We were again relaxing with a cup of tea as he unwound from his day. We talked a little about happenings at work; then he asked, "What do the numbers 2012 and 5125 mean to you?" I replied, "Nothing that I know of. Could they be lottery numbers?" He said, "I don't know, maybe. They just kept coming into my mind all evening at work." I asked, "What do you feel they are in reference to?" He thought a moment then said, "I'm not sure, but I think 2012 is a date, like the year 2012, and 5125 is the passage of a number of years, a span of time."

I pondered the significance of this. By now I was learning not to overlook seemingly odd questions. I had just been reading through a little metaphysical newspaper we had picked up in Sedona a few weeks before. An article in it claimed we are making a transition into a new age over the next twenty-five years. I only glanced through it, but it went into explaining planetary alignments and cycles of some sort in connection with this "New Age." For some unknown reason, I tried subtracting 25 years from the year 2012 and came up with 1987, which was last year, the year of the Harmonic Convergence. I wondered aloud if that was what the 2012 could be in reference to. Dennison asked, "What is the Harmonic Convergence?" I had to admit I was not too clear on that myself. "It was some sort of a big deal last August where the planets were lined up in a rare configuration, and it was supposed to change the earth's energies and bring in a new age of enlightenment. Don't you remember there were a bunch of people gathered in Sedona and on the Hopi reservation?" He didn't remember, which wasn't too surprising, especially since he doesn't keep up with current events.

A few minutes passed as he finished his cup of tea and leaned back on the sofa and closed his eyes. Suddenly he said, "I see a statue of a priest of some sort. He has a bald head, and he's wearing a beautiful headdress and large earrings. I think maybe he is an Egyptian Priest or something." I wondered if it was the same priest he saw last night.

He remained silent for a little while, his eyes still closed. I got a notebook, in case he came up with anything more.

"What is Me-yan? May-yin? Something like that?" I tried to put the word in an Egyptian context, but could think of nothing. Finally I asked him if he could spell it. He spelled M-A-Y-A-N. I exclaimed, "My-yan. Do you mean Mayan? Could that statue you saw be a Mayan Priest?" Immediately he said, "Yes. . . . Did the Mayans ever tell about their priests going up in UFOs? Did they leave any records where they had contact with Star People?" I replied, "Not that I've ever heard of!"

He was quiet for a few moments; then he said, "They're telling me many were taken away in UFOs. The priests were very psychic and had tremendous powers. The Star People worked with them and taught them many, many things. They gave them a calendar system more accurate than any ever known. It also predicted the future. Many priests were taken away in UFOs and are now coming back to make contact. There's also going to be several things found, discovered buried, that will prove this and several other things. The world will be amazed." He went on to say the Mayan calendar and the year 2012 were connected. He then asked "What is the Mayan factor?" I couldn't even imagine, so I said, "I have no idea." He went on talking, as if I hadn't even spoken, *The Mayan Factor* is a book on which the Harmonic Convergence was based. While most of the people who were gathered for the Convergence were meditating, they were paying attention to the wrong thing. While their minds were focused on one thing, another thing was happening. There was like a time warp. A change of energies took place that will bring in a new world within the next twenty-five years. These energies will be focused on bringing us in touch with Nature. One with Nature. There will be floods, droughts, earthquakes, etc. As people get more and more in tune with Nature, it will balance the natural disasters."

I knew once again something extraordinary was happening. Someone or something was speaking to and/or through Dennison. I decided to try asking a few more questions and see if "they" would answer them. I still had some unanswered questions regarding the UFOs after the session last summer. I asked: "Can UFOs travel faster than the speed of light? Otherwise, how can they travel the vast distances required if they are traveling from other galaxies?"

"UFOs can go forward and backward in time. Time is not linear. That is why they can appear and disappear with ease. That is also why they can't declare themselves and interact with us yet; it would cause

something like a crack in time. It would speed time up for us. We exist where time only goes forward. Only when our collective minds can change, our energies raised, can we transcend time's barrier and interact with them."

I wondered, "Where do they come from; where do they live?"

"There are UFOs under the ocean and inside the earth. Aliens have cities there. I think they are under volcanoes, too."

"What are they doing here?"

"They are like genetic farmers. They watch, abduct, and examine people for many reasons . . . to observe humans and to keep records of their progress. To collect genetic material, eggs and sperm, to save to use to rebuild the earth if we destroy ourselves. To use to seed other planets. To make humanlike beings that inhabit physical bodies to learn the lessons that being entrapped in a physical world can bring."

"What happens to such beings when they die? Do they have souls like ours?"

"Yes, all return to The Source."

As before, I felt "they" seemed to be without feeling. I wanted somehow to feel they watched over us in a benevolent, parental way, not in a remote, scientific way. "How can they claim to care for us and yet be so unfeeling?"

The reply came, *"They understand that souls are forever; only the body dies. They see the overall picture. They do not experience emotion as you do. You are like an experiment; earth is a school for souls. Their ultimate goal is to guide you into raising your energies. When or if that happens is up to you. You could possibly destroy yourselves, and if that happens, they'll just reseed you here or somewhere else.*

"You are going through a critical change now, in order to force growth. Many won't survive, unless they can learn quickly to raise their energies, open their minds to the spiritual world. Remember, this world is not real; it is created with your beliefs. When you die, it becomes real.

"Something to remember is that illness exists in the mind long before it manifests in the body. To treat the body for illness, you must first treat the mind. That's your information for now."

We spent the next few minutes discussing what we had just experienced, trying to analyze it and fit it into our belief system. I noted how toward the end it seemed I was talking directly to "them," instead of to "them" through him. He said the whole thing seemed dreamlike, as if he were sort of observing from a distance and only getting part of what was being said.

I asked if he had ever seen a UFO or had any memory of a strange event. He couldn't remember ever seeing a UFO, and admitted he had never really given them much thought before these strange episodes. He went on to describe a strange event that had happened in his early childhood and which had greatly disturbed him. The memory was still clear in his mind.

"I was just a kid of maybe six or seven. My aunt, my mother's sister, had been killed in an automobile accident. She was a wonderful woman who lavished us kids with a lot of attention, and we had loved her a lot. It was a shock to lose her. This was the day of her funeral, and all of us kids had to stay at home with my older sister while the adults went. It had grown dark, and the folks hadn't returned yet. I was still outside playing, when I saw what looked like a fire, maybe a camp fire, under a large cedar tree that sat on top of a small hill a little ways from the hogan. It startled me, because I knew no one could have gotten up there without passing the house, and we or the dogs would have known it. Why would anyone want to camp in our yard, anyway, and even I knew at that young age that only a fool or a white man would build a fire right under a tree. I called my older sister, and she and the rest of the kids came out, and we all looked at it. It wasn't exactly like a fire, because it didn't flicker, and it was brighter than a fire, more white. We didn't have electricity; nobody on the reservation did in those days, and there were no close neighbors. The light seemed like it was right underneath the tree, and it lit up the branches all the way to the top. My sister grew frightened and said, 'We'd better all go into the house. I think maybe it's our aunt's Spirit, coming to tell us goodbye.'

"The next morning, we all went out to the tree and looked around. There was no sign of a fire, no burned spot, nothing. I always thought maybe my sister was right; it was my Aunt's Spirit or something."

It was the night of December 5, and Dennison was still working swingshift. He had just come home from work, and we were again relaxing and talking of our day. After a pause in the conversation he said,

"Jose Galloes or Jose Argalloes or something like that; that name keeps coming to my mind. Do we know someone by that name?" I replied, "I've never heard of him; maybe it's someone at the Mill." He was thoughtful for a moment, then he said, "No, 'they' are saying he was a High Priest who gathered people together for the Harmonic Convergence.

"There's books that the Mayans made that are hidden away in oiled skin bags. Many are made of metal, like brass or copper. They used metal left there by the Romans and Phoenicians; those people that came over there. There's a connection between the Mayans and the Egyptians. They are going to discover something soon that proves it.

"Macci?. . Macca?.. There's a pyramid there, where a lot of this stuff is still hidden. One priest was buried with a lot of knowledge and power. Secrets were written on stone and buried with him."

There was nothing more until December 22. Dennison was home, after working graveyard shift. I was sitting on the bed talking to him as he lay relaxing, getting ready to go to sleep. He asked, "Is there a place called Maxi-Peechoo, or something like that, in Peru?" I said," Yes, there is a ruin by that name."

He went on to say, "I feel it is a vortex area; so is the Great Pyramid in Egypt. Jose Arguelles, that is the name of a High Priest. He was a High Priest to the Mayan, and he's now like a High Priest to a part of the New Age movement.

"There's something they are missing in translating the Mayan Calendar. It has to do with the UFO connection with the Maya. They are so busy calculating and working out the computations and charts, that they are overlooking a very important factor: the Aliens interacted with the Maya and are still interacting with us. You see, there are different species of Aliens. Some are very highly evolved and are overseeing Mankind, trying to guide him and help him. Some come and blend in with humans. They are kind of interbred. They mostly go to places where Man is still in a primitive lifestyle, like Natives.

"Mankind is on the tip edge of a MIRACLE. . . . If this so-called New Age Movement, this 'new' way of thinking can take hold, then there will be a transformation. If it does not, Mankind will again be destroyed.

"Mankind must learn to transmune with Nature."

A few days later I was in a bookstore in Flagstaff, and I was amazed when I came across a book entitled *The Mayan Factor,* by Jose Arguellos!

Elaine

DECEMBER 1988

WE HAD BECOME ACQUAINTED WITH a woman in town who was very interested in crystals and their alleged mystical properties. She owned a small business in town and carried a few pieces of Dennison's jewelry, including some of his new crystal pieces, in her store. As our friendship grew, I ventured to tell her a little of Dennison's experiences. She was very receptive to hearing them and soon introduced us to a couple of other receptive friends of hers.

One day, our friend, Elaine, asked Dennison if he could call upon some of his early training from his Grandparents, to be a Medicine man and help a friend of hers. She went on to say she felt Dennison was surely gifted and receiving guidance from higher sources. Her friend was dying of pancreatic cancer and was in a lot of pain. Elaine wanted to ask her friend's son and his wife and some others who were close to the dying woman over to her home and have Dennison lead the group in sending her prayers as well as giving emotional support to the son. At first he said "no," but she kept at him until he reluctantly agreed to do a small "ceremony" for the group to help us send our prayers for this woman.

We all gathered the following evening. He burned some sage and some cedar on some hot coals scooped from the wood stove with the ash shovel. He had us all bathe in the fragrant smoke in a sort of purification. He added more herbs as we continued. A piece of the dying woman's jewelry was given to Dennison to help him focus in on her. As he held the jewelry, he began to describe what he "saw." "Did she ever have a horse? I see a young woman and a horse she used to love to ride." He went on to describe a woman he had never seen and a vivid scene of her with the horse. Everyone was amazed at his accuracy, since he had never met this woman, nor her son and his wife. After this, he asked each one who knew the woman to describe something in particular about her. While she was vividly in everyone's mind, we then all joined hands in a circle and prayed and sent her energy for her soul to use as it saw fit. It was a very moving ceremony, and everyone left saying how nice it would be to get together like this and share love and prayers more often.

A few days later, we ran into the son and his wife. They told Dennison they had talked to their Mom the day following our ceremony. She told them of a strange light that had appeared outside her bedroom window and hovered for several minutes the night before. They wondered if Dennison knew what it could have been and if he had anything to do with it. He had to tell them he had no idea what it was.

I would like to think we all had something to do with it, for it brought her great comfort. It would be a perfect way to end the year.

Odds and Ends

JANUARY 1989

THE FIRST TWO MONTHS OF 1989 found us agonizing over whether Dennison should quit his job with the paper mill and go into art and silversmithing full time, or not. He hated his job, and it was hard for me to see him come home exhausted, literally covered with the white, powdered lime from the kiln. It was a miserable, hot, and dangerous job in the caustics department, and it was slowly killing him. On the other hand, he had worked at the mill for nearly eighteen years. Early retirement was not that far away, and he knew he could tough it out if he had to. Financially, we were no further ahead than we had been a year earlier. Quitting was a major decision. Could we make a living if we devoted all our time to art and jewelry making? It represented the unknown.

We didn't realize it at the time, but our lives were taking a turn into a whole new way of living and thinking.

Much of the information Dennison received now was more of a personal nature. Many were teachings on healing techniques, such as the use of crystals and various stones and the use of vibration and tones to aid in healing. He was told how to sense energy and how to call on and send healing with his hands. Afterward, he would try doing the things he had been told about, on me, and it was amazing what he could do.

The first time he used crystals on me, I felt an immediate change, as if I had taken a tranquilizer. When he used his hands on me, they grew very hot, as if he had been holding them over a stove.

One Friday afternoon, I began to feel the onset of a dreaded bladder infection. Money was a major consideration, so I didn't even attempt to call a doctor, determined to beat it by drinking cranberry juice. By late evening I was in so much misery that I couldn't sleep. It would be Monday before I could see the doctor, and I was beginning to feel frantic. Dennison offered to try to help me. I was more than willing, so he set to work, using first some stones, then his hands. Miraculously, within minutes I could feel the cramping spasms beginning to subside. After he finished, he went outside and returned moments later with a container filled with juniper berries from a tree in our yard. He prepared a tea from these and had me drink several cups of it throughout the rest of the evening. By the next morning, I felt great. I used to have frequent bladder infections, but since that time I haven't had another.

I told Elaine and a few other friends about what happened and how he used the stones and his hands. It wasn't long before they were coming to him, wanting him to try to help them with small complaints. Word of mouth spread, and before we knew it there were several people coming to him on a regular basis, because he could make them feel better with his prayers and his inner guidance.

He was told that illness begins in the mind before it manifests in the body. To treat the body, he must also treat the mind. He began to find as he worked on people that he would sense or see certain things or incidents, which he would ask them about. By this process, he would get to the heart of their problem and be able to work on the cause as well as the problem.

Over and over he would marvel at what was taking place, not fully understanding how it was happening or why he was being called to do it. It was obvious to me that he was being trained and guided from the "other side."

There were also a few experiences which fit no category.

One evening in January, he was working graveyard, so he decided to take a couple of hours' nap before leaving for work. I decided to lie down with him. After a few minutes, he asked, "When you were a little girl, did you ever run and run in the dark?" It was such a bizarre question. I searched my mind, trying to think of what he could be referring to. I finally said, "I can't recall anything; why do you ask?" He said, "I was just going to sleep, and I saw you as a little girl running and running in the dark. I think you were hiding or something. You were lying in some bushes, out of breath and laughing." Suddenly my mind went back to wonderful, warm summer nights as a child, when my parents and some neighbors would sit on the front porch and talk. The kids in the neighborhood would gather and play a version of hide-and-seek, which we called spooky-spooky.

Then he asked, "Did your family ever own an old green Chevy? I see a woman standing beside an old green Chevy, holding a baby. I think it's your mother. She has blond hair, and it's kind of long and curled under. She is wearing a green skirt and jacket." Again I had to probe my early memories. He continued, "I think you had a puppy, and it got run over or something." Once again I was transported back into my early childhood, when my dog went chasing a school bus and was indeed run over and killed. My mother was going to a funeral and was getting ready to take me and my baby brother to a sitter. I was devastated, and as she held me and dried my tears, I got her white silk blouse dirty with my dusty hands and tears. Over and over again, Dennison came up with other obscure incidents from my past—things he could not possibly have known, things forgotten even by me. He said he saw scenes come before his eyes, much like movie sequences. For some unknown reason, the incident left me in tears. I felt almost as if I had actually gone back in time and relived the past. Old emotions, long forgotten, surfaced later after he left for work, and my night was filled with half-remembered dreams. I suspect I needed to go back and get in touch with my inner child.

Another incident happened on January 11, again after going to bed. At first, Dennison began to speak in a sort of mumbling whisper, as if talking in his sleep. I asked, "Did you say something, Babe?" For a moment there was silence, then he began to speak again a little louder, but it was in a strange language, not Navajo. It sounded a little like Spanish, but no familiar words. I asked, "Lovey, are you awake?" He continued to speak in the strange language, seemingly saying the same phrases over and over. I was beginning to feel frustrated and a little irritated. I waited a little while, then said, "I can't understand a word you are saying. Please speak in English, if you have something to say." He was silent for a little while, then spoke normally: "Is Linda taking medication of some kind?" I replied, "I don't know. I don't think so though." He went on to ask, "Did she tell you she went to the doctor?" This came as news to me, and to be honest, I highly doubted it. I told him, "I just talked to her earlier this evening, and she didn't mention it." Linda was my closest friend, and we had shared all our frustrations, dreams, and troubles, on a very regular basis. Dennison insisted, "I just saw her going to a doctor, and then I saw her taking a pinkish pill. A voice told me to tell her not to take any more; they would do her serious harm. They said it was urgent she be told." I asked why he had been speaking in that strange language, and he said he didn't know; it just started coming out. He felt it was a doctor of some sort "on the other side."

The next morning I called Linda at work and related the strange events. She was silent for a long time. Then she told me she had indeed gone to the doctor the day before, not even telling her husband. Her teenage son was having some serious problems, and her husband, the boy's stepfather, was having trouble dealing with some of the situations. In turn, he was putting pressure on her to control the boy. Between the two of them and the pressures of her job, she was at her wits' end and felt she was "losing it." She had then gone to the doctor, hoping to get something to help with the stress, and he had given her a prescription for some antidepressants, and yes, they were pinkish.

On January 22, we were invited to Elaine's to attend a get-together with some friends. She wanted to introduce us to a man calling himself a "New Age Preacher." This man was new to the area and in hopes of starting some sort of a church. Dennison wasn't at all interested in going, so I was trying to convince him that it wouldn't hurt. It wasn't that I was interested in the church, but I liked Elaine and didn't want to appear we were being judgmental. I was also curious to know what a New Age Preacher was all about. As we talked, Dennison heard a voice in his head say, "You must not ally yourself to any one way of thinking. You are not ready yet. A mind can easily be misled. The light will be shown again. The Force will be given out again to those who are chosen. The time is yet to come."

We didn't go to meet the preacher, and it wasn't long until he moved on to a more receptive community.

A Leap of Faith
FEBRUARY 1989

It was now February 7, and we were still trying to make up our minds as to whether Dennison should quit his job at the paper mill and pursue his art and jewelry full time. Each day he so hated going into work, but he had support payments to make from his previous marriage, and I had my oldest son living with us. It was a big gamble to try it on our own, and we had no back up. We had tried to save during the past year, but it seemed something always came up to take it.

The night before, he had a very lengthy dream of a basketball player. At one point during the dream, the basketball player said to him, "I'll show you how to shoot the ball." He then took his stance, licked the fingers of his right hand, and in an elaborate series of moves, got ready to shoot the ball. He stopped and turned to Dennison and said, "Even with all that, the best sometimes miss. But you never know until you shoot." The next morning, Dennison went to work and gave his notice. We had $60.00 to our name. It was a great leap of faith, and we were terrified.

Lessons
FEBRUARY 1989

THE FOLLOWING EVENING we were both tired and went to bed early. Our friend Elaine was thinking of carrying a new line of hypnosis tapes to help lose weight, quit smoking, relieve stress, etc. She wanted us to listen to a demo and give her our opinion, so I decided to put it on. Neither of us were really concentrating on the content, but instead we lay there discussing our doubts and fears and hopes for the future. A few minutes later, Dennison turned over to go to sleep, and I turned off the tape midway through it.

Soon his breathing was regular, and he seemed to be asleep. I lay there worrying for us both. Suddenly, he began speaking. "The act of creating is a meditation. When you create, you are at one with the Creator. A person can get in touch with his inner self, find himself, through creativity.

"Creativity is like a yeast; the more you do it, the more you want to do it, and the more ideas you have. The more you create, the more you grow."

After saying this, he was silent and soon was snoring lightly. I didn't try to wake him up, but in the morning I asked if he remembered saying it. He had absolutely no recollection of it. I wondered if he was under hypnosis or asleep when he came up with this? It seemed too profound to have come from a dream state.

After Dennison quit his job, our lives began to take on a magical quality. Our first step was to design several unique pieces of jewelry, much of it crystal with a Native American flair. We took these to Sedona and sold out completely on our first trip. We reinvested most of our money into more supplies and had orders waiting to be filled. We were often up until 2:00 or 3:00 a.m. working on jewelry.

With Dennison home all day working, the small trailer we had been living in became too small. We knew we had to find a larger place to live, preferably a house with a workshop or a garage. So far, we had been working in our small living room/kitchen. However, our finances were stretched to their limit, and a larger house would mean more money for rent.

While standing in line at the post office, I overheard a woman telling the post mistress she was looking for someone reliable to rent her home and would be willing to rent it cheap, if only she could find good renters. I interrupted the conversation to ask more about the house, and before the end of the day I had rented her beautiful, large, two-bedroom house with a garage/workshop. The house was unfurnished, but she was willing to rent it to us for the same rent we were currently paying. I was thrilled with the home and was more than ready to sleep on the floor, if I needed to.

The next day I called our landlord to give him a month's notice. He said, "You know, I think I will rent this place unfurnished from now on; it's too hard to find good renters who will take care of the furniture. Could you use it? You've been such good renters, I would be willing to just let you have it, if you want it. Go on and take all the furniture in the trailer, as well as the washing machine in the laundry shed and the bar-b-que grill and picnic table. In fact, I have an extra twin bed and dresser in my garage I'd like to get rid of, if you want to come over and get those, too."

It felt like we were being taken care of by some invisible force, and we were in great wonder of it.

Meditations and Visions of the Future
APRIL 1989

BY LATE APRIL, we had settled into a busy routine of making jewelry, going on a selling trip somewhere, hopefully selling, paying a few bills, buying new supplies, and doing it all over again. It was very exhausting, and the wolves were always at the door. We never knew from day to day if we would have any money for bills or not. Fear and determination kept us going. Mostly because we felt so lost and adrift with no guidance, we began to meditate and pray, hoping for something to point us in the right direction. On one hand, we seemed so taken care of physically, but on the other hand, financially we were barely hanging on, without a clue how to proceed.

We had been meditating every morning for several weeks, and Dennison often "received" very interesting information, though never any advice on how to relieve our financial burdens, nor a direction to move in. At first, I didn't keep notes on it, because I felt like I was too busy with other things to keep up with writing the notes, so I just let it go. Then, for some reason I became uncomfortable with this attitude, so I resumed taking notes. That day, he saw the following:

"I saw a staircase, and I began to climb it. As I stepped on each step, it would light up with a number. Soon I reached a room. It was fairly large and decorated real fancy, all in red. In the center was a platform with a beautiful throne on it. It was covered in red velvet and was made of gold and set with red jewels. I crossed this room to another staircase and began going up again to another room. There were seven rooms in all and seven thrones, each a different color, like orange and green and blue and purple. At the end of the last staircase was a huge, golden, carved door. I opened it and was met by a bearded man wearing a long white robe and some sort of a headdress. His hands were outstretched, palms up in welcome. There were several other robed figures standing behind this man on a balcony. They were all looking over the railing. So I went over and looked down over the railing to see what they were looking at. I could see the Earth far below, and I could see people going about their daily lives. I asked what they were looking at, and they told me, *'We are watching Mankind and waiting for them to open their minds, so we can work with them.'* My guide then took me to another level, where there was a huge room full of

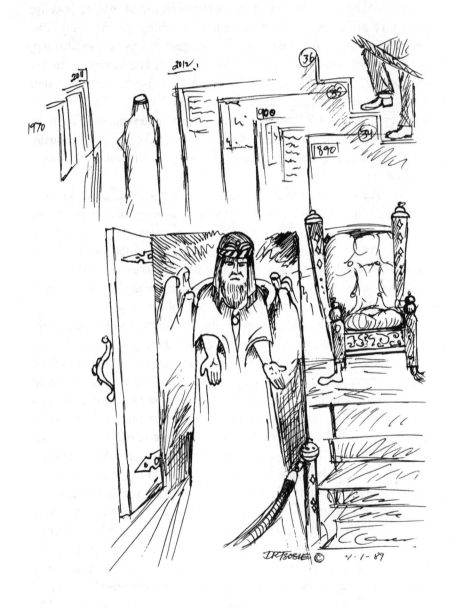

Watching Over Mankind

shelves. On these shelves were large volumes of books; each volume had a different year written on it. My guide said, *'This is everything that has happened on Earth since the beginning of Mankind; anything you want to know is here.'* I noticed the volumes only went to the year 2012. I asked, 'Is there any more after 2012?' His reply was, *'That depends on Mankind.'* The guide then said, *'I have to go now, but you can come here any time you want to know something.'"*

The following day, as he entered meditation, Dennison asked again to return to the place he had been yesterday. After meditating, he felt the need to write the experience.

4-2-89

On this meditation, the interesting part was a lady that I met at the doorway. As I opened the door, there was a pretty lady in a light blue veil with her hair wrapped in a bun on top of her head, with pins in it and a very clear, see-through shawl over that part of her hair.

She said, "How are you? Come and follow me. The question you have in your mind is down this corridor on the next level, come." I followed her as we went down these glass stairs. At the bottom was a glass floor. There were lots of people wandering around, but it seemed like they paid no mind to our presence as we went on by into a very large building with a high ceiling. There was lots of information on the shelves which surrounded us. I saw large volumes and words that I couldn't recognize. So I told her, "I am looking to find out what happened in the year of 2012; does it exist yet?" She said, "It may happen or not happen, depending on what people like you do." I didn't really know what she meant, but as she was talking, one wall became a screen, and she said, "This may or may not come about, so watch very carefully, my son, and think in your mind how this could happen and how you could help to prevent it."

The screen divided in half; on one side was the earth as it is now, on the other side was what may happen later. One part was dry and burned, with smoke and volcanoes, empty and desolate. The only life I saw was people flying in some type of hovercraft, flying around looking for something. It looked very sad. I'd never seen anything like it. I had never considered it could be possible. What happened to our people, to

A Guide to the Future

mankind?! She said, "This can be avoided, if people will change their way of living. You will meet more people like yourself, who will be called Earth Keepers. They will help you, and later, more will be open to what you have to say. Things can change if people will see what is happening and what is going to happen."

Then I just turned away and left, because I had seen enough of what can't be possible.

Now I wonder what are Earth Keepers? Am I supposed to be one of them? What is their job? Are they just people like us that care? Do we need to get stronger? I don't think I can do anything that would change things that much.

A Troubling Dream

JUNE 1989

TWO MONTHS LATER, on June 20, 1989, I recorded a particularly vivid and unusual dream of Dennison's:

"I was dreaming I was on like a sort of a flat boat, except it was flying. You know, like a space-age machine that can hover above the ground while you sit on it. I was looking down, and the whole area was devastated. It was like a horrible thing had happened. There were charred bits of wood and twisted metal and things smoking and smoldering. I was with some aliens; we were looking for survivors, I think.

"I felt terrible inside, and I don't like to even think about it. Even now I hurt inside, like it really happened."

A Lesson in Automatic Writing

AUGUST 1989

THE NEXT SIGNIFICANT EVENT happened on August 17. Dennison had been working on jewelry all day. He does a lot of fine cutting with a small saw to create many of his jewelry designs; it is very tiring on the eyes. He was sitting on the sofa with his eyes closed, resting them and listening to the evening news on the TV. He said he suddenly saw a little old man with a long white beard, much like the old man (leprechaun) he saw previously. This fellow was sitting on a stone wall with a tablet of paper in his hand, making circles with a pencil on the pad. A voice said, *"Go ahead and try it, and see what happens."*

Dennison felt compelled to get up and get a piece of paper and do as he was shown. As he began to make large circles, he felt as if something or someone was guiding his hand. At first he resisted, then he just relaxed and let it happen. He watched in amazement as the following was scrawled across the paper.

There you are.
What you may
not know is very hard,
hard for you to understand.
You are very afraid to make
a move in your new world,
but do not be afraid. You must
understand people need to know
what you have to offer and
you must love them all.

He got up off the sofa and handed me the scrawled message. We both were puzzled over what it might mean. Perhaps "they" were trying to comfort him in a way, because he was still resisting what was happening to him.

Teachings About Mother Earth and Feminine Energy
AUGUST 1989

THE NEXT DAY, August 18, Dennison was working in his shop. A buzzing sound began to intrude itself into his consciousness. At first he thought it was the fluorescent lights; then he thought perhaps it was the radio. Being mainly occupied with his work, he let it go and continued working. Suddenly, he felt a tap on his shoulder and he looked up, then turned completely around. No one was there. At this point he heard a voice in his head say, *"Get a pencil and paper and jot some of this down."*

"There is cosmic energy that is creating much now in both the human and the animal world. It is affecting all walks of life. You can see it happening now. It began in 1988 and increases in 1989, continuing into the end of the century. The causes are very understandable to those who are in harmony with Mother Earth.

"Mother Earth, as you know, is a living organism, just like you. She loves, She feels, She senses, and She hurts. She is trying to heal Herself now. This generation is being affected by this. Many people are being forced to make changes in their personal lives, especially in their relationships. Those who are not afraid to grow spiritually will understand and be able to adapt. Those who don't grow spiritually will find their lives aren't working, and unless they seek their spiritual selves, their lives will continue not to work until they self-destruct.

"As Mother Earth heals and grows strong again, the ill shall become well and the weak shall grow strong. Each in its own way shall be given new life; just seek it out. Earth energy is feminine energy. As the feminine energies are increased, women and especially Mothers will be affected, so please make them aware that it is just to make them grow and be strong with Mother Earth. Many Mothers will become assertive, because they want recognition and validation of their worth.

"Mother Earth provides for all of you; use it to fill your needs, but when you take, you must give back.

"All knowledge is available to mankind, if he would just open up to it, but first he must reconnect with Mother Earth and become more spiritual within. Realize he is One with all things. Psychic ability is just being spiritually connected. There is a lot of psychic energy available now, but many misinterpret it and misuse it.

"There are going to be some earth changes to come. Many people will be afraid, because they don't know what's happening. If the time comes and it's necessary, people will be shown safe places to go ahead of time. There is no need to fear.

"Mother Earth is using all available energy to heal herself. This is partly what is causing the earth changes. A balance must be regained. Mankind is being given a chance to heal himself. You are being forced to change, because the energies are changing around you. Women are changing, taking charge of their lives, healing themselves, as Mother

Earth is healing Herself. Their female energy is being opened up, because women are instinctively in harmony with Mother Earth. This is causing stress in many relationships, as women who now feel empty, unfulfilled, invalid, and without purpose will begin to feel a need to get in touch with their feminine self and with Mother Earth. They will become more assertive as they reclaim their 'power.'

"Even the female animals are changing—their behavior, their breeding habits, their migrating habits. The water too shall change. Mother Earth needs water for Herself and for Her cleansing. She is calling for moisture, and the Universe will give it to her. There will be a time of imbalance, droughts where there once was moisture, floods where there were droughts. Eventually a balance will be found. Unneeded things will be forced to the surface and discarded.

"Spiritual energy is primarily feminine energy. Mankind has been dominated by male energy; society is male oriented. You all have both male and female inside you. This should be in balance. Many men view the female as being silly, weak, erratic, and emotional. They deny any feminine aspects of themselves and put down feminine qualities in women as well. If such men begin to open to their spiritual self, the feminine self seeks a balance. As they become more sensitive and begin to feel this feminine aspect of themselves, they will fear they are becoming weak and overly sensitive, losing control of themselves and their physical world. They are quick to shut off this feminine energy and retreat back into their old masculine self, stopping their spiritual growth.

"The best thing Mankind can do is love. Love each other and love Mother Earth. She needs all this energy she can get. That's why you are needed now, to gather the people together who are willing to understand. Show them how to get in touch with their Mother, how to love and share with each other. Separately you are weak; together you are strong."

As we discussed what he had written, Dennison expressed, "Why am I getting all of this? Where does it really come from? I never in my life thought like this. It's like my mind has a mind of its own. It's like it's going somewhere I don't even know, and I'm being dragged along, even if I don't want to go."

An Introduction to Joseph Campbell
AUGUST 1989

LATER IN THE EVENING, AS I WAS READING, Dennison said, "It seems like my mind is out there flying. There's so much information to know. For instance, do you know why teenagers are the way they are nowadays?" I replied absently, "No, why?" (My mind was still on my reading.) He went on to say, "In the old days there were myths, like the Greeks had. Legends, which were teachings about life." Now he had my full attention. I knew right away these were not his own thoughts, and I asked him to wait as I found a note pad. He continued, "There were initiations from childhood into adulthood. You knew when you were there. For instance, in the past, a baby went from diapers of infancy into shorts of childhood, and then into knee pants until he was an adult, when he could wear long pants or a suit and tie. He was then considered a man, and he was let in on the secrets of being a man. (At this point I asked him to try and slow down, so I could be sure I was getting everything.) In other societies, there were initiations and rituals. A boy was circumcised at a certain age, or there was some other ceremony to test him and bring him into manhood. There were secrets that men shared. The same was true for girls, in another sense. When her period began, she had a ceremony to welcome her into womanhood. She changed how she wore her hair, how she dressed, etc. Now there are no standards for dress. Kids choose what they want to wear. There is no line between childhood and adulthood. There are no initiations, no rituals recognized by society. They have no boundaries, no way to compare. That's why they turn to drugs. In that state they 'fly.' They find a sense of something greater than themselves. The need for mysticism is in a sense satisfied. They create their own rituals, their own brotherhoods, in the form of street gangs, creating their own initiations into manhood." (This stuff was very profound and unlike things he had gotten before. I had to keep reminding him to slow down, so I could capture it all both in my mind and on paper.)

Dennison paused, as if gathering more information, then continued, "Marriage is more than a simple love affair. It is an ordeal. A sacrifice of the ego for the sake of the relationship, where the two become one.

"If you see your lives together simply through your relationship with your children and remain together for them, you are fooling yourself.

After they leave home, you will go apart, for there is no spiritual bond to hold you together, because you interpreted the union through the child.

"Marriage is a sharing of oneself, a harmonizing of one's mind and actions with the other's. Recognizing and experiencing that they are one. Seeing one's partner as a part of one's self. Knowing that a true partner is someone to grow with. In the end, both have spiritual growth.

"The Marriage Ceremony has lost its force. Now you can just stand in front of a judge and in ten minutes get married. In some societies, the Marriage Ceremony lasts for three days. The couple is glued together!"

After another pause, Dennison continued, "I was thinking about the movie, *Star Wars*. You know, it was really about Mankind and the danger of losing one's humanity to technology. Man is just a number, a part of a whole, run by inhuman, unfeeling machines. Luke Skywalker represented the part of ourselves we are in danger of losing. Darth Vader represents technology and the danger mankind runs in losing himself to technology. He is a robot; his human self is stunted. When his mask is removed, you see a man who has not developed as a human individual."

Again Dennison paused. I remarked, "Man, this stuff sounds like something out of a college thesis. I can hardly believe you are saying it. What you were just saying about *Star Wars;* I never really looked at it like that, but I can see how it could be what George Lucas was trying to say. I wonder where this is all coming from?" He said, "Just a minute, let me go see. . . . The ideas came from two books, one was *The Masks of God* and the other was. . . . I can't quite get it. . . . I can't quite get it. . . . It's not important; George Lucas just combined the concepts used in those two books."

He continued, "You know, the power of illness and the power of wellness are equal. If you are ill and you say, 'I want to get better,' you will. But if you follow that by saying, 'I am really sick right now,' you will have just canceled the positive statement of wanting to be well. The energy forces are the same and equal in strength. If you say, 'I want to be well; I am getting well,' and never say or think, 'I feel bad; I am sick again,' you will get well. Illness is caused by a *belief* in illness and wellness is a *belief* in wellness. The same is true of old age. *Believe* you are growing old, and you will begin to act and feel accordingly. This is also true about wealth. It takes as much energy to be rich as it does to be poor. Money is simply a form of energy that has been manifested in the form of money."

Dennison took a deep breath and stretched, and the receiving of information was over. Within moments he was deeply asleep.

Two days later, on August 20, we went to visit my Mom. We were folding up the covers on the sofa bed, where we had just spent the night. Out of the clear blue, Dennison said, "Remember the other night, I was getting that stuff about *Star Wars,* and you asked where the information came from, and I told you one of the books, but couldn't get the name of the other? Something just came to me. The other book was called *Hero with a Thousand Faces.* " I asked if he knew the author, but he said he couldn't get a name. I made a note of both book names and put it in my purse, intending to check on whether such books existed the next time we were in a book store—especially after finding *The Mayan Factor* that way last year.

Another month passed before I had a chance to look for either of the books. We were at a New Age bookstore in Scottsdale, which had just recently opened, selling jewelry. I noticed they had a large book listing all available books by title and author. I asked to use the book; then I got the piece of paper out of my purse where I had written the names of the books Dennison had mentioned. I first looked for *The Masks of God,* and within a few moments I had found a book with that title listed, written by a man named Joseph Campbell. I was very excited by this discovery and tried to get Dennison's attention, but he was talking to the manager. So I looked up *Hero with a Thousand Faces* and found a book with that title too, by the same author! I was really impressed by this time, so I interrupted Dennison and quietly tried telling him what I found. He just said, "Pretty neat," then went on with his conversation. When I got my chance, I asked the manager if they had either of the books. He said "No," but referred me to a new book they had just gotten in by the same author entitled *The Power of Myth.* We looked at the book, and Dennison opened it up immediately to a page that had a picture of Darth Vader on it. I scanned the page and found it carried much of the message Dennison had gotten the month before. As we flipped through the book, I kept coming across other things which sounded similar to what Dennison had gotten. The manager then told us there had been a series on PBS conducted by Bill Moyers regarding the things covered in the book. He added that there were video and audio cassettes of the series available, and he had them on order. At this point I was mainly interested in the book and ended up trading jewelry for it.

When we returned home, I got out the notes I had taken the month before and began comparing them to the book. I found amazing similarities and even verbatim passages. Much of the book reflects the same information Dennison had gotten. Talk about impressed—I was blown away!

We do not get PBS; in fact, we are living in a place where cable is not available, and we receive only one TV channel, NBC. Please remember Dennison doesn't read much, and certainly not books like Joseph Campbell's. In fact, we later received the videos as a gift, because he couldn't read the book. Even with the videos, I was constantly having to explain parts of them. We live in a rather isolated area and don't have ready access to current movies, books, etc. Up until this time, neither of us had ever even heard of Joseph Campbell.

Since the above incident, I have come to realize how very important these books and others by Joseph Campbell have been to our education, which we seem to be receiving.

The Roswell Incident
NOVEMBER 1989

ONE NIGHT, WHILE VISITING A FRIEND, we watched a program on TV entitled "Unsolved Mysteries." This particular program dealt with an alleged UFO crash in Roswell, New Mexico during the 1940s. The evidence presented was pretty convincing that our government was covering up the incident. As we drove home, we pondered the implications and why the government would cover up such a thing. It just didn't seem logical that they would or could keep such a secret for so long. There was always someone, somewhere, who would expose the truth. Look what happened to Nixon.

The next morning, Dennison came out of meditation and asked for a pencil and some paper. He wrote furiously for awhile, then handed me a pretty garbled story. At first, I could make neither head nor tails of what he or "they" were trying to convey. After many questions, the following story emerged:

After he entered meditation, Dennison had asked a question about the validity of the previous night's TV program and what really had happened.

"After a couple of minutes," he said," I could sense someone close to me; then I saw a dark figure walking in circles around me as I lay on the floor. Then I saw this bright blue light with two yellow spots flashing in the center. The light said, *'Forty of your human life years have passed since we touched your earth plane with our ship. This ship crashed while trying to avoid hitting one of your earth vehicles. When we came to recover the shells of our people, we found your government had the shells and would not release them to us. We contacted certain people within the government and made an agreement to let them study our people and technology for a time, in exchange for certain favors.'"*

At this point I questioned Dennison about what sort of favors were exchanged and what sort of technology was gained, and who in the government was contacted etc. He said, "I had impressions and also saw where information was given on traveling forward and backward in time, technology way beyond what we had at the time. That an agreement was made where these beings and some of our government and our military actually built hidden, underground facilities where some of this technology is put into use and experimented with, for military purposes. In return, our government gave permission to them to take (abduct) people for certain tests. Our president as well as high ranking military officials were involved."

This sounded too incredible, and my first reaction was to reject it as some of the far-out fringe, UFO fear-based stories. I wondered why such a thing would come through Dennison. To be sure, in my first drafts of the typewritten form of my notes, I did not include this part for fear of turning others off. Only my knowing Dennison and his lack of knowledge in this area kept me open to hearing the rest.

"It is now time for your government to release the shells to us, but they have asked for more equipment and information from us first. So far we have not come to terms, so we cannot provide this." (Dennison said,

"I sense there is a man in the government with a white beard who is dealing with this. He has all the information on what has happened. The government is hiding him.")

"We have tried to contact many people, but they react with great fear. We cannot use them. There has been contact with other people of earth, but they cannot provide the information we need. Your government is like a machine for war. Anything they can't take apart or figure out is a threat to them, and they fear us. It is necessary to recover the shells, because there is a danger of their being made public. If mankind as a whole finds out and believes they are aliens in the classic sense, they, like your government, will fear us and see us as a threat. If that happens, we cannot help you later when it is needed. Mankind must grow spiritually before they can understand us and accept us. It is not time to come yet, but we may have to anyway. If we do, it will be in a human form." (I sense they are building shells or body suits to contain their energy forms, which are made of human genetic material and will look like humans.)

"There are some highly evolved earth people we are working with now, who may be able to help us to reconnect. Time will tell."

Later that evening, after we had gone to bed, Dennison started to get more information. He began by saying, "Something is telling me this whole area, from here to Payson, to Happy Jack, to Show Low, this higher ground was once a refuge. The refuge will be used again, if needed. You will find signs of people who lived here before. Many civilizations have found refuge here on higher ground." I told him I had more questions about the earlier information received during his meditation and asked if I could ask some questions. He replied, "Go ahead." I grabbed my notebook on the nightstand and began:

"What were the bodies recovered from the Roswell crash?"

"There was no form within the form. We are energy. We use shells like a rubber suit, to manifest on the earth plane."

"Why are you here, and what do you want?"

"We have always worked with and watched over man. A lot of other energies work with us. A lot are not needed yet."

"Are you the same as the Watchers we've talked to before?"

"Yes, we are Earth Keepers, Watchers."

"You say you are energy inhabiting a form; aren't we also energy inhabiting a human form?"

"You call it human form; we call it God's form. You are given a shell similar to the shells we use, but you were given other functions, nerves to feel, a heart, veins, an energy within a human body. Actually called an element that grows from one atom."

"Are we related to the Watchers?"

"You too are energies, but live within the human form and cannot leave until the shell dies."

"If you are energy, then why do you need space vehicles?"

"In order to pass through space and time, we've got to have a vehicle."

"Where are you from? Where do you live?"

"We are from the Source; we are of the Universe."

"Are other entities which people channel, like Lazaris, the same as you?"

"No, they are from the Astral plane; they are teachers, we are Watchers. We keep the earth and guide the progress of humanity."

"Much is spoken of the so-called earth changes; how much time do we have before they begin to take place?"

"As much as is needed. A space of time is given where you can grow. There will be time for spiritual growth before the changes come. The visions of earth changes are given to encourage people to change, to seek the spiritual. Time can be changed, too, if people want. It is in the thought, in the mind.

"If man doesn't change and grow, the earth changes will be brought to force growth. Only human minds will change.

"The earth changes, the volcanoes, droughts, etc., will happen slowly, over a period of time. They will be easy compared to what must come first. There will soon be some happenings to make people grow. Mostly in the economic and social systems. The governments, money systems, religions, all must fail, and mankind must learn to work together, to become one again. These will be the hardest to get through. If these don't change man enough, the bigger changes will come in, like wars and bigger wars. The big wars will change the climate, will change the atmosphere. The earth changes, the natural disasters, will be simply what's needed to help Mother Earth reclaim her own self."

"Will the wars be necessary?"

"It is hoped not, but the way it looks now, the earth must again be destroyed so the spiritual ways can be brought back again."

"What will happen to all the people who are destroyed with the earth changes?"

"The same as happens now when they die. Only spiritual people will hold together in one system. If they don't work together, they will be overpowered by uncivilized people fighting together. Foreign wars, big city riots, seem far away, but eventually they will come closer. That's when you'll need a refuge to go to. You can't live in the cities any more then. There will be shootings, riots, severe pollution, street gangs."

"What can we do now to prevent this?"

"Open people's minds like you are doing now. If you need help, a means will be there. Eventually people will come to you, after you've reached out far and wide.

"You are all being loved. When being loved, you earn it, too. It may be hard, but it is necessary. This road isn't easy.

"Stones are important. You'll know which ones. They'll come to you as they are needed. Symbols are very important. People will need different symbols. They'll be given to you.

"I must go now.

"The health you were worried about, look back at it as you were five years ago. In another five years look back again. You've grown."

Guidance and Teachings
DECEMBER 1989

IT WAS LATE IN THE EVENING ON DECEMBER 28, 1989. This was a particularly difficult time financially for us, now with Christmas over. No one was interested in buying until late spring or early summer for the tourist season. It is a slow time for everyone, particularly in these rural communities. I was lying in bed, wondering how we were ever going to pay our rent on the first of the month.

Some friends of ours in California wanted us to go visit them. They felt we could possibly sell to some of their acquaintances as well as to some shops there. Our problem was a lack of funds to even make the trip, not to mention the necessity of making several payments within the next two or three days. Our friends had offered to loan us some money, which we would pay back if we sold something there.

As was typical, Dennison lay there sleeping, and I lay there worrying. He sort of mumbled in his sleep, then said clearly, "The Watchers are here." I wasn't sure if he was dreaming or if he was actually speaking to me, so I waited a few moments and then asked, "The Watchers are here? What do you mean?" At first he was silent, and I figured he was just talking in his sleep, when he said, *"Do you have any questions?"* I took a deep breath and asked the first thing on my mind.

"Should we move from this area, maybe to a city like Tucson or Phoenix or Albuquerque, where we would have more opportunities to generate business?"

"You are needed here; there is much work to be done. You will be guided when the time is right to move."

"Well, things are getting pretty tight financially, and we aren't able to sell much jewelry or art work around here. We need to pay bills and eat too."

"You create your physical reality with your mind. The key is the mind. Remember, all matter is energy; the thoughts you have and the thoughts you send out are also energy."

"I understand this, but I guess I don't know exactly how to make it work."

"You must first clarify your intent."

"Would going to California next month be a good thing for us?"

"If you intend it to be, it will."

"If we go, we will have to borrow money from Rob and Jeannie. I guess I'm worried about making enough money to pay them back and still make it worth our while to go."

"Why do you worry about repaying Rob and Jeannie?"

"If we were unable to pay them back right away, I would feel terrible."

"Rob and Jeannie were guided to do this. Others will be guided to help in ways needed when it is time. Have no fear."

For some reason I felt like I was talking to an indulgent parent and more than a little foolish for all my selfish and trivial worries. At the same time, I felt a great relief, as if we were being very taken care of. I also felt we should be doing our part in return. We were now doing "gatherings" periodically, with some of our friends and their families, thanks to Elaine, but this didn't seem like much. I asked, "Are we doing what we should spiritually? Is Dennison carrying out what you intend for him to do?"

"Right now he is directing his energies toward the physical world of making a living, creating jewelry, paying bills. Be patient; he will become more spiritual when he is able to put aside his physical concerns."

"Is he doing what he should with his gatherings?"

"He is doing all right, but he is doing them by himself for the most part. We could do much to help him, if he would open up and let us come in."

"How should he go about this?"

"Meditate, open to receive guidance. Ask us in."

"Does he meditate enough?"

"We would enjoy talking to him more; we miss him. We would like more meditation, but he must want it too."

"Is there anything I need to know?"

"Is there a problem?"

"No. . . ."

"Do you have any more questions?"

It's funny how any other time I have many, many questions I'd love to ask, but now I could think of very little. At last I asked, "Dennison's first experience was with the so-called Record Keeper crystal. Was the experience produced by the crystal?"

"Yes, in a sense the stone facilitated the event. Certain stones were imprinted with information. That stone was meant for Dennison, to activate his mind."

"During his experience he saw a beautiful valley. He called it a hidden valley that exists now. Is there really such a place?"

"Yes, but not in your earth plane. Not in your vibration. It can be accessed from certain places on earth. It is called The Valley of All Knowing. When a person is ready, he can go there to learn."

"Are Watchers also what are sometimes called Masters of Wisdom?"

"We are called Watchers, Earth Keepers, Masters of Wisdom, Knowers, Seekers, Wise Teachers, Elders, many things."

"Do you become a Watcher after having incarnated enough times to have learned your lessons and evolved higher. . . ?"

"Some Watchers have incarnated. Many have not. The ones who incarnate, choose to do so to help Mankind progress in some way. Some are chosen to go to fulfill a certain purpose. Dennison was one who was chosen."

I felt a shock go through me at this revelation. "Dennison is a Watcher?!!"

"Yes. He is just beginning to awaken to his purpose."

"What is his purpose?"

"This he must grow into. He will be guided."

"Is his spirit a human soul, or is there any such thing as a difference in souls?"

"All are part of The All Knowing. Dennison's soul is not the same as a human soul; he is intermingled with the human soul."

"I don't think I really understand. When and how did this take place?"

"When the body was born, he entered into it with the human soul."

"I guess I still don't really understand exactly. Did he seem different to his family? Was he gifted?"

"Many in his family perceived he was gifted."

"Are there others like him?"

"Yes, there are many, many others incarnated at this time. Each with his own purpose.

"There is a stone, some stones with information, which will be coming into Dennison's life. He is tied to them, connected to them, and is receiving information from them now. Later, when the time is right, they will come forth. The information from them must be given to the world. You must keep better notes. It is very important to keep this information in order. Keep up with all that is given. Get your notes in order!

"Call him."

"What?"

"Call Dennison."

I said, "Dennison? . . . Dennison." He gave a deep sigh, stretched, and seemed to be just waking up. I asked him if he knew what had happened. He said, "I was sort of aware of some of it. Your voice seemed far away. . . ." I asked what he was experiencing, and he said, "I felt or saw the Watchers as a string of bright lights, all connected, yet separate. When they spoke, it was sort of like a group discussion; then one would give the answer, or else all of them would speak in unison. When the answer was given, I felt it go through me. I really don't remember very much. It feels just like I woke up from a dream."

A Lesson in Energy
JANUARY 1990

WE WENT TO A BIRTHDAY PARTY FOR A FRIEND ONE EVENING. His wife, who had been at Elaine's house last year when we prayed for her friend with cancer, asked Dennison to please do a small ceremony, a blessing of sorts, for her husband, before everyone went home. Dennison led us all in a prayer, and we each gave him our best wishes. It was simple and beautiful, and he was deeply touched.

Later, after we went home and were in bed, Dennison said, "Someone is telling me, *'A group of people that is of one mind, one thought, charged with emotion, can bring in an unlimited amount of energy. A thought charged with emotion carries the energy of your innermost being. If a circle of individuals share an emotion and allow it to flow through each individual to the next person, the circle's energy begins to rise in vibration. Great things can be accomplished with group energy in an emotion-charged meditation. You can use this for powerful healings, individual goals, peace, earth healing, etc. If anyone in the group has mixed emotions, doubts, or personal problems that are foremost in his mind, the energy will be decreased. You create your own physical reality with your mind. Remember, all matter is energy. To manifest what you want in your physical reality, you must first clarify your intent.'"*

A Strange Encounter
JANUARY 1990

ON JANUARY 16, AFTER COMING OUT OF MEDITATION, Dennison said he had seen blue swirling; then he saw a tablet with symbols written on the pages. Each page flipped over to reveal another page of symbols. He attempted to look closely at the symbols, trying to decipher their meaning, but was told, *"It's not important now; just go with it."* As each page turned, he felt himself go deeper and deeper into a trance. He felt paralyzed, and then he had no memory of the next few minutes. Later, as he struggled to come out of the meditation, he could see himself from behind, as if he were outside his body. Just for a brief moment, he glimpsed a man in a white robe exiting his body. Then, suddenly, he was back inside again and coming out of his meditation.

A Search for the Holy Grail
FEBRUARY 1990

IT WAS FEBRUARY 9, 1990. Neither of us had seen the latest Indiana Jones movie, *The Last Crusade,* so we rented the video for the evening.

I was doing some needlework and keeping an eye on the movie. Suddenly Dennison asked, "Where is Greece?" The scene in the movie was of Jones deciphering part of a stone tablet. I thought maybe I had missed something that was said about Greece. I replied, "I think it is below Italy. Why?" He stated matter-of-factly, "Somewhere over in Greece there is a stone tablet that's engraved. There is also a message engraved on the side of a mountain, and the sun is reflecting off it. You can only see it when the light hits it a certain way and only from a certain direction, I think north. The tablet is hidden there, but somehow it is also in another dimension or something. . . . I don't really understand."

Somewhat taken aback and a little confused, I asked, "Is this something you read or heard?" Impatiently, he said, "I'm there right now! I'm on the north side of Greece on a mountain, and I'm looking out across a valley with a stream and some hills. It's very green down there and very beautiful. I'm just looking down from this mountain and something says, *"Greece."* I see this stone tablet and the writing on the side of the cliff on this mountain I'm on. Is there a mountain named Tana?" I told him I surely didn't know, that I would need an atlas or something to look it up. He said, "I keep getting the name Tana." I asked if it could be the name Tanya? He paused and thought and said, "I don't know, maybe, but I think it is Tana. . . . Now I get Oro. . . . Maybe it's Oro or something . . . Tana . . . I don't know. I sense someone carried a message that far and couldn't go any farther, so he hid the tablet and etched the message in the cliff."

Since we were watching a movie about The Holy Grail, I asked if this had anything to do with the Holy Grail. He replied, "I don't know, maybe."

Puzzled, I made notes of what had transpired and finished watching the movie without incident. I tried asking questions later, but he seemed to remember little of what he had gotten. I was later to find this was the beginning of information which was to come in puzzling bits over a span of time and still continues to come periodically.

A Search for the Holy Grail

A few days later, on February 14, we stopped to visit some friends while on a selling trip. I noticed a World Atlas in their bookcase and took advantage of the opportunity to look up Greece and to see if I could find a mountain called Tana or Oro or Toro, or anything similar. I didn't find a Mountain called Tana, but did find the name Oro on several mountains in Greece. Next I looked in the glossary and discovered the word Oro meant mountain in Greek.

Later, when we were driving home, I told Dennison what I had found, and he replied by asking, "Is Babylon in Greece?" I told him, "No, I think it is in Egypt or Iraq or something; some place in the Middle East, anyway." He said to me, 'Funny, every time I think of that tablet, I get the word Babylon. Something is telling me there were two brothers who left Babylon with some sort of scripture or sacred writing or information; something sacred. One of them got as far as this mountain in Greece and could go no farther, so he wrote a message on the side of a cliff. I see a lion. Something to do with a lion. A guardian to a gateway of some sort or to something? . . .

The next evening we were at home. I was talking on the telephone to a girlfriend and Dennison was sketching and watching TV. As I hung up the phone, he came over and showed me some strange-looking writing, much like hieroglyphs. Below were some cartoon-looking figures on his sketch pad. I looked at him in puzzlement and asked, "What is it?" He replied, "I don't know, I just did it." I asked, "What on earth for?" and he replied, "I don't know. I just felt like someone took hold of my hand while I was sketching, and my hand started making circles at the top of the page. I was curious what was going on, so I just turned the page and waited to see what would happen. Then pretty soon my hand felt like someone was guiding it again, and I made this first line of symbols.

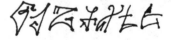

"Nothing happened for a little while, and I felt 'they' were waiting for me to recognize what it meant. Pretty soon my hand made the next line, but this time it was letters, only I still didn't know what it meant.

arimisha lui cardiie beliluz

"Then my hand made another line of symbols, and I couldn't figure it out either—

so my hand made another line of letters. This time I heard someone speaking in a language I didn't understand. The last word sounded like it was pronounced 'hee-nee.' I felt somehow I should know what it meant, and 'they' were impatient with me because I didn't remember.

ISHA RINDENTII BILLEHDII HUNII

"After a couple of minutes my hand started to draw these figures.

"Then I thought I'd better show it to you and see if you had any idea what it means."

I knew at this point that Dennison was getting some sort of message in symbol form, but I was not well versed in meanings of symbols and was at a loss as to what it could mean. It was frustrating that "they" didn't just come out and say what they wanted to convey. I see now that in trying to find possible meanings to the drawings, we were led down many paths, which opened the doors to learnings we might not have otherwise searched out.

I asked Dennison, "Did you have any sense what it was all about? Did 'they' explain anything, or did you get a sense what it was all about?"

Dennison was very still for a few minutes, as if having some sort of inner dialog; then he replied, "I sense it was a difference of opinion. A conflict over a belief. It started out small, but it grew as more and more people became involved. There was a sacred box with a treasure in it that was the center of the conflict. This box was taken and hidden away."

I asked if the boat on the river was showing this, and he replied, "Yes. It went from a place in the East to the north side of a mountain." I queried, " How do you know this?" and he drew:

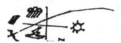

with the cloud symbol at the top representing the North, then the sun to represent the East, a bird to represent South, and a black rectangle to represent where the sun sets in the West. After he drew the direction symbols, he drew the shape of the door to the cave, but this time broken.

He said, "There was a hidden treasure, and the place was broken into, and it was taken away to the mountains, and later it was taken somewhere else." I asked what was in the "cave" that was stolen, and again he began to draw another series of pictures.

First he drew three tablets linked together. Below he drew a key, and above he drew a fancy, equal-armed cross. Above this, he drew a tie or ribbon-looking thing that was separated in the middle. He drew little arrows on either side of the separation, as if to call attention to it. Below these things, he drew four objects with numbers or symbols on them.

From there, he drew an arrow down to the river and drew an X. He drew another X below the boat and another X high on the mountain and another X farther away from the mountains, toward the Stonehenge-looking area.

I asked what the triangle within the triangle above the cart represented, and he drew little lines above it like energy or light coming from it and a + above it. I asked him what the + meant, and he said he felt it was sacred.

After this, I asked what the three tablets were that he had just drawn, and he drew two seated figures with three tablets in front of them. The one on the left had a symbol of a circle with a cross under it drawn on it, reminding me of an ankh. I asked him what the seated figures were, and he drew the head above them, which looks like a king with a crown, or maybe a bishop. He said, "I think they are high priests. The word Priest-Kings comes to my mind."

I was beginning to realize there was much more to this than I had first thought. I was getting side-tracked and complicating things with my questions, so I went back to the beginning and asked what the lion represented.

Dennison drew what looked like a country on a map, with water on three sides. It reminded me of Italy without the boot. Next he drew a lion's head above. I wasn't at all sure what it could represent, so he went on to draw a person who was holding a shield and a sword and wearing a rather Roman-looking helmet. On the other side of the lion, he drew a building with stairs up to it and pillars and some numerals on the front.

After this, he drew an arrow from the lion to the building and another from the lion to the person, as if to show they were in some way connected.

I asked what the dragon meant, hoping to get some clue to this puzzle.

Dennison drew a small island to one side of this country and a boat on the water.

He said he felt it sailed from somewhere else, where they were in conflict with the people represented by the lion, to this island. Still hoping for some clue to this thing, I asked what was in the box they were fighting over.

Below everything else he began to draw a hand, and below the hand he drew a cup. As he drew the cup, he began to breathe hard, almost a sob. He drew a liquid in the cup and a drop of perhaps blood coming from the palm of the hand. I immediately associated this with the Cup of Christ, or the Holy Grail. He continued to draw. Below the cup, he drew a maze-like stand holding up the cup.

To the right of the cup, he drew a triangle with an arrow pointing upward inside of it. Next to it he drew a square or diamond shape. Inside was another arrow with a circle below it. Then he drew an arrow connecting the two and said, " They are separated now, but they were once one, and they need to come together again."

After this, he drew a candle sort of leaning toward the drawings. Perhaps to shed light on the drawings?

Below, he drew what looked like a coiled piece of string or cord.

Then, once again, he drew a tie, only this time it was only partly separated.

Next, he drew a bottle with a cork in it and a tie around it.

Below that, he again drew a box, this time with the lid open. Then he drew an arrow toward the first box, the one he had drawn in the beginning.

The whole thing boggled my mind, and I couldn't seem to get hold of anything that had meaning to me. I felt I was going in circles, and I needed time to think and do a little research At this point, I wondered out loud who this information was coming from. Dennison turned the tablet to the next page and began drawing a face. When the face was finished, I asked if the person had a name and Dennison replied, "He calls himself Reshee or Resheed (phonetic spelling). I asked what he had to do with this story, and Dennison said, "He says, 'Abela, a brother.'" I tried asking more questions, but nothing was forthcoming.

The whole procedure had been incredible to watch. His hand moved smoothly, almost mechanically, stopping and pausing now and again. The sketch pad was rough newsprint, and the felt tip pen would sort of bleed into the fibers of the paper when he paused, creating a sort of dot to dot effect. The tip of the pen never left the paper except to begin a new figure.

I became obsessed. Like a good mystery it compelled me to try to find a solution to the cryptic message. The name "Gisor" was one of the first things I recognized. Several years earlier I had purchased and read the book *Holy Blood, Holy Grail,* by Michael Baignet, Richard Leigh, and Henry Lincoln. It was a complicated story that had meant little to me at the time, so I had given it to my mother. The book talked about the Knights Templar, and I remembered the name Gisor was an important name in the Order. I also noticed the ornate cross in the drawing looked something like a Templar cross.

I recognized the name "Cairo" and wondered if it was the name of the "city" or settlement that was drawn beside the river. I also wondered if the word "Reshep" written next to it might be actually Reshed or Resheed, the name given the face he had just drawn. I was also fairly sure this was some sort of story or combination of stories about the Holy Grail.

The first thing I did was to get the book, *Holy Blood, Holy Grail,* back from my mom and reread it. After doing so, I found Jean De Gisors was the first Independent Grand Master of the Knights Templar and lord of the fortress of Gisors in Normandy. I also read of a division which took place within the Order in 1188, when it split into two factions. This seemed to have been symbolically consummated by the cutting of a large ancient elm tree at Gisors. The reason for the event is shrouded in mystery. Could this be what the severed tie or ribbon in the drawing represented?

The Knights Templar were known to have spent much time in the Holy Lands when the Order was first formed. They had actually lived near the ruins of Solomon's Temple in Jerusalem, for several years. Some speculate that secret information, hidden knowledge as well as some treasure, was brought back to France and hidden away. The book concerns the legend of the Holy Grail and a secret society that has existed for twenty centuries. It talks about a line of Priest Kings in France who trace their lineage back to Judaic origin and ancient Egypt.

One chapter in particular caught my interest, where the authors talk of the Twelve Tribes of Israel and a conflict between the Tribe of Benjamin and the rest of the Israelites. In the wake of the conflict, most of the Benjamites went into exile. This exile supposedly took them to

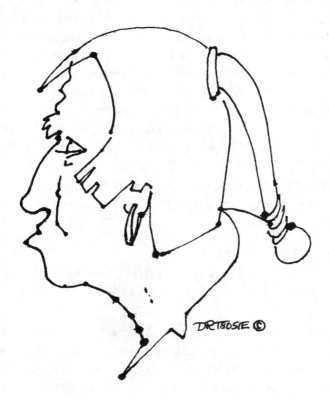

Resheed

Greece and the central Pelopponesus. I looked the Pelopponesus up in an Atlas and found them located on an island at the tip of Greece. The shape of the island and the main part of Greece extending down by the island looks very much like Dennison's "map" in his drawing.

The book was fascinating this time, and very informative. I highly recommend reading it. However, it probably raised as many or more questions than it answered, and the real meaning of the cryptic message was still very much a mystery.

A Spiritual Brother
FEBRUARY 1990

A FEW DAYS LATER, ON FEBRUARY 19, as we were eating breakfast, Dennison asked, "What is meant by a spiritual brother?" I replied, "I suppose it would be someone who has the same spiritual values or outlook as you do." Dennison continued, "Something tells me a spiritual brother is coming into our lives. I sense it doesn't have to be a male, just another person. I think they are from other countries; they aren't from here. . . . Yes, they aren't from America. I'm being told this person is being prepared now. They say I will know this person when I see him. There are four of us. We will eventually come together. I will know them when I see them. We're supposed to work together in the future, somehow.

"Now they are saying I'll be getting lots more information from now on. I need to start writing my thoughts or recording them. It is very important to do this."

Messages While Driving
MARCH 1990

ON MARCH 14, we were driving to Phoenix, nearing the outskirts of the city. It was nearly 11:00 p.m. Dennison reached over and turned off the radio. After a moment, he asked, "Have you ever heard of or read about Light People or People of the Light?" I replied that I thought so. He continued, "There's people called Light People who carry the flame of the Source. They come from the Source, and they are Keepers of the Torch. They will be coming into mankind's awareness soon. In fact they are already working through some people. They are here to teach healing with the hands. Greater gifts than are now given. Healers will work with light energy through their hands and will be able to do things you can't even imagine now."

By this time I had found some paper and a pen. In the dark, I began taking notes, only guessing where I was writing. Dennison continued, "Have you ever heard of Mutt People, or maybe it's Mud People? I think it must be Mud People, because they are associated with Mother Earth. They have greenish eyes, kind of strange eyes. They are coming to this plane to care for the earth, but no one knows who they really are. Most are not on this level yet; they are working on other levels. Both they and the Light People will be working through certain people who are pure in spirit. Channelers will soon begin talking about them, the true Channelers at least."

After a moment, he went on to ask, "What are Star Clemingers?" I replied I had no idea. He answered himself by saying, "They are people who commune with the stars. The stars talk to them. There's a lot of information given through the stars' energies. The stars speak, but few will listen." I mentioned the Star Gazers of the Navajo, virtually a lost art now. Dennison went on to ask, "Do you know the names of the stars in the Pleiades?" I told him I didn't, but felt it would be pretty easy to find out. He then said, "Keep an eye on the stars in the handle of the Little Dipper; from them will come a message for all mankind to see. The two end stars will be sent out to search. They will eventually come back together, and that will be a message to all mankind. That will be put out as a life line." Dennison was again asked if he knew the names of the stars in the Pleiades. He asked why he would know their names. He was told, *"You should know them by heart; you worked with them many times in the past. If you can name them in the proper order, communication can be established. You can also meditate with the morning star. It is very important you meditate with these stars. You've got to connect certain stars in order to communicate, and you need to know their names. You should know their names."*

By this time, we were well within the city traffic. Dennison was dividing his time between watching traffic, watching street signs, and getting information. Still the information kept coming. *"A time of change is being forced upon mankind. You are going to change yourselves. There will be changes in the social structure; that's beginning to happen now. Socioeconomic changes. Soon to follow will be problems with the earth's energy sources. Gas, water, oil . . . these resources will not be plentiful. That will be the first signs. There will be a lot of messages in the sky. Watch the skies for these messages, these warnings. There will be severe cold from the North. Dry, extreme cold. There will be droughts."*

I later asked him if it felt the same to get this information while driving as when he got it at home. He said, "Somewhat, but I feel a lot of pressure in my head. It feels heavy. The information seems to come in on several levels at once. There is a voice in my head as well as a 'knowing,' an expanded sense of what is being said. Then there seems to be something on a subconscious level that just comes up later."

We were on our trip home from Phoenix when once again Dennison began receiving more information.

"I see two lions on either side of a gate or door. Above the door are two keys crossed, and above the keys is a bird . . . a dove, I think. I feel like it is a temple or cathedral of some sort. I feel someone entered through the gateway and took something. Whoever was guarding the gateway lost the battle, and they entered and took everything. Some things had a lot of power. They don't understand how to use it.

"There were two brothers, I feel like, . . . who were involved in carrying some sacred information somewhere. . . .

"Someone took something from Stonehenge that was hidden there. It was taken and hidden somewhere else.

"None of this stuff makes any sense. They are saying a Mayan priest is the key to the whole thing. He had some tablets he buried somewhere. I don't know if it has to do with this other, but I feel somehow it does.

"Every time I think of the drawing, I see a man in a white robe, like a priest, shaking his finger and pointing at the lion and the dragon. They are the keys to understanding the drawing.

"What is *Allihoostipher* (phonetic spelling)? It is a name of some sort. A Lemurian Priest? . . . A Mayan Priest? . . . Is there a such thing as the Lanayan People? or the Winged People? the Butterfly People?"

At this point, Dennison was told, *"If you want to look back in time, a lot of this will make sense to you."* Dennison replied by saying, "How can I possibly look that stuff up?" The reply came, *"If you don't use your powers to the greatest extent and try to expand them, then why have them?"*

Time to Move Again
MARCH 1990

WE HAD BEEN IN OUR WONDERFUL HOME for just over a year, when the owner sold it and informed us we would have to move within the next six weeks. It was hard to go, because this place had suited our needs so well. I felt like my feet were dragging all the way.

Once again, money was a factor. Coming up with the required first and last months' rent and cleaning deposit were way out of our budget. Finally, we found a double-wide mobile home for rent. What was most appealing was the fact that it sat on a two-acre fenced lot in a secluded area, bounded on two sides by National Forest. The home itself was in desperate need of cleaning. I offered to clean the place if the owner would waive the cleaning deposit. I also asked if he would trade art work or jewelry for the last month's rent. He agreed, and we set to work.

Curiously, four years ago while Dennison and I were dating, we had looked at this place from the outside. At that time, it was for sale. We were going for a drive in the forest when I noticed the house and said to Dennison, "Wait a minute; would you mind backing up? I want to go back and look at that house." The reason I had him stop was because I recognized the back yard as a scene from a recurring dream I had been having for several years. In my dream was a cluster of rabbit cages, a chicken coop, a shed, and a tree house. These same buildings, even down to the tree house, were there in the backyard, looking very much as I had dreamed them. Now, four years later, we were going to be living there. Somehow it seemed prophetic.

More Automatic Writing
APRIL 1990

ON APRIL 22, I was packing some things, and Dennison was working on jewelry. He came into the house with the following written on a piece of paper. He said he had felt compelled to write it down.

"There's much talk about prophecy, and there comes a time when there will be people calling themselves prophets, returning angels, and guardians of time. These will be more misleading, and there will be much misunderstanding. You may yet cipher this out. In time you will know what this means.

"People should not react so harshly to this. Believe these were written and it has been said it would come to pass."

I was a little confused by the meaning and asked several questions to try to clarify this message. He said the feeling connected with the information was that there are hard times ahead. As a result, there will be many "leaders" and "prophets" who will arise, and frightened, confused people will easily be misled. In the future, we will come to understand what this means. We should not to be too alarmed by this, for we have been warned ahead of time, for it has been prophesied or written that it would come to pass.

Trade Embargoes
MAY 1990

IT WAS MAY 2, and we had retired for the night. I was reading, and Dennison had turned over to go to sleep. Suddenly he spoke and said, "Remember the Trade Embargoes?" I asked, "What??"

Dennison turned over and said, "Something just said, *'There's going to be Trade Embargoes. They will lead to shortages.'* Remember the Boston Tea Party and the trouble in the harbor?" I replied, "That was during the Revolutionary War; is that what you are talking about?" He said, "I don't know. They are just saying it to me. There's going to be something like that again soon. The Government is going to cause it, but this time I think it's going to be over oil. I saw some ships in a harbor firing at each other. I think there could be a gas shortage. People are going to be fighting over oil. I think it's going to happen pretty soon."

The Gulf War broke out later that same year. Was this message a reference to it?

To Heal the Earth, You Must First Heal Yourself
MAY 1990

AGAIN, A FEW NIGHTS LATER, ON MAY 10, we had just gone to bed, and Dennison was snoring lightly. He began to mumble, and I thought he was talking in his sleep. After a moment, he mumbled again. This time I said quietly, "Did you say something, Babe?" He replied, "I walked the streets of poverty at one time. I saw people who were hungry. I saw them die of starvation. I knew they put themselves there. I could take the poverty from them on the outside, but it must be taken from the inside before they can really get away from it. Their way of thinking must be changed first.

"People must learn to live again, but the thing that's stopping them is materialism. Love of material things separates families, neighbors, nations.

"People gather to heal Mother Earth's hurt, but they must heal themselves first, before they can heal the Earth. If they can heal themselves, the Earth could take care of Herself.

"They gather for Earth Day and leave tons of trash behind them. It's lip service. Their minds must be healed first. Work on the people first, and the rest will follow. When man learns to love himself, he will learn to love his Mother Earth."

A Vision of War
AUGUST 1990

IT WAS THE 18TH OF AUGUST, and summer was quickly slipping away. We had decided to go camping with another couple before our long winter season was upon us. It began raining shortly after we set up camp and continued the rest of the day and into the night. We ended up sleeping in our van. Sometime in the night, Dennison woke up, saying he heard a bell, like a church bell. I listened intently, but could hear nothing but the soft patter of rain. (We were far away from any civilization.) Later, he again woke up, saying he could clearly hear a woman's voice saying something to him, but he couldn't quite understand her. After lying awake for awhile, I looked at his watch and saw it was 4:30 a.m. The rain had stopped and the eastern sky was beginning to grow light. We decided to get up and take a walk to the top of a nearby hill and greet the dawn with corn pollen.

The air was sweet with the scent of rain and damp earth. Mist was gathering in the low places. We came upon a herd of deer and watched them for several minutes before continuing our walk.

After we reached the top of the hill, we offered our prayers and watched the sun bravely try to show itself through the clouds. We then sat on a wet log and meditated for awhile. Suddenly Dennison broke the stillness saying, "I see airplanes dropping bombs. I hear sirens and lots of noise, like a big battle is going on. . . . Now I see lots of black smoke and fires. It looks like a desert, and there's soldiers dropping like flies. They are dying for no reason."

It was after this that President Bush decided to get "tough" with Sadam, and the Gulf War followed.

The Watchers

SEPTEMBER 1990

IN JULY OF 1989, WHILE ON A SELLING TRIP, I picked up one of the free papers offered in some of the shops where we sell our jewelry. I like to pick them up to look for potential markets for our jewelry. Later on, at home, while glancing through the ads, I came across an ad for a UFO Conference to be held in Phoenix in September. Normally, I would have no desire whatsoever to go, since I considered them to be sort of a fringe element, attracting "weirdos" and "true believers." I considered ourselves to be neither.

What caught my attention was that the ad stated a woman named Betty Andreasson would be the keynote speaker during the opening evening banquet, and she would speak on her encounters with "The Watchers." I felt a sort of shock or thrill go through me as I read this. Could these beings possibly be the same "Watchers" Dennison was talking to? Years ago I had read "The Andreasson Affair," a story written by UFO researcher Raymond Fowler, about Betty Andreasson and her abduction experience. At the time, her experience didn't fit my beliefs about UFOs, but I had been impressed by the woman's sincerity. Something real and very strange had happened to her. Now it appeared she was coming out with more information, and I wanted very much to hear what she had to say.

I called the toll free number to inquire if a person could attend the evening banquet without attending the conference, and if so, how much. A recording told me it would be $25.00 per person. That meant $50.00 for the two of us. At that time, it was more than we could afford, so I wrote to the promoters of the conference and asked if they would forward a letter to Betty Andreasson. In my letter to Betty, I explained my husband had been having experiences with unseen entities calling them-selves "Watchers." We were very interested in knowing more about her experiences. I also explained we would likely not be able to attend the conference, but wanted to know if she would have a book or any forthcoming information on her experiences and if so, how could we obtain it.

It was now September, and the conference was only a week away. I had no response from Betty Andreasson and had no assurance she had even gotten my letter. A friend from San Diego was visiting her brother, who lived nearby, and so she was spending the day with us. She asked if Dennison had had any more experiences. (I had shared my journal with her the previous summer.) As I caught her up on the latest events, I found myself telling her about the UFO conference and the woman who was going to be speaking of her experiences with "The Watchers."

Excitedly she exclaimed, "Well, we have to go!" Reluctantly I explained, "As much as I'd love to go, we simply don't have the funds for the trip, the dinner, the motel, etc." She brushed this off and picked up the phone and called her husband and explained the situation.

Even though her husband is open-minded, he is also very logical and rational in his approach to things such as this. I fully expected he would laugh at our craziness and put a stop to her generous plans. Instead, he good-naturedly went along with her suggestion, saying he'd never experienced such a thing and it sounded like it could be fun. Within minutes, she had made reservations for the four of us.

Friday found Dennison and I in a crowded hotel lobby, waiting for our friends to catch up with us. We found a quiet corner in a hall outside the conference room, where a small table and a couple of stools had been set up. Since no one was around, we took advantage and sat down to wait.

A few minutes later, a young woman came to the table with a box of tickets. I asked her if they were the tickets for the dinner and lecture. She smiled and said, "Uh-huh." I had her search for our reservations, and as she looked, she asked, "How do you like the conference so far?" I explained, "We just got here a few minutes ago. We're here just to listen to Betty Andreasson speak." She smiled, saying, "Me too, mostly; she is a personal friend of mine. She's a very special lady." A few moments later she asked, "Is your husband Navajo?" I gave her a puzzled look and asked, "Yes, how did you know?" She smiled and asked, "Did you write a letter to Betty?" Even more surprised, I answered, "Yes, I did, last July." She said, "I think Betty would like to talk to you. She said a Navajo man had written her, and she was hoping he would be able to come. Let me go ask her if she wants to talk to you."

A couple of minutes later, she returned, saying Betty would very much like to talk to us. I felt I needed to wait for our friends to catch up with us, so Dennison went to talk with her. He returned just as the doors opened to the conference room for the dinner to begin. When he found us he said, "Betty and her husband invited us to sit at their table with them." But by the time we made it through the buffet line, we found someone else already sitting there.

Both Betty and her husband, Bob Luca, spoke after the dinner, and what they had to say was very interesting, but didn't really bring any light to what was happening with Dennison.

Later, Betty found us in the lobby and talked a little more to Dennison, interested in what he was experiencing. Over and over, we were interrupted with others wanting to talk with her. Finally, she asked if we would be coming to her lecture the following day. This was another

$40.00 each, and we simply didn't have the funds. Regretfully, we told her, we needed to return home and wouldn't be able to attend.

Afterward, we went to the motel room we shared with our friends, changed into our swim suits, and spent the rest of the evening enjoying the warm summer night out by the pool.

Early the next morning we said good-bye to our friends, and they went on to San Diego. We went back to the conference room to purchase a copy of Betty and Bob's lectures of the previous evening, before heading back home. While we were waiting in line, Betty found Dennison and generously offered us the opportunity to attend her lecture free of charge. Amazed at her perceptiveness, we gratefully accepted.

During the lecture, Betty played excerpts from her hypnosis sessions, where "The Watchers" broke in and spoke directly to those doing the hypnosis. It was riveting. By the end of the lecture, we felt there was a connection with the beings Betty had experienced and the voices Dennison was experiencing. The messages were remarkably similar.

We went home feeling amazed at how this had all come together with so little effort—almost as if it were "meant to happen." The result of talking to Betty and listening to her lecture gave Dennison a lot more confidence in his experiences. It also took a lot of the fear out of it, he didn't feel so alone. Betty's story of "The Watchers," by Raymond Fowler, came out several weeks later, but it was nearly a year before I was able to purchase it.

A Dream of the Little People
OCTOBER 1990

It was the morning of October 19. We had just gotten up and were having coffee, when Dennison asked, "What's a Chichila?" (phonetic spelling). I repeated the word and let it rattle around in my mind, trying to come up with a similar word with a meaning. I thought of a chinchilla and asked him if it could be what he was thinking of. He asked what a chinchilla was, so I explained it was a small furry animal, kind of like a mink, and was raised for its fur.

He laughed and said, "No, that's not it. I had a weird dream last night about some funny-looking people. They told me they were Chichilas or

The Little People

Cuchilas or something like that, but humans knew of them as Gnomes. I could see the upper half of their bodies real clear, but toward the bottom they sort of disappeared into sparkles. They wore funny clothes and strange hats. What was so strange was that they or maybe their clothes seemed to have flowers and twigs and moss growing out of them here and there. The one who spoke to me had a long white beard, down toward his feet. He had a band that hung diagonal across his chest with small bags, sort of like medicine pouches hanging off of it. The little guy said, *'I hope you aren't afraid of us. We're part of Nature.'* Then he placed his hand on his hip and shook his finger at me to make a point, and he said, *'You need to tell people that we're real. Tell them! There's another world out there. They can't see it, but it's there, so tell them. You guys worry too much. In time, everything will come back to you.'"*

Dennison went on to ask me, "What do you know about a round reed?" I thought about this for a moment, "I can only think of hollow reeds that grow in the water." He said, "No, not that kind of a reed. Kind of like the ones you hang on the door at Christmas." I laughed, "Oh, you mean a wreath." "Whatever you call it. What do they really represent?" I told him I really wasn't sure, but thought it might mean without beginning or end. He went on to tell me that as he was falling asleep last night, "I saw a wreath in sort of a spiral, made up of scenes of Nature, with trees and flowers and streams, all green and beautiful in the center, but as it came out, it began to turn gray and dead. It was like scenes of the countryside becoming dead and desolate. I think it represented how Nature started out and how it is becoming now. Soon the circle will be complete, and Nature will reclaim things again."

10-19-90

Wreath of Nature:
Represents a beginning of a time of good, a time of growth,
and a passing of Nature as it was. It's coming into a complete cycle
of completion, of time to grow again. Once again nature will take over
and all will grow again. Stands for peace and growth.

The Best Birthday Gift Ever
NOVEMBER 1990

NOVEMBER 3 WAS DENNISON'S BIRTHDAY. We had some friends over for a potluck and an enjoyable evening. When everyone began to leave, Dennison put a leash on our dog and looped it over a chair on the porch, so she wouldn't get in anyone's way as they backed out. We said good-byes to everyone and went to bed. Dennison had gotten many wonderful gifts, but it seemed the best one was yet to come.

It was nearly midnight when I woke up hearing the dog whining. I realized she must still be tied up on the porch. I could hear Dennison was waking up too, so I asked, "Did you unchain Maya?" He said, "Oh no, I forgot! I'd better go do it." When he returned to bed, he told me he had been dreaming that he had a rainbow cord coming from his body and extending out into the universe. After a little questioning on my part, he began to elaborate, saying that there were actually many cords, and each cord was made up of threads of color. These cords came from various points all over the body. For example a "cord" of orange would be radiating out of the body, and within that orange were many very delicate threads of many iridescent colors. Then, from another spot, emanated a cord of blue, with the tiny iridescent threads within. Rainbows within rainbows.

These delicate, filament-like threads extended out into the universe, penetrating all things. Everyone and everything in the universe has these rainbows of energy extending out and connecting with all other things. These threads are connected to the Source, The All Knowing. Messages are sent and received through the threads. All thoughts, all feelings, all knowledge, everything passes along these threads. This is true of you, of me, of everyone and everything. All is experienced by each other on some level. When negative thoughts and emotions travel along a thread, it is felt and experienced by the Universe collectively. It is like a sour note in an otherwise beautiful piece of music. Eventually a negative thread will be disconnected from the Source, and since this thread also receives from the Source, the owner of the thread is deprived of that connection. When enough negative threads in a person are disconnected, that person becomes spiritually dead. Love is what will rebuild the threads. We are literally ONE with all things. To a great degree, mankind has disconnected many, many threads. More and more we lose touch with the Creator.

When a baby is born, it is still connected directly with the All Knowing through the soft spot on the top of its head. As the soft spot closes up, the connection becomes less and less direct, and more and more the baby becomes a part of our physical world.

As Dennison was talking, he was seeing and feeling his connectedness with all things, and the feeling overwhelmed him repeatedly, his voice husky with emotion. He went on and on, getting information on one subject, then another, explaining things to me as best he could.

"There is only one fear on which all fears are based: the fear of death. The extinction of self. Yet this is such a foolish thing to fear, because we are dead already, and we only really live when we die. Our world and our lives are an illusion that we have collectively created. We are energy, existing on many levels. Our human form, our body, is only a shell, a vehicle, and it begins to die the moment we are born.

"It is through Nature we must learn to love again. There is a lot of love in planting, nurturing it, watching it grow and flourish. Machinery has been created, but there is no love in it, no life. Man used to walk, ride horses or wagons to travel. He was directly involved with his environment and with the earth. He was in communion with it. He planted, smelled the soil, felt the seasons, watched the skies, *communed* with the earth. Now he sits in an air-conditioned conveyance to travel. Even the tractors are enclosed and air conditioned. There is very little contact with the plants and the earth. Or he buys food in the stores, already prepared. We have lost touch with its source. We are cut off from the earth, and, much the same way, man is cut off from each other. This must all change.

"Even the spoken language limits us by putting labels, encapsulated concepts, boxes. We automatically limit ourselves with language and concepts."

Ideas and information and visions continued to pour forth all night. It was after 7:00 a.m. before we went to sleep. The night was full of wonder. The whispered awe in Dennison's voice at times, the mind-stretching concepts at other times, left both of us full of wonder at the simplicity and the beauty of life, as well as the frustration of how foolish mankind is. Dennison felt one with all things, and through him I too felt it, to a lesser degree. Our own existence and fears, as well as that of all mankind, seemed trivial and almost absurd in the way we view things, compared to what *is*. Strange, no matter how hard you try to hold on to the feeling, the *knowing,* slowly it fades, and once again you are back to your old fears and outlooks, only somewhat tempered by the memory of the experience.

The following is what Dennison wrote after the experience:

We have a life-line that is connected with the All Knowing. The energy of our Creator is so fragile and so tender that a small negative thought or a simple misguided word can make a tear within these small lifelines. These are made of small webs, like telephone wires, that just interlace throughout the universe. All the different rainbow colors create the energy field around us and around every little thing in the world, stones, plants, trees, and all mankind. Through these tiny lines we interact with life and each other and all created things, with our thoughts. We bring things into our lives, and these lines that are connected to our bodies make it seem so simple that you would think life would be a breeze, if we just sent the right thoughts and the right words. We could radiate healing energy and love toward one another and throughout the world. By not knowing and not believing, we block all things out with our negative thoughts and our physical concerns.

We came away from our Mother Earth and our Creator when we quit planting our own food. The crops in our fields that we loved so much, the love we put into a small vegetable garden when we planted the seeds and put them into the soil with our hands. The feeling of the dirt and the warmth of Mother Earth in our hands is for the most part gone. The nourishing caring is all gone.

Even in our own lives there is so much change that we don't live for ourselves anymore. When we try to, we feel guilty for being selfish. We forget we are just here to experience life and enjoy the physical world. We must learn to detach from the concerns of our physical world if we wish to become spiritual. Let's follow our hearts and learn to love and be happy.

Our mind is a wonderful thing, or it can be our enemy. Our mind controls our hearts if we let it. When we fear, fear controls us. We fear because we are afraid of dying. Afraid of the nonexistence of the ego. We fear being alone, fear not being good enough, not having what we really want in life. Love is letting go of fear.

Meditation . . . *Your Ego Versus Yourself*
DECEMBER 1990

ON DECEMBER 8, WHILE WE WERE MEDITATING, Dennison received the following:

"I saw a big, I mean really *big* book, the size of this room almost. It was bound in green leather with gold lettering and gold edging on the pages. It opened up to a page, but I couldn't really see what was on the page, because the book was lying flat and the page was so big, or I was so small, I couldn't take it all in. I tried backing away, but I was too far away to read it then. The pages had a beautiful design on the border, and the writing was strange, kind of like this, where I could see it. Then I saw what I first thought was a big box, or maybe a wall with a picture on it. Maybe it was another big book, standing up, with a picture on the cover.

"The picture is of two bees facing each other. At first I thought they were fighting. They looked a little different from each other. One had large black stripes; the other was lighter-colored and its wings were whitish and its antennae were smaller. Over their heads appeared crossed swords and a candle above. There was a wreath-like circle of flowers around them. Between them was a triangle with two other triangles inside. I sensed the bees represented male and female. Underneath, small writing appeared, which said, "The feminine side of you leads you to your spiritual path. Your ego versus your self.""

Meditation . . . *a Wise Teacher*
DECEMBER 1990

TWO DAYS LATER, ON DECEMBER 10, as Dennison and I were meditating, Dennison began speaking:

"I see a waterfall, very, very beautiful, coming down this cliff. There is thick vegetation all around, moss hanging everywhere . . . trees, ferns, flowers of every color. A pool of water that goes out into a calm sea.

Your Ego versus Yourself.
The feminine side of you leads you to your spiritual path.
The bees represent the male and female.

There's large rocks and boulders all around. There's people gathered, some playing on the rocks and in the water. Some are sitting in a circle, and there's a man talking, like a teacher or somebody. He's wearing a blue robe and a green cloth on his head, sort of like a shawl, with pieces of metal going down the sides, and a piece going down over the nose, and a metal band around the head holding it on. He has a tie-like shawl over his shoulders, like a priest would wear, and a beautiful crystal necklace.

"I'm sitting in the circle with some others. I'm wearing a long shirt-like thing with no collar and no sleeves, and it drapes down from the neck in front. I have on a green bracelet on each wrist made of something clear, sort of like colored glass. My hair is square cut.

. "I can't see the face of the teacher. It's as if the sun is reflecting in my eyes. I can just make out the rest of him. He's speaking in a strange language. At first I can't understand it, then it's as if I begin to understand parts of what he's saying.

"He calls each of us by name. He calls me Jos Malaya (phonetic spelling). He tells me to hold out my hands. I do it, and he puts some drops of liquid, like large drops of water, on them. I feel it seep through my fingers; it feels like water, only thick and a little sticky, sort of like honey.

"He calls me 'his child.' He says, 'There will be a time when we'll come back together again. A time when you will all be *home* again. You must now work to bring that into being. You must teach others how to love, how to share.'

"He kept saying a beautiful word, 'Guyos Billibaugh' (phonetic spelling), which means giving of yourself with open hands, with no intention to receive in return, only to love. As I hear this, I know I am not to charge for healing. It's like I'm two people, one here and one there. The one here says, 'I have to charge; I have all these damn bills, and it takes time away from my art work and jewelry to work on people. How can I pay them if I'm supposed to heal and teach, and I don't charge. I can't even eat now much of the time, much less keep up with my bills. I can't do my jewelry or art work, much less go out and sell it, if I'm busy all the time working on people for free!'

"He replied, 'Are you in need right now? You know you must not fear.' Again, that other part of me argues and says, 'How can I not fear when I have bills and no money?' He simply says, 'Don't fear. Play a

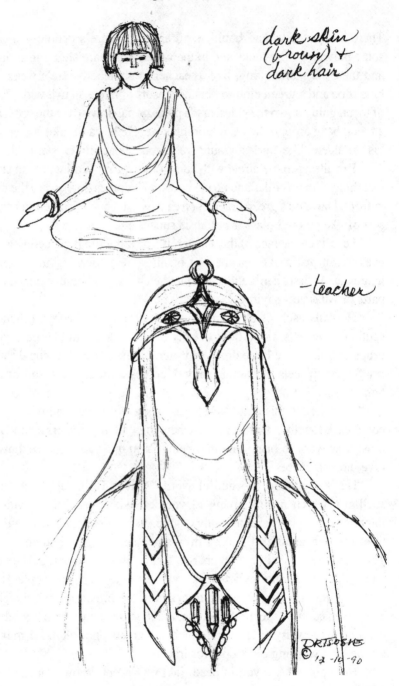

dark skin
(brown) +
dark hair

~teacher

A Wise Teacher

little, and love. You will gain a following as you continue working; it's only natural. Some people will love you, and some will fear you. Love those who don't understand, and show them the way. One day you will stand alone. You must not be afraid.'

"He held out a small yellow flower and placed it in the palm of my hand. It had four petals and a brown center. As I held it, it turned dry, and I crumbled it with the palm of my other hand. It turned to powder, like pollen. Then it dispersed into the air like sparkles of glitter. He said to me, 'This is your only tool. All you need.'"

A Dream of Thankfulness and Forgiveness
DECEMBER 1990

THE NIGHT OF DECEMBER 21, Dennison woke me to tell me of a dream he had just had:

"I dreamed we were walking across a flat land. The ground was covered with fine grass. There were no trees, no rocks or hills, as far as the eye could see, just level and flat. Someone with us said, 'I need a Coke.' There was nowhere to get a Coke, but I felt I wanted to make everyone happy and wondered where in the heck I could find a Coke.

"Way up ahead I saw three figures. As they got closer, I could see they were carrying a box in their hands. As I approached, I noticed they were wearing robes and were very small, about four feet tall. I asked them if they knew where I could get a Coke. They replied, 'There's none here; you're going the wrong way.' I replied, 'Where the heck am I? Am I on earth or what? Who are you?' They said, 'Thankfulness and forgiveness. It's time for thankfulness and forgiveness. You are going the wrong way.' So I asked, 'What way is the right way? Where am I supposed to be going?' They replied, 'To the East. Just turn around and go the opposite way.' Then they handed me a skin bag of water and said, 'This is all that you need to drink.'"

Dream Guidance from Grandfather

Several weeks later, on February 3, 1991, Dennison again woke me, saying, "Are you awake, Babe? I was just dreaming about my Grandfather." I struggled to wake up and gather my wits. "Hmmm? A dream about your Grandfather? That's nice ... do you remember what you were dreaming?"

"I was on a mountain. One of our four sacred mountains. There was a little lodge made of cedar. I went inside, and my Grandfather was there in front of a fire. I sat down across from him. He greeted me and said, *'Your heart is heavy, and so is your mind.'* I acknowledged this was true. (Our business had been severely hurt by the recession and then the war. Dennison had been agonizing over whether he should put aside his spiritual work and his art and jewelry making and go back to work at the paper mill.)

"My Grandfather began singing some songs (prayers); then he took two stones, one black and one white. He tied them together and tied them to an eagle feather; then he handed it to me and told me to hold it over my heart. After that, he reached into his pocket and pulled out a silver dollar and placed it in front of me. He placed another eagle feather, a perfect one from the wing tip, beside it. It was the most beautiful feather I've ever seen. The tip was sort of silver white and golden brown. It had a handle of carved wood, like cottonwood. Designs were carved in the sides, and it was inlaid with colored stones, the colors of the rainbow. The bottom of the handle had a silver piece screwed into it. There were brown threads, like horse hair, coming from this. Grandfather said, *'The eagle is very powerful medicine. He flies higher than any other bird; his spirit touches the Sky Father, the spiritual realms, but he can also touch Mother Earth, the material world. Reach over and turn over the dollar.'* I did what he told me. *'See, this has an eagle too. Which do you choose?'* I reached and picked up the eagle feather. My Grandfather laughed and said, *'I knew you had savvy.'* I noticed the eagle feather had pollen on the tip. Grandfather said, *'The pollen represents the essence of life. If you are healing someone and use this, you will know what's in their heart and you will feel what they feel; then you can heal them.'* With this, he began to sing some more songs. I heard four sharp whistles, like from an eagle bone whistle, and when I looked up, Grandfather was gone. In his place were two eagles, one with a white head, and the other was golden. The first one had a crystal in his right foot; the other had a medicine pouch in his right foot. The first one spread his wings and flew to the East; the other walked gracefully over to the silver dollar and picked it up and flew to the West."

Pure Poetry
FEBRUARY 1991

THINGS HAD BEEN ESPECIALLY DIFFICULT for us, financially. Dennison had been in a deep inner turmoil, struggling with his Spiritual calling and the demands of the physical world. He often felt alone, without council or support, to the point of strongly wishing to return to his former way of life. He had never written poetry, nor had he ever read it. Recently I came across several "poems," written over a period of several days, beginning on February 15. They are beautiful and reflect his inner struggle in a way he would otherwise never express. I want to include them here.

A SMALL NARROW PATH

At some time in our lives,
there is a difficult path

A road that is dark and narrow
with not knowing what is ahead.
Yet this is part of our path that
we chose to walk.

I walk this path and I stumble,
I know I must go on,
I know the road will widen
and grow brighter.

So why am I afraid, if I know it's good
once I pass this narrow part of my
path, why am I afraid?

INSIGHT

I have come to a point where a strong warrior must also seek strength and wisdom.

Grandfather, I thought I was strong and very knowledgeable in my time. I thought I had everything I needed, yet now I am alone and the world is no longer together and one with the Spirit.

Our Great Mother is once more overpowered. How long can She take this? What does She say in her heart that we must hear?

I know She cries, Grandfather. Why can't we hear these things anymore? What things must we remember of our past? What tools or prayers were used to speak louder than the thunders? I have looked to the East and to the South, the West and the North and see no sign or guide to tell us what to say or do. Is it too late to change? Is it so, Grandfather?

I Long To Be Wise

I long to be wise and one with the Spirit,
but what does it take to be wise?

I wish to be wise like the Old Ones,
yet I do not speak the words or sing.

My heart beats like the drum, the songs
and chants echo in my ear. Still my lips
remain mute.

The air and the wind seem to whisper to me,
my feet want to shuffle the pollen dance.
Yet I cannot move.

Why do I still smell the Sage burn
when my heart is heavy with sadness?
What has happened to the ways of my youth?
Where can I turn when I am troubled?

How I long to be wise and one with the Spirit.

Mother Earth

Mother Earth, you are the wise one.
You nurture us without exception.
We feel safe when we sleep close to you at night.

Legends say we emerged from inside your heart.
That is why we are a part of you. I know
you feel and have emotions just like us. Yet we
rip up your body for our greed. The rivers and

*springs are the blood in your veins. Yet we fill
them with our filth. How is it, Mother, that
you have been so patient with us?*

*Today you have touched me with your
strength and your wisdom. Teach me to feel
with you, and let me be one with you again.
Teach me to be like you.*

CIRCLE OF LIFE

*A circle, a circle of creation. The first
foundation of life. In this circle, the Spirit
moves clockwise. From its center, life is born,
life gathers again.*

*In this circle, the elders taught their wisdoms.
Thus our ceremonies are done in a circle.
If we gather in a circle, we will always be strong.*

*We once left this circle to travel in the four
directions. Now it is time to join with the elders
who have long been waiting.*

*Grandmother waits with her sacred pollen of
life, to bless me. Grandfather is in his sacred sweat
lodge to cleanse me. I hear their voices, their prayers,
the beat of their drums.*

*Long have I waited to be held and loved in this circle of
my Elders. To be where Mother Earth meets Father Sky.
At last I am home in the circle of all creation.
I am One with all things.*

EAGLE DREAM

In my dream I saw an eagle.
Was it really a dream?

In the eagle's eyes I saw my eyes,
In his wings, I saw my arms,
In his feet, I saw my feet.

When he expanded his wings with
the wind, I too felt the strength
against my arms.

When he leaped into the heavens to soar,
I too felt my heart leap and soar with him.

With him I knew I too was one with
the universe, with the Great Spirit
and with Mother Earth.

Premonition of a War in Africa
FEBRUARY 1991

ON FEBRUARY 16, we were driving to Snowflake, when Dennison asked, "Is there a canal somewhere around the Persian Gulf?" I tried to think, but I had no idea. I told him, "I don't know of any." A few minutes later he asked, "What's that area called that's near by Saudi Arabia?" Again I had no idea what he could be talking about. He said, " I keep seeing a body of water, like a sea or something, and a narrow area, like a canal. I sense it's near Saudi Arabia."

Again he was silent awhile, then he asked, "What is the country right across the water from Saudi Arabia?" I told him, "Africa is close; can you be talking about Africa?" He thought about this, then asked, "What are the people in Africa like? Are they fighters like the Arabs?" I said, "Yes, a lot of them are Arabs." Dennison said, "I keep getting that there is a country close to Saudi Arabia, just across the water from there, and they will surprise everyone by entering into a war."

Dream of a Riderless Horse
FEBRUARY 1991

ON FEBRUARY 24, Dennison had an odd dream: "I dreamed of a black horse that was running. He was lathered up, foam streaming from his mouth. He had an odd saddle on his back with a tall saddle horn. The saddle horn was in the shape of a dragon. Blue ribbons streamed off the saddle and bridal.

"Behind the horse, tied to a rope, was an empty suit of armor, which the horse was dragging."

Hitler
MARCH 1991

WE WERE HAVING DINNER WITH A FRIEND the evening of March 2. She had made some German food, and Dennison remarked something about "Heil, Hitler." A few moments later, he asked what "Heil Hitler" really meant, and we both said it meant "Hail Hitler." The conversation went on to something else when Dennison said, "There was another name besides Hitler . . . Armetis . . . Armedes . . . something like that." Our friend said, "How about Amadeus, that's German." Dennison went on to say, "I don't think so; he was a Roman officer of some sort. He wanted to be a commander of the military or something, but he was passed over and never got his chance."

Our friend looked questioningly at me, wondering at the odd turn of the conversation. I realized Dennison might be getting information given to him so I asked, "What significance was this Roman soldier?" We both felt a little shock when Dennison said, "He reincarnated later as Hitler." Our friend asked, "Will he be reincarnated again?" and Dennison replied, "Yes." I asked, "Why?!" and the reply came, "He is again incarnated because you still have something to learn from war." I asked, "Does that mean there is still going to be a big war to come?" The answer came, "That's up to you. If you want it, then it will come. The energies are now high for war. You have tasted the success. . . ." Our friend asked, "If there is enough energy put out for peace, could such a war be prevented?" He replied, "That is also up to you." I was thinking about what he had said about Hitler being reincarnated. It seemed like he had insinuated he was alive now! I asked, "When will Hitler come back again?" The answer came, "He will make himself known when you are in your 60s." "That's only fifteen years from now, does that mean he's alive now?" He replied, "Yes, he's 18; he will come to power when he's 35." Our friend asked, "What nationality is he?" "He is an Arab." "What is his name?" "He is known by the name of a Season. Do not fear. You will be guided. If you fear, then you cannot receive."

I asked, "What of the predicted earth changes, are they also going to be happening too?" He said, "The predictions of great catastrophes won't be as bad as many say, with one exception. There must be a replenishment. There is a heaviness, the Earth cannot breathe. The heaviness must be broken up so She can breathe. The cement, the asphalt shall be broken up." "You mean earthquakes?" "Yes, earthquakes."

The phone rang, and the session was over.

A Dream of Solomon's Temple
MARCH 1991

IT WAS MARCH 4, and Dennison and I were working on jewelry when he asked, "Was there such a thing as Solomon's Temple?" I replied, "Yes, there surely was." He then asked, "What was it?" I explained, "I really don't know too much about it except what I read in *Holy Blood, Holy Grail.* Solomon was a king who was known for his wisdom. He was also supposed to be quite wealthy. He built a temple, and there was a lot of treasure associated with it. The Jews kept their Holy relics in there too, like the Ark of the Covenant, I think, but I don't really remember for sure. The temple was later taken by their enemies, and the treasure was never accounted for, and some think it was hidden away in the Temple somewhere. The Masons also claim some sort of connection to Solomon or his Temple, I think. Centuries later the Knights Templar stayed near there for several years. Why do you ask?" Instead of answering,

Dennison asked, "When was Solomon King, and where?" "He was king of the Jews sometime before Christ, and the Temple was in Jerusalem." Dennison thought about this for a few minutes, then said, "I dreamed about Solomon's Temple last night. 'They' told me I needed seven stones to get inside. 'They' said it was very difficult to get in; many have tried and failed. I asked them why in the world I would want to get inside for? 'They' said there were many secrets inside, very advanced knowledge. I think there is some sort of stone in there. Was there a stone that was associated with the Temple or King Solomon? 'They' told me there was a stone inside I need to communicate with."

A Dream of the Crusaders
MARCH 1991

A FEW NIGHTS LATER, ON MARCH 11, Dennison had another strange dream:

"I dreamed of a breastplate with a green stone in the center, surrounded by brownish-looking stones. It was hanging in an old church somewhere. There was a tomb or a casket-looking thing sitting in the floor. Hanging near it were banners with dragon symbols on them. There were also many statues around the room.

"'They' said to me, *'The crusaders weren't heroes; they were sacrificed for a cause.'* I also saw symbols sort of like crosses, but the arms were equal, like the + sign, and the ends were rounded, in kind of the shape of the top of a heart, but I sense they weren't really crosses, but were a stylization of bones, like the crossbones beneath a skull. It was the symbol of a secret order. I also saw XXIII; what does that mean?

"I keep getting the number nine or ninety-nine . . . I think it means King Charles the Ninth or something. I sense he was like the end of an age. The end of a bloodline, or something like that. A bloodline ended, and he began a new era. There's some missing history. Something missing or hidden. I don't know, I think maybe the Church did something, and written history was changed to something different than what really happened.

"A long time ago, I think that kings were like priests; they ruled by Divine direction. Some had like high lieutenants, which later became the

Knights Templar, special fighting holy men for a cause. They protected a bloodline, which the people considered Holy Rulers because of who they were. The bloodline had to go underground, remain hidden, because of all the bloodshed. If they were to make themselves known now, France could rule the world because of who they are.

"The kings and rulers nowadays don't mean anything, they are just figureheads; their power died out with the last king of that bloodline. The Knights who were an order became a secret society, but they don't mean anything any more, either. They were broken up by the Church.

"The bloodline still exists, and it will make itself known when the time is right. Now people are still locked in their old beliefs, and the bloodline and what it stands for would threaten their beliefs. It would just turn them over completely. Priests and bishops would mean nothing. What the churches teach means nothing; it's all wrong. They twisted the truth to suit their needs and made it a religion. Slowly, slowly the truth is coming out."

I recognized the overall information as being much the same premise of the book, *Holy Blood, Holy Grail* by Michael Baigent, Richard Leigh, and Henry Lincoln. The book speaks of a royal bloodline, the Merovingians, who ruled France from about the 6th century AD until about 700 AD. The last of the direct descendants of the first ruler, Dagobert, was assassinated on December 23, 679. It seems his death was secretly arranged by the Church, and history altered the circumstances to hide the fact. The book, *Holy Blood, Holy Grail,* speculates the Merovingian bloodline is descended from Jesus. There is also some evidence that Dagobert had a small son who was taken away into hiding, and through him, the bloodline still exists today.

I find it curious Dennison keeps getting these things, especially since he has no previous knowledge and little interest in it.

The Talking Stone
MARCH 1991

AFTER RELATING HIS DREAM, we ate breakfast and left for Sedona to try and sell some jewelry. Perhaps the following happened because the green stone in the breastplate in the dream was still fresh in Dennison's mind, or perhaps he was being guided to discover a new teacher.

We were selling jewelry in a New Age shop. While I was taking care of business, Dennison wandered around the store. He saw a display of unusual looking stones called Moldavite. It was a translucent emerald green and looked a little like lava rock. He picked up a piece, and much to his surprise he heard the sound of horses galloping. He was completely taken aback. He asked the owner of the shop if he could take the stone outside for a few moments. She said, "Sure, go ahead." He stepped out into the courtyard in front of the store and quieted his mind, and as he put it, "opened myself." This time he "saw" a chariot being drawn by two horselike creatures, one black and the other white. Their bodies were like horses, one's head was like a lion, the other like a bull. Riding on the chariot was a woman in a white, Grecian-like gown and a blue gauze cloak hanging from one arm and shoulder. The word Zeus came into his mind. He thought of purchasing the stone, but the price was well over $60.00, and he felt he couldn't afford it.

The store owner, noting his interest in the stone, told him the only place they were found was in one area of Czechoslovakia, and they were thought to come from outer space, like meteors. She also said they were thought to be the stone of some of the Grail legends. It was very strange how all of a sudden stuff about the Holy Grail kept coming up, so I went over and looked at it and held it for a few minutes. It gave me an uncomfortable prickling in my hand, followed by a hot sensation like a flush over my whole body. I wasn't particularly attracted to it and put it back in the display and we said our good-byes. After we left, Dennison told me of the strange experience with the stone, and I urged him to go back in and buy it, but he wasn't really sure the stone had actually been the cause of the experience and felt he couldn't justify the expense, especially if it wasn't.

Later in the day, we went into another New Age store to try and sell some jewelry. This shop loved our things, but they said they couldn't afford to buy any at this time. We walked around, and I noticed they too had a display of Moldavite in a locked cabinet. I quietly suggested to Dennison that we might be able to work out a trade if he could find another piece that he could feel something with. He asked to see the stones, and, while holding one, he saw many bright particles of light, like fireworks. We negotiated a trade and left with our new stone. Later, while we were having dinner, he remarked he felt strange, as if he was walking on an air mattress.

We were driving home when he asked, "Where is Artesia?" I thought he had noticed a road sign, and I looked around to find what he was looking at. After a bit of confusion, he explained it seemed the Moldavite was talking to him, or at least something was talking to him through the stone. He said, "It is telling me about a place in Egypt that was considered a sacred place. I 'see' a cavern and an underground pool of water. The stone says it was a natural well, and the water is full of certain minerals. It's saying ceremonies and sacrifices were carried out there. Egyptian women used to take their babies there and dip them in the water. People filled containers with the water and drank it for health problems. There are some type of stones under the stream that make the water so powerful."

This was interesting. I wondered if it would be possible to ask questions and get answers, so I asked Dennison to ask the stone where the Moldavite comes from. The reply was, "From outside your galaxy. Your galaxy is where earth and the other planets and stars you know about exist. Beyond your galaxy are other galaxies, and other life exists there. A star burst, that is what I showed you when you first picked up your stone. Pieces were sent through time to be manifest on the earth plane to be there when it was needed to aid in the transformation of Mankind."

A little later Dennison said, "I'm being asked if I am in touch with the largest crystal ever found. It is in Hawaii. He says I should be in touch with it; it has a lot of important information in it."

The stone continued to "chat" with Dennison, asking him such things as, "Are you familiar with the Osage Indians? They used crystals a lot in their healing and ceremonies and were considered very powerful healers. The same was true of the Cherokee." Dennison felt rather uncomfortable about having a stone "talking" to him and kept expressing how no one would ever believe he was talking to a *rock*. He exclaimed, "Lovie, I feel like I'm weird talking to this stone and having it talk back to me. Please don't tell anyone."

As we rode along, I thought about his incredulity at a stone being able to seemingly talk with him and ask him questions. I realized I had come a long way in my own acceptance of the extraordinary. It didn't really seem all that strange to me that a stone could impart information.

More from Jospeh Campbell
MARCH 1991

THE NEXT MORNING while Dennison was working on jewelry, the stone once again began talking to him. He quietly continued with his work. Suddenly the stone told him, *"Stop that, and listen! That's not important."* He stopped his work and started to get up and find a pencil and paper to write down what was being said. The stone said, *"Now what are you doing?"* Dennison replied, "I'm getting something to write down what you are telling me." The stone said, *"Just keep it in your mind."* Dennison told him, "You don't know my mind; it will rattle around in there, and I'll forget." The stone told him, *"Okay, get your paper, then."* The following is what Dennison wrote.

When you are older, the concern of the day is over. You must turn to the inner soul. If you don't know where it is, you'll be sorry.

Realize you must be aware of this. This is how you must think. Please note this first.

One of our problems today is that we are not well acquainted with the literature of the spirit. We are more interested in the news of the hour. Your spirit should be kept in a hermetically sealed-off area, where the news of the day does not impinge upon your attention to the inner life and to the magnificent human heritage we have in our traditions. Plato, Confucius, the Buddha, Goethe, and others speak of eternal values, that have a lot to do with the centering of our lives.

As Dennison was getting this, I was talking with my mom on the phone. I saw him get a pencil and paper and start writing like crazy. When I hung up, I went over to see what he was writing. He finished and handed me the paper and said, "The stone was just telling me this, and I wrote it all down."

I was quite impressed to say the least, especially the use of such words as hermetically, impinge, and references to Plato, Goethe, etc.

These were not in Dennison's reality, much less his vocabulary. I was especially impressed at the correct spellings. Just for curiosity, I asked him to read back what he had just written. He couldn't even pronounce the words.

About a week later, after the above incident, I was pondering what had been written. It seemed very hauntingly familiar. Suddenly I felt certain it was something of Joseph Campbell's. I found our book, *The Power of Myth,* and after just a few moments, I found it in there. Dennison has never read the book, even after his earlier experience of getting Joseph Campbell information. Perhaps because of his heritage, he seems to almost casually accept the validity of what he receives without needing confirmation, and even seems a little detached when evidence is presented. He seems more worried about what others might think of his experiences.

Teachings from the Stone
MARCH 1991

LATER THE SAME DAY, the stone began to "pick" at Dennison to make a point. We were making medicine bags out of deerskin and rabbit fur, when the stone asked Dennison:

"Are you a witch doctor?"

"No!"

"Do you sacrifice animals?"

"No! Why do you ask?" (I spoke up at this point, as Dennison had been relating the conversation to me. "Maybe he was referring to our working with these skins.")

"What happens to the insides?"

"I don't know; I didn't skin them."

"Could you use the insides?"

"I suppose, but I bought the skins like this."

"Why do you make the bags?"

"To make money."

"Is money that hard to get?"

"Yeah, I guess so. We have to do many different things to get it."

"What will you do when the animals are all gone?"

And later the same day the stone asked,
Are you religious?"
"Yes."
"Where is your Altar? A man of God should have an Altar."
"I have an altar in my healing room."
"You don't use it. Would it not be better in the room where you sit? Where do you keep your healing stones? They should be kept in the sunlight. Keep them separate, for your use only, and cleanse them after each use.

"Do you ever talk with the stars? They have a lot to say. It is best to go out on a full moon and look in some water at the reflection of the stars. A still pond, a bowl of water, or even a pail of water. The water is a conductor of energy. The water and the stars talk a lot to each other.

"Trees also talk. You can communicate with them like you do with me. They have spirits also.

"Birds are messengers. They travel far and see a lot, and they carry messages and have powerful energies. Each species have their own energies.

"The wind talks, too; just listen. The whole universe is in full communication. You have to listen with your spirit."

By this time, Dennison had returned to making jewelry. He complained that the stone was chattering at him constantly, and it was driving him up a wall. Dennison is a quiet man, and this constant dialog was too much for him. He put the stone away in a drawer in the bedroom so he could concentrate on his work. To be honest, I suspect he's still more than a little uncomfortable with the idea of talking with a stone.

As I pondered the conversations with the stone and Dennison's discomfort with the idea, I thought I remembered that the Oracle at Delphi in Greek writings was supposed to have been a stone. I looked in my *Women's Encyclopedia of Myths and Secrets* and learned also that the long sought after Philosopher's Stone was said to be able to communicate with certain individuals. I found there was a name given to stones that talked, *Baetylic Stones.* Such stones have been talked about throughout history. Quite often these stones are said to have fallen from the sky and were thought possibly to be pieces of meteorites. The Talmud and other Jewish writings speak of such a stone being used by

Moses to communicate with God. It was kept inside the Ark of the Covenant!

That evening another in the string of seeming coincidences relating to the Holy Grail and our new stone happened.

A girlfriend I hadn't talked to for a long time called from out of state. As I caught her up on the latest events in our lives, I told her of our new stone and how we came to purchase it. I also cautiously told her of how it seemingly conversed with Dennison. She asked what kind of stone it was. I told her "Moldavite," and she exclaimed, "That's really weird! I just got through buying a book on Moldavite."

I asked her what the book had to say about Moldavite and its alleged properties. She got her book and read, "Moldavite is from a subgroup of an enigmatic class of natural glassy objects known as Tektites; from the Greek word *Tekos*, meaning Molten. Most other Tektites are black or brownish black in color, but the Moldavites are deep emerald green. It is not known where tektites come from, but one school of thought says they may have been formed by a meteor or comet impacting on the earth." Then she went on to say, "It also says somewhere in here that the stone is associated with the Holy Grail legends. Some also think it is the basis of the stories of the Philosopher's Stone. It looks like there's quite a bit in here about that, as well as about the Holy Grail."

As we got ready to end our conversation, my friend offered to purchase a copy of the book for me.

This whole thing is surely something to ponder. Was this really a coincidence? Why did the Holy Grail keep coming up?

Strange Information About the Holy Grail
MARCH 1991

A FEW DAYS LATER, ON MARCH 13, the stone again was speaking to Dennison, and he in turn dutifully repeated to me:

"Have you given much thought to what you call beings from other worlds? They are called People of The Light.

"The Holy Grail is no longer on the earth; it was removed to another plane of existence by The People of The Light, because it was endangered by Mankind. It will be returned to the earth by these so called "Aliens" when the time is right. If it were to be brought back now, Mankind would destroy it by fighting over it.

"There is another stone you are connected to, but you won't be working with it until it is needed, later; it's not time to get it yet.

"You are here to help bring the Grail into the earth plane. You have been given a very powerful tool from God to use for this purpose. The tool is Love. You must love everyone, and you must teach others to love. Send them out to spread the word of love. Love energy is God's energy. God is Love. You want to heal people; it is with love that healing comes.

"Beyond your solar system are other solar systems, other galaxies. Your spirit came from another galaxy to incarnate on the earth as a human to help spread love, and to be there for Man when the Great Change comes. Until that time, spread love. Unconditional love. Love for all things, love for the earth, the trees, the animals, and for Man.

"You should remain in a position to help people and remain in the mountains in some place of power, where people would want to go.

"Another world is in existence beside this one. At one time they were as one. As Mankind became more and more negative and fearful and fought more and more, they separated. There exists but a veil between these worlds. The time is at hand when the veil will be lifted and the two worlds will again join together. The problem is that this world you live in is about three-quarters negative; the other world is positive. When they come together, the two opposite energies will for a time cause great disturbances. The more negative your world is at the time, the worse the disturbances will be. The more love and positive energies, the less the disturbances will be. That's why it is so important to spread as much love as possible. When the two worlds come together, the forces, the energies, will be great. There will be holocausts, cataclysms, quaking, destruction. Those who are negative and fearful will destroy themselves. Those who love will be guided. They will survive by working together. Places will be needed where people can go."

Get Ready to Go Canadian
MARCH 1991

THE FOLLOWING DAY, Dennison was working on jewelry when he looked up and said, "Funny, I clearly, clearly heard a voice say, *'Get ready to go Canadian.'* What do you think that could mean?" I told him, "Maybe we will be getting some jewelry orders from someone in Canada." I decided to write it down in case it related to something later.

More on the Holy Grail
MARCH 1991

THE STONE CONTINUED TO DISPENSE INFORMATION AND TEACHINGS, but not as often. On March 26, the stone was talking to Dennison, and as Dennison told me what it was saying, I thought it a good opportunity to ask some questions about the Holy Grail, after what the stone had told him a few days ago.

"Ask the stone what exactly is the Grail? Is it an actual physical object, like a cup? What does it represent?"

"The Grail is abundance for all Mankind, a time when all man will believe in the same Source. It is the return of Nature, the return of the Golden Age, the return of the Gods to Earth. Paradise regained. Mankind will be one with God. Man will be able to heal himself, heal with his hands, perform miracles.

"The Grail is also a bloodline. There was a time when beings you called Sons of God and Angels walked on earth. They were from another plane. They wished to manifest in the physical form, and they combined with Mankind, to create beings who were half 'God' and half man.

"Do any of these beings or their descendants still exist today?"

"I can't answer that. If people were to think certain peoples, certain races, or certain families were part 'God,' it would cause serious problems. It would be a threat to some, create new religions, new governments or rulers for others. The same as would happen if the Grail were brought back now. Many would fight over it for the power it possesses. The Grail is no longer on the earth plane. It was taken away

to another plane because mankind fought over possession of it. It was given to mankind for their benefit, but its powers were misused. Kings possessed and used it to enslave people, to destroy enemies, to create personal wealth.

"The 'Gods' who inbred with Man could have benefited Mankind so much, but they misused their powers.

"There were three stones and a tablet with two sides associated with the Grail. A higher spirit energized these stones to create outward, to symbolize a true teaching. The object, once energized, can go in and out of physical existence. Two of the stones are like a magnet that can be energized to attract certain energy.

"The Grail was given into the care of a Sacred Teacher, like a Priest. Given to two Priests to hold as sacred knowledge. Power seekers attempted to take it, and the tablet was taken apart. One part remained with one Priest, and one was hidden somewhere. Two of the stones were lifted out of the earth plane. The rest of the tablet remains intact; one stone remains with the tablet. In order to regain power, the other two stones must be united with the one to create a triangle. The one stone that was left is a Moldavite.

"The Priest who was entrusted with the knowledge was named Isaiah. When they tried to take the tablet, he hid it somewhere in the side of a mountain. He was to take it to a certain spot, but he didn't make it. It is still hidden.

"There are many forbidden and hidden things to go through to find it. Only an anointed person could retrieve it. So far no one has come. . . ."

"Was Jesus Christ one of the half 'God' and half Man beings, or of their bloodline?

"Jesus was a very great Teacher. There have been many great Teachers. I'm talking of Great Beings. Healers beyond the power of Jesus Christ, who could shoot fire from their hands and eyes. They could fly . . . they possessed real power, but they misused it. They could have benefited Mankind so much. These powers will be brought back in time."

"When will this happen? Will it be in our lifetime?"

"It won't be complete in your lifetime, but you will hear about it beginning to happen. It will show in some places first. Great healers will come; man will heal with his hands.

"Have you heard of 'Aloids?' There will be beings called Aloids that will come into existence at this time who will interact with Mankind and be accepted by Mankind. They will look more like humans, but they are what you call aliens. They are made from samples of human genetic material taken from earth beings. They look like humans, so they can interact and be accepted by humans."

"What are the Watchers? Are the Aloids a part of them?"

"We call the Watchers planetary beings. They are associated with the regenerating of Mankind and oversee the resources on the planet, reassuring there will always be Mankind."

"Who or what are you?"

"I am one of the cosmic energies. Why does Mankind fear so much when there is nothing to fear? They create their own fears when none are there. That's a lesson yet to be learned by him.

"You must truly, truly learn from the animals. Watch how they change, their habits, their habitat. This will be a sign to humans. Animals sense things and know things you don't know. They are in constant contact with the All Knowing. They will be among the chosen few. Animals are God's children. They love unconditionally. They were brought here to replenish the earth for your benefit."

The stone answered no more of my questions. As I pondered the information, it occurred to me that the Grail being spoken of sounded much like the Biblical Ark of the Covenant, and I wondered if it might be one and the same. I wish I had paid more attention to the Old Testament teachings I had gotten in early childhood. I can't remember what happened to the Ark of the Covenant, nor when it was in use.

A Dream of the Ozone Layer
MARCH 1991

ONE MORNING DENNISON AWOKE and said, "I dreamed of the ozone layer. It was like watching a movie."

He was silent for a long time, lying with his eyes closed as if again seeing the dream. Finally, he continued, "They showed me the ozone layer, like thin, thin, delicate tissue paper, even brittle in places. Then they showed me holes forming, as they explained that outside the ozone layer are harmful chemicals and rays. The layer acts as a buffer to keep these things out of our atmosphere; it filters out the harmful rays from the sun and keeps clean pure air within the earth. The holes in the ozone layer are now allowing in harmful rays and these, combined with the increased effects of the sun, will heat up the earth.

"Many things are causing this to happen. Pollution from cars of course, but the greatest danger right now is coming from several large chemical plants, power plants, and factories. It's worse in the North. Coal burning plants are an extremely serious problem. These plants are causing acid rain. Near the North pole is where the ozone layer is the most damaged. All the North is at great risk. We'll be seeing effects of this more and more.

"Other countries are becoming very industrialized, and their factories are doing a lot of damage, and we have no control over what they do. Many of our factories are setting up factories in these countries and are not complying with our environmental standards. This is creating many problems."

It seemed a curious dream in that, even though he was concerned for our environment, he was not particularly environmentally aware or knowledgeable. Also, how many people ever dream of the ozone layer?

More Teachings
APRIL 1991

THE FIRST OF APRIL, we were driving home from Snowflake, when Dennison said, "The stone is saying, *'Did you know the Japanese are working with growing very clear and very high quality crystals? They can create a lot of energy. They are also experimenting with using crystals and sunlight to create energy for electricity, etc. They now have a satellite in space with a bed of these crystals. They are right on track; they just need to use other crystals with them to ground energy and direct it. Like amethyst or rose quartz. Layer the crystals.*

"'In the near future Mankind is going to return to more holistic forms of healing, the use of herbs, and more natural ways of living. There is going to be a new medicinal plant discovered that will become very popular and be of a great benefit for healing. Shamanism and Native

American spirituality will lead the way, as it becomes more and more popular. People will be put in touch with their power animals. They should be taught always to wear something which represents that animal, a piece of fur, tooth, feather, or a pendant, even a picture in their pocket.

"'You should collect several long, thin sticks and tie them into a bundle and use it to gently strike a patient's body when healing them after a sweat, to stimulate their nerves. This aids total body function.

"'Sound is also important to use in healing. Humans are addicted to sound. It affects their nervous system and emotional well being. Some sounds are very beneficial, like drumming, chimes, natural sounds like water, etc. Many sounds have a very harmful affect, like very low frequency sounds, some music, angry words, machinery, etc.

"'Drumming is very effective in healing, especially if you can surround the patient with three or four people drumming. It also helps induce an altered state of consciousness, which is very important when healing. They have their minds open then.

"'Your Grandfather is working with you; there is a lot he still needs to teach you. You'll be given some powerful chants soon.'"

A Dream on Ancient Scrolls
APRIL 1991

IT WAS THE MIDDLE PART OF APRIL, and we were camping with some friends. As we were eating breakfast, Dennison said, "I was dreaming I was in a cave. There was this . . . there was something in there that at first I thought was a beehive. It was a very large square frame, filled with small cylindrical cubicles, like a honeycomb. It covered a large portion of the cave wall. Inside each cubicle was a metal cylinder; the end of each one had a symbol that I sense was numbers. I took out one of the cylinders and opened it. Inside was a rolled up, parchment kind of paper. It was yellowish, like old newspaper, and thin and fragile. I tried carefully to open it, but it crumbled away, no matter how careful I was. I noticed on the parchment was tiny, fine writing of some sort, kind of like hiero-glyphics. At first I couldn't read it, but then I found I could read part of it. It said, *'Mankind must solve his own problems just now in order to raise himself spiritually.'* The rest just crumbled away. Something said, *'These are some of the Akashic Records.'* I wondered what Akashic Records were. Then I looked around me and I saw a long, flat slab of stone, like a table or an altar. On it were several round stone dishes with old candles melted in them. That's all I can remember."

Later in the day the stone began "talking" to Dennison, telling him about the Akashic Records. *"They are records of Universal Teachings and knowledge from the beginning of Mankind. Much of it is kept on another vibrational level. Much information and many teachings were channeled to people in ancient times from Universal Beings. Much of this information was gathered by the Romans. They got it from the Egyptians, from China, and even Australia. It was copied down by priests. A lot was not copied correctly. It was stored in a place that was later destroyed. Some of this information was hidden away and has not been found. A lot of it contained prophecies from ancient times up until about fifty years into your future—a lot of philosophies and sacred teachings. Some of these hidden works are still in existence and will soon be found, when the time is right for them to be brought forth.*

"It is possible for you to get into the Akashic Records and bring forth information, but it is very difficult. Many have tried, but few are able to do it. Try low frequency or high volume rhythmic vibration, like drumming. You have to make yourself small like an ant and go down into the earth. It takes a lot of practice.

"There's going to be some great spiritual teachers coming to America in the future from all over the world: African, Tibetan, Chinese, etc. Even Native American. They will all be gathering together.

"You need to get a large crystal, a very large crystal, a natural, clear, or partly cloudy one with records on it. The more prominent and raised the record and the larger the crystal, the better it receives. Record Keeper crystals are just receivers of universal knowledge. It isn't recorded in the crystal, the crystal acts as a receiver and transmitter of universal information."

Fish and the Ozone Layer
APRIL 1991

LATER IN THE DAY, Dennison said, "The stone was just telling me that the fish are in great danger, because there's holes in the ozone layer and more showing up.

"The fish, especially the Dolphins and the Whales, which spend a lot of time near the surface of the water, will soon be adversely affected . . . sunburned. The holes in the ozone layer will also affect the food chain in the water. The algae, which some fish eat, won't grow, and small fish will starve; then there won't be small fish for the larger fish to eat, and so on. Large pods of whales will be seen in areas where they have never been seen before, because they will be trying to escape the effects of the sun's rays. What will you do? Put them all in aquariums?

"There is a way the holes can be repaired, using chemicals in the form of fog, but you'll have to figure that out how for yourselves. Learn your own lessons."

A Dream of a Yaqui Indian
APRIL 1991

THE MORNING OF APRIL 18, we lay in bed half asleep, hating to get up. Dennison yawned and stretched. Sleepily, he asked, "Where do the Yaqui Indians come from?" I told him, "Down in Mexico, I think Chihuahua or somewhere like that." He went on to say, "I dreamed I was with the Yaqui Indians. They were living in caves on the sides of a canyon. I could hear people talking and some chanting and drumming in the distance. There was a well that went down into an underground cavern. There was a ladder going down inside, and there were women and kids climbing out, with skin bags full of water. There were rope ladders on the sides of the canyon walls, leading up to the caves.

"I noticed an old man sitting by himself in front of one of the caves. He was thin, but his body was strong, well-muscled. He was wearing a necklace of different colored beads. They were long and thin, made out of stone, or maybe ceramic. They were carved with strange writing or symbols on them. I stood in front of the old man, and he untied the cord from his neck and dumped the beads on the ground in front of me. He told me to look at them and see if I could read their meaning.

"I studied them for awhile, and they began to gather together and swirl in a vortex until they vaporized. Then, out of the vapor, a woman appeared, wearing a leather dress adorned with beautiful beads and jewelry; she had a headband set with an amethyst in the center. She looked sort of Egyptian, and I thought of an Egyptian Princess. She was holding a golden or copper wand with a green stone set in the tip. She waved the wand over the old man and then me and then toward the other people. She spoke to me and said, "The old man is a Caller. He called me forth. There are messengers coming. Listen to the wind. There are lots of messages in the wind, if you will listen carefully. It's telling of changes. The animals are changing; you will begin to notice it. There are some birds that won't return this summer. Their migrating habits are changing, too. The sun has changed a little; the light is different. Even the stars have changed a little, but no one has noticed." The image disintegrated, and the beads fell to the ground. The old man reached over and picked up a blue and green bead that had some writing on it and handed it to me, then scooped up the rest of the beads and put them in a leather pouch."

The Inca

APRIL 1991

LATER IN THE DAY, Dennison was working on his jewelry when he asked me, "What do you know about the Inca?" I had to admit, as I thought about it, that I knew very little. I told him I thought they lived in South America around the time of the Maya. He asked, "What were they like? Were they spiritual? Do they still exist? Are they like the Tibetans?" (A friend had recently told Dennison she felt the Navajo were somehow connected to the Tibetan Buddhists and how similar many of their beliefs and some ceremonies were, even to the use of sand paintings for healing.)

I told him I was sure their descendants were still living in small villages in Peru, but I knew very little more. Then I asked why he wanted to know. He replied, "The stone was just asking me, *'Do you know about your brother, the Inca?'"* I told him to ask the stone to tell him about the Inca.

After a few minutes he told me, "The stone said, *'You are much more closely related to the Inca than the Tibetan. The Inca are your brothers in the South, and you are closely related to them. They were sun worshipers, and they built pyramids and temples; they were very wealthy and grand. You will be meeting with them in the future.'* Somehow I feel we will be connected."

Dream of a Catholic Priest
APRIL 1991

ON APRIL 20, AS WE WERE EATING BREAKFAST, Dennison said, "I dreamed about a Catholic Priest in an old church. He was wearing a long, dark brown robe with a cord tied around the waist, and sandals.

"It was night, and there were candles burning in the church. The Priest was hiding things in the walls of the church. He made holes in the walls, and then he was putting gold objects like gold candlesticks, gold cups, bowls, and things, inside these holes and then closing them back up again. He had holes in the floor, too. He hid a fortune in the walls. There were also some documents that he hid, too.

"The Priest killed one of his brothers who found him hiding the treasures, and he hid the body in the walls of the church, too. I guess the Priest was being transferred somewhere else, and he knew he couldn't take these things with him, so he hid them and planned to return later and get them. He never did."

A Dream of Volcanoes
APRIL 1991

APRIL TURNED OUT TO BE A VERY EVENTFUL MONTH for dreams and information. I wondered if it was somehow due to the Stone?

On April 29, Dennison had another vivid dream. I sat writing a letter and drinking a last cup of coffee. Dennison remarked, as he put breakfast dishes in the sink, "Last night I dreamed of two volcanoes that were erupting. One was out in the ocean. It was the largest ever recorded in history. It was causing lots of problems, and somehow several coastal cities were under water. There was also another volcano on land, connected in some way with the one in the ocean. The skies were dark with ash, and the cities were covered in ash for hundreds of miles. Cities were being evacuated, and people were moving to higher ground. 'They' were saying the ash from the volcanoes would cause weather changes. I don't know where it was."

Dream of a cave containing artifacts from our forgotten past

I looked up from my letter and turned the tablet to the next page and began to take notes. He was quiet for a moment, thinking. Then he continued, "I also dreamed last night that I was in a cave, and I found these metal cylinders in there. The cave was huge, with high ceilings and stalagmites hanging from them and some coming up out of the floor. There were some metal-looking cylinders hanging from the ceiling and some more on the floor, too. There were some long, crystal-looking rods coming up out of the floor, with some round, very large, donut-shaped things stacked on them. They seemed to give off a greenish glow.

"On the floor were some baskets, very finely and tightly woven, like none I've ever seen before. Woven into them were strange symbols or writing. There was also pottery, earthen pots different than anything I've ever seen.

"A little farther back in the cave were sort of oval-shaped stones laid to form pathways, and dwellings made of stone and mortar. There were chambers leading away into the cave. Then I saw 'boxes' made of sticks—twigs mortared together. Somehow they reminded me of what an insect would build. These boxes were long and stacked, one on top of the other. As I looked at them, I realized the sticks seemed to form shapes, like symbols or writing. I also realized these boxes were burial chambers or coffins.

"I had the feeling this place was *very* ancient, and it does exist and has never been discovered. I am the first to see it.

"I also have the strong feeling our history and beliefs about the past and of this world as we know it are wrong. Something is very wrong, and we can't see it. We need to change our thinking, need to learn the truth, before we destroy ourselves. This cave is something we don't know about, something in our past we've forgotten, and now don't believe ever existed."

A Dream of an Airplane in Trouble
MAY 1991

ON MAY 5, SLIGHTLY BEFORE 2:00 a.m., I woke up and realized Dennison also seemed to be awake. I rolled over on my side, my back to him, in order to get comfortable and resume my sleep. Dennison turned and snuggled against my back. A few moments passed; then I felt his solar plexus quiver. The quiver subsided, only to begin again. Slowly, the quiver increased its intensity, and I noticed his chest muscles were now involved in the quiver. I was becoming a little alarmed and said, "Lovey, what's happening? Why are you shivering like that?" He said, "I don't know; I guess I'm cold." This didn't make any sense, as it was not a cold night; he was covered, and we sleep in a heated waterbed. In fact, I was a little too warm with him snuggled against me.

I expressed to him that it was *warm* and asked if he felt ill. He said, "No, I'm just very, very cold." By this time, his thighs had begun to quiver and his upper arms. I had him turn his back to me, and I put my robe on top of his blankets and snuggled him to me. I noticed his buttocks were quivering now, and so were the muscles in his back, even his neck muscles and cheeks. What was odd was that his skin felt normal in temperature. Not too hot, nor too cool, and he had no goose bumps, just continuous quivering. Not exactly shivering. By this time, I was very alarmed and unsure what to do. I worried he was about to have some sort of a seizure. The only thing that kept me from total panic was his insistence he was only cold. Slowly, the quivering began to subside until it was just occasional, isolated twitches. I asked him if maybe he had a dream, and he replied, "Yeah . . . I was flying an airplane. . . . It was a twin engine, and one of the engines was out and the other was sputtering. I could see the wing of the plane; it was white with red on the tip edge. A number was painted on the wing in red. There were two pedals on the floor and a tiny steering wheel. I was pushing the pedals to try and keep the plane level and not lose control. I was exhausted with trying to keep the plane under control. I kept pushing a button on a panel on my right, trying to get the engine to start, but it wouldn't.

"There was a hole in the floor of the plane beside me, and *cold* air with ice crystals was blowing in. I could look down and see snow-covered peaks and tree tops just below me. I could see ridges in the snow. There was someone sitting beside me in the seat to my right, and some people behind me in the plane. The people were all scared and yelling for me to please not crash. I told them if I could make it over these mountains, I knew where there was a level place we could land."

I had a very hard time going back to sleep, but Dennison was soon asleep again. The rest of the night, he continued with momentary quivers.

The next morning, I asked him if he had had any more dreams, and he said, "I dreamed of flying in space. I could see the Milky Way, and above it was a large city. It seemed to waiver between material and non-material. As I got closer, there were three huge circles of colored metal. One was green, one blue, and one white. Through these, I could see the city—more beautiful than any on earth could ever be. It seemed to be made of crystal or glass. The buildings were *sooo* perfect. Some were rectangular in shape and some square, some tall and some short, but somehow seeing them was very satisfying. I sensed there were beings there, but I couldn't go any closer. Then I knew I had to leave, and I really hated to have to go. I hope I get to go back there."

The Power of Symbols
MAY 1991

MAY 20 DAWNED with the smell of summer in the air. I made coffee and toast, and we sat on the front porch, in the early morning sun, watching the hummingbirds and listening to the joyful sounds of the earth awakening. Dennison spoke, saying, "A little while ago, while you were making coffee, the stone was explaining that certain symbols, like the cross, the triangle, the square, and the circle, have a lot of power, and if used properly, they can manifest things you want. Even so-called Christian symbols, like the dove and the cross, had earlier meanings and were used in different ways to create certain energies. The serpent or dragon had a very powerful meaning.

"The human body is a reflection of Mother Earth. We humans have certain points of spiraling energy that go in different directions, either clockwise or counterclockwise. We call them Chakras. The earth also has such points. Certain stones and metals affect these chakras, both in the earth and in humans. There are certain places on the earth, such as Stonehenge, as well as many other sacred places, that relate to these points. Some of these places, if seen from above the earth, form the shape of a dragon. These points relate to and are connected to certain stars and receive energy from these stars. The star pattern also forms a serpent or dragon. The coils of the serpent mean different energies. Each hump and even the way the tail coils and the number of circles or coils create certain energies. Four humps are very powerful.

"Another powerful symbol is the Tree of Life. It is directly related to man's spiritual connections to the earth and the Creator.

"The old earth religions and the ways of the primitive peoples, the spiritual practices and teachings, are what kept the world in balance. We must learn them again if we are to survive.

"The excavating of old ruins is not a good practice. The energies created by a society still exist, even after they are gone. These energies are disturbed when the excavations take place and can lead to different problems. If you want to see how these past cultures lived, there are certain kinds of mushrooms that were used by many ancient peoples. If you eat these and then go to old ruins, you can see these energies and how these people lived.

"There are still many things that exist on the earth plane that are yet to be discovered, such as the Cup of Christ—things which people's belief systems will manifest.

"As people come to *believe* in something, when the belief energy is strong enough, it will be manifest.

"Our history is all wrong. Our beliefs are all wrong, and things must come about to shake our belief systems before new beliefs can come in."

You'll Be Meeting Some Japanese
MAY 1991

THE FOLLOWING AFTERNOON, as we worked on jewelry, Dennison casually mentioned, "The stone was just saying we'll be meeting with some Japanese. It said, *'There are going to be some Japanese coming into your lives soon.'* I sense a man and maybe a woman. Definitely a man. I think somehow we'll be working with them in some way."

More on the Ozone Layer
JUNE 1991

THE STONE SEEMED TO BE GROWING LESS COMMUNICATIVE, almost as if it were running down or something. I think Dennison was a little relieved.

On June 3, while meditating, he was instructed to put his Moldavite together with a small crystal. He got the following information after doing so.

"The ozone layer is becoming like a spider web. Very fragile, with many holes. Its purpose is to filter out harmful rays from the sun, as well as other cosmic particles. The effects are just beginning to be seen and felt.

"All plants have a protective coating; a film that helps keep insects out and protects them from harmful things in the environment. The harmful sun's rays, which are now able to pass through the ozone layer, are burning away that protective coating. This allows natural moisture in the needles or leaves to evaporate too rapidly and lets in environmental pollution from cars, from industries, and from many other sources. This will damage, weaken, and even kill the tree. Insects are also more able to do damage. There will be much, much more of this thing showing up in all vegetation and crops in affected areas. The vegetation itself gives off a lot of moisture, which goes into the air to form clouds. When enough vegetation dies, this eventually will affect the weather, and droughts will follow.

"The seas are also affected. There is a moss-like substance that grows in the sea, which the fish and mammals eat. This too is being damaged by these harmful rays. The fish are going hungry and turn to eating garbage that is dumped in the sea. This is killing them. The rays are also burning the whales and dolphins. That damage will begin to show up soon.

"There are a lot of insects that aren't coming back. Though it might not seem important, they are very important and part of the balance. They aid in the pollination of plants, but more important, their excretions and saliva aid in plant growth.

"In drought areas, as the soil dries out, cracks form. As the cracks dry out, they go deeper and deeper into the earth, and then the water table inside the earth evaporates through the cracks.

"Eventually, crops will have to be grown in giant greenhouses with filters to filter out harmful rays. Artificial, underground water tables will have to be created.

"When logging is done, certain trees should be left. These trees reseed and fertilize the area and keep the balance. Trees also attract clouds. They actually give off certain chemicals, pollen particles, and even moisture, which attract clouds and create rain. When trees are cut, the clouds don't come, and the area dries out, and the weather pattern changes. (I immediately thought of Snowflake, where I lived for ten years. It was a standing joke about the "hole in the clouds" right over the town. The whole time I lived there, the areas all around Snowflake would get lots of rain and snow, but there wouldn't even be clouds over the town. Old timers there told of deep snows in the winters and lots of rain in the summers, of the creek running through town frequently overflowing and causing flooding in the past. I recalled Snowflake in the past used to be nestled in a thick cedar forest, but in the early 1960s, the BLM took bulldozers and pushed the cedars over for miles and miles around the town to create grazing land for cattle.)

"Every several thousand years, there is a new cycle, a shift of the energies. Even the stars shift; their energies affect the earth. You are nearing the end of a cycle. The prevailing energies on earth are magnified during this time. If there is a lot of spiritual energy, it will be magnified and in turn create more spiritual energies. TV programs, movies, literature, and the arts will become increasingly more spiritual. People will begin to help each other, greed will begin to stop, abundance will be shared. If materialism and fear is strong, it too will be magnified, and you will see an increase in wars, poverty, prejudice, street gangs and violence. That is why right now it is so very important to open people up to being spiritual. If there is enough spiritual energy at the time of the shift, the material world will eventually self-destruct, and the spiritual world will go on to a higher vibration.

"You are needed now to open people's minds. Give them sage and cedar, fans, medicine bags, stones, crystals, and love. Teach them prayers, ceremonies, love, and hope. If you need more supplies, they will be provided. Each person you touch, touches other people who touch others. A network is created, and as the energies magnify, these people will reach out to help each other. More and more people will help you, so your work can continue. There will be people who will come forth with funding for a retreat, if you wish. You can buy land and build it."

Greed

JUNE 1991

ON THE 7TH, when Dennison went to meditate, he again put the two stones together and received the following.

"Mankind is entering into the Mammalian Age. By the end of this century, man will be able to communicate with many species of animals, such as Dolphins and Whales. This will be achieved telepathically.

"There were times in Man's distant past when he was able to communicate with certain species, especially reptiles. That is because he was once related to the reptiles. Man was tried out in many different forms, until the best-suited form was found.

"He was Created to be caretaker of the earth and the animals. He was to take only what he needed for himself and oversee the rest. He was given the power of reason. But when he began to reason, he began to fear. He had a sense of self, and reason told him he could cease to exist, so he feared. He feared he might starve, might not survive, so he became greedy, and he fought his brothers over his fears.

"Time has brought man to where he is now, and his greed is about to destroy his home. He is about to be tested to see if he is worthy to keep his position as caretaker of the earth. He is, after all, a Mammal too, and very little different than any other Mammal. He believes he is superior, that his brain is superior, but it's not. All Mammals are equal; they are brothers. There is very, very much he can learn from the animals.

"Man is about to enter into a time of testing, where he will be forced into a position to see what he has done to the planet he was put in charge of caring for. He will thirst and he will hunger, and he will have to learn to share or die. His greed, the greed of big business, has created this. Man's desire for material things supports the greed of big businesses. Your thinking is locked into getting more and more of material things, and each thing you acquire supports the greed. This way of thinking and living has to be done away with before the end of the century, the end of this cycle of Man.

"At the end of this cycle, there will be a doorway that opens into another vibration. The religions would call it a time of judgment. All Mankind must pass through this doorway. Those who are spiritual and open will continue to grow and create a balanced and harmonious world; those who are caught in the materialism and greed will stay until they self-destruct.

"There are beings called Guardians coming into existence on this plane now. They will be working through certain earth people who are open to receive. The Guardians are some of the so-called aliens, and the earth people they are working through lived in Atlantis during the time there was a separation of power. The Guardians are coming to bring this power back and to oversee that it is not misused and separated again."

As the weeks went by, the stone began to communicate less and less. I'm not sure if it was Dennison's resistance to having a stone communicate with him or if it simply had finished its purpose. Little did we know that this was to be the last information given through it.

A Miracle
JUNE 1991

IT ALL BEGAN EARLY ONE MORNING IN JUNE. A friend of ours called and asked Dennison if he could do a healing for her daughter-in-law, whom we had never met.

Dennison asked, "What's the problem?" She elaborated, saying, "My daughter-in-law is six and a half months pregnant. They recently did a sonogram and found her baby has a massive tumor on one lung. It is so large it is crowding the baby's other lung, her heart, and her kidneys. Her head is filling with fluid and is too large. There are many, many other complications. The doctors are amazed the baby is still alive and that her mom has carried her this long. Now she is too far along to terminate the pregnancy, and the baby is too small to survive if they try to take her now. In fact, they give her very little chance of surviving, even if she is carried to term and surgery is attempted."

Dennison told our friend, "I don't know if there is anything I can do. I've never had any experience with something like this." Our friend pleaded, "If you could just do a prayer for them or something. Give my kids something to hold on to. They are both so frightened, and it's really hard on her having to carry this baby to term, knowing she'll likely lose her anyway. It's their first baby, and they've been so excited. . . . If you could maybe just talk to them and help them to cope with everything. My son is just shutting down. Shutting everyone out, so he won't have to feel."

With reluctance, he finally agreed, not really sure what he could do, hoping somehow to give comfort. He set a time for the following evening for the family to come over.

The next day, he fasted and prayed to be guided in how to proceed. That evening the family arrived, and after a few minutes of talking and getting acquainted, Dennison explained what he wanted to do. He had us all go into one of the bedrooms, where he had set up a massage table and a small altar. He had the young woman lie on the massage table, and her family and I formed a circle around her. He began praying over her, and as he prayed, he later told me, he felt his hands being guided and heard "someone" telling him what to do. He followed these instructions, ordering me to get him a wooden bowl full of spring water and an arrowhead. The best I could come up with was a salad bowl and some bottled spring water. The instructions continued, and as he worked he had us all touch her with our hands and send her energy. We all felt a powerful, tingling energy in the room. Later, when all was finished and we sat in the living room talking, Dennison casually asked the young woman if her father was deceased. Surprised, she answered, "Yes." He continued, "Was his name Bill?" Even more surprised, she again answered, "Yes. He died two years ago." Dennison commented, "I feel like you were very close." She blinked back tears and nodded yes. He went on telling her, "There was a man there with me, standing down by your feet. He had dark hair with a lot of gray on the sides and a small mustache. He said his name was Bill, and he wanted me to tell you that you worry too much. And to tell you everything is going to be okay. He wants you to believe that." She really began crying with this news. Through her tears she said, "That's exactly how he looked! He used to tell me that a lot, that I worry too much and everything is going to be okay."

A few days later we got an excited phone call from the young woman telling us she had just had another sonogram, with the doctors keeping an eye on the baby's progress. To everyone's amazement, the tumor had shrunk considerably, and the excess fluid build up in the baby was greatly decreased. The doctors now had hope the baby might be able make it to term and to survive a surgery.

In September, the baby was born and had a successful surgery within hours after her birth. There followed many crises, many prayers, and many tears over the next several months. But, at the time of this writing, she is a healthy, intelligent four-year-old. The doctors say she is a miracle.

The family kept thanking Dennison for all he did, believing the baby was alive largely because of him. His reply was, "It wasn't me. I don't know how to heal anything. I was just hands. Creator did the rest. It's all up to Him."

After helping heal the baby's tumor, word spread rapidly as the family told many friends, and Dennison's reputation grew. More and more people with more and more serious problems began to seek him out. The responsibilities that go with helping such people were daunting, and he shrank from the task being asked of him. Over and over he questioned why he was being asked to do what he was doing.

One day, we were in Flagstaff selling jewelry. As we returned to the parking lot, we saw an elderly Navajo man trying to work on his pickup truck. Dennison walked over and asked if he needed some help. The old man looked up and smiled, and offered his hand in greeting, "I guess my starter's gone out. I could use a ride to an auto parts so I can get a new one." We took him to get a new starter and helped him install it in his pickup. As we conversed, we discovered he was a medicine man from the area of the reservation where Dennison had grown up. He remembered Dennison's grandparents and his dad. He asked if anyone else in the family became a medicine man. Dennison found himself telling him a little about what he had been doing and some of what he was experiencing. The old man was thoughtful, then replied, "There's a lot of people who would say you shouldn't be doing this stuff for White people. . . . I guess it's because you're married to a White woman, but you should be helping your own people." Dennison protested, "I have Indians who live in town that come and see me; I see anyone who needs help. I don't ask what color they are." The old man brushed this aside and said, "You should come out and help with some ceremonies. Learn the songs and stuff. They always need helpers. That's where you belong, with your own people."

Dennison was troubled by what the old man had said, and he began to question if he should try going back to the reservation, if only occasionally, and involve himself in working with his own people. This wasn't a White man's thing, this was the Native way, and Native people knew and understood how to work within the system. Let the White people go to their own medicine men, their own doctors. And finally, maybe he shouldn't do this at all. Why did he feel such a need to help when asked. What did "they" want of him anyway?

The next day he spent several hours praying about what to do. He was told, *"It's not your destiny to follow only one path. You are to be there for all people. Traditional teachings and beliefs bring with them boundaries and dogma. They are your foundation, but you are learning to go beyond them.*

"You are here to help open people's minds and hearts, to help mankind get back in touch with Mother Earth and the Creator. You are here to teach love and to live love. That will be accomplished by many methods, not only healing. There must be no boundaries to get in your way. The only one you answer to is Creator."

Still feeling the sting of the medicine man's criticism, he replied, "I feel guilty I'm not helping my own people." Gently he was reminded, *"All people are your own people."*

A Dream about a Hawkman
JUNE 1991

EARLY THE MORNING OF THE 12TH, Dennison awakened me and said, "I just had a strange dream about a Hawkman. He had the body of a man and the head of a hawk. He had wings as well as arms. His chest was bare, except for several necklaces that looked like they were made of feathers, or maybe paper. He had on a knee-length skirt. His legs were bare and ended in bird-like feet, with black talons and three toes.

"He was standing on the edge of a canyon, watching a caravan of people on the other side, getting ready to go down into the canyon. They were carrying a covered platform. I sensed they were taking someone or something to be buried."

And Hidden Tablets

WE WENT BACK TO SLEEP, and when we woke up at our normal time, Dennison said, "I was dreaming again. I saw an old man crouched on the side of a mountain. He was beside a crevice in the rocks, chiseling something into the face of the rock. He was wearing a brownish-gray, rough-woven fabric that went over one shoulder and tied around the waist. His hair was thin, nearly bald.

"He was supposed to take some sacred tablets, sacred documents somewhere, but he couldn't make it to his destination, so he hid them in the crevice of the rocks; then he marked where he hid them. I saw day and night, day and night pass as he sat there chiseling in the rock. At night, a sort of yellow glow came out of the crevice. I couldn't see exactly what he was chiseling in the rock, but I knew it could only be seen when the sun struck it from a certain angle.

"When it was hidden, it was at shoulder level, but now it is down low, hard to spot. So far it hasn't been found.

"Someone asked me, *'Do you know any of the stories about the tablets hidden on a mountain?'* I could only think of the movie of Moses and the Ten Commandments. They told me, *'Your history is all wrong; the Bible is not correct either.'"*

Tidbits
JUNE 1991

ON THE 17TH, as Dennison was working, he said, "Something is telling me it's time to focus on what we want. The energies are shifting, and it's time to set goals and focus on them. It has something to do with the Mayan calendar.

"There's something to do with breeding, too. I can't really get what they're saying. Something about the breeding habits of women, as well as female animals, will change. Not as many young will be born.

"These energies are also affecting world governments. The governmental systems will be in an upheaval. Great changes will be taking place in the highest parts of many Governments. President Bush will start it. The final outcome will be for the best."

This was before the breakup of the USSR, and after it happened, I couldn't help but wonder if this was a reference to it.

A Dream of a Strange Shower
JUNE 1991

THIS MORNING WE WERE TAKING OUR SHOWERS and getting our day started, when Dennison said, "This reminds me, last night I was dreaming I was in this cylinder-like thing. The walls were transparent, and I could see outside of it. I seemed to be on a low platform, in the center of a room. The wall in front of me was a little curved, as if the room could be circular. I was naked and paralyzed or something, because the only thing I could move was my eyes. I noticed there were these tubes along the wall of the room, with curved ends on them. They reminded me of mechanical arms. The cylinder I was in was bathed in light. The light slowly changed colors, going through all the colors of the rainbow. As I stood there, a thought came into my mind, *'This is for your soul.'*

"After a while, I noticed there was a vibration that seemed to come up from the floor of the cylinder and vibrate through my body. Then the lights stopped and warm steam filled the room, like a sauna. After this, there was a cool shower of water, almost like a mist. And then there was warm air that dried me. Then the cylinder lifted off of me, and I found out I could move. So I stepped down into the room, and a door seemed just to open up in a wall in front of me. I headed for the door, wondering where anybody was and what I was doing there. Then all of a sudden I woke up.

"During the dream, I kept noticing a smell like nothing I can describe, yet very familiar."

A Dream of a Strange Shower

A Dream of Light People
JULY 1991

A COUPLE OF WEEKS LATER, ON JULY 10, we went camping. Dennison woke me up early in the morning, saying, "I was just dreaming about some beings called Mangoids. They are Light People in human-looking bodies. I saw them, and they looked like regular people, except they seemed to glow slightly. They carried this large . . . like a ball that was a glowing bluish color. They were going to certain people who were critically ill or severely injured, then healing them with their hands. I was being told these Light People were coming into the earth plane soon, and they would be healing certain people and teaching these people to in turn heal others with their hands; to be healers, because in the past they had been great healers, during the time of Atlantis. People will soon begin to hear about some of these healings.

"I also dreamed about riots. Really bad riots. Fighting in the streets, buildings destroyed. I think it was street gang and race related."

The following May (of 1992) marked riots, buildings destroyed, and fighting in the streets of Los Angeles.

A Dream of a Cave and a Hidden City
JULY 1991

A FEW NIGHTS LATER, ON THE 15TH, Dennison again had an interesting dream. I wished my dreams were as interesting as his.

"I dreamed I saw a kind of narrow cave in some rocks on the side of a mountain. I stepped inside to look around, and the floor gave away under me, and I slid down, down, down. I tried to stop myself, but it was slippery and muddy and full of loose rocks. Finally, I came to a stop, and in front of me was a wall that looked like it was made out of stones fitted together. It was obvious that it had been built by someone. There was enough light coming from the top to see a little, and as I got used to the dark, I looked more closely at the wall. I found a place where it had fallen away, and I could see a room on the other side. It looked like it had a tiled floor, and there was what appeared to be gold objects and precious stones and some other things in there. I followed the wall a little farther in, to see if I could find a way into the other room to get a better look.

"A little farther on, the wall looked like it had collapsed into rubble, and I climbed through it into the room. Then I noticed there were hollowed out places in the wall, forming a kind of bowl with a rope-like thing hanging out. I felt inside the bowl and found something oily and decided it was a light of some sort, so I lit the rope. This illuminated the room, and as I looked around I saw a stairway and decided to see where it led. As I climbed it, I could hear like a woman singing or crying. I followed the sound, only hearing it now and then. Sometimes it sounded like the sighing of the wind.

"Suddenly I realized I had gone a long way, and I now had no idea where I was. Strangely enough, there was light enough to see where I was going, and I noticed I was walking in a tunnel of the cave. I saw a glow like a light up ahead of me and kept walking toward it. Soon I could hear the sound of someone hammering. I followed the sound until I came to the edge of a huge cavern, and below me was a little man like an elf. Beside him was a huge crystal. It was nearly as tall as the ceiling and glowing a bluish glow, which lit up the cavern. The little guy was chipping away on some crystals. Then I noticed a path around the edge of the cavern, and it led to what seemed to be an opening to the outside. I followed this and went outside. I came out at the edge of a large body of water, like a sea. There were cliffs above me. As I looked along the cliffs, I noticed the ruins of an ancient city of some sort. The walls were white, with huge pillars on many of the buildings. Even now it was beautiful, as it spread along the shoreline. Somehow I felt I had been there before. I thought of going over to it, but part of me just wanted to find a way out of there. I began looking for a way out, when suddenly an old man in a long white robe and white hair was beside me. He said, *'Do you remember where you are?'* I told him, 'No, I don't.' Then I asked if he knew the way out of there. He said, *'Follow me,'* and began to lead me up some stairs that I hadn't noticed before, which went up the canyon wall. As we neared the top, I suddenly noticed he was no longer there. I went the rest of the way by myself, and as I got to the top, I found myself back in front of the narrow cave on the side of the mountain."

A Call from Canada
AUGUST 1991

ON AUGUST 7, we got a curious phone call from a Cree woman in Canada. She said her Cree name was Asanee Watchew Iskwiw, which means Mountain Woman. She said she had been feeling a pull to go to Arizona, but hadn't known why. Then a friend had sent her a peice of Dennison's jewelry and a letter saying he was a Navajo healer who lived in Arizona. After receiving this, the need to go became even stronger.

She went on to explain her son had had leukemia and the Rainbow Society was making it possible for them to travel to a Native gathering near Santa Fe, New Mexico in a motorhome. She wondered if she, her kids, her brother and his wife, and a Cree Elder, who was traveling with them, could travel on down to meet us.

The following week they arrived, and within a few minutes after their arrival, it felt as if we had found long lost family. It was a sort of recognition of the Spirit, and we all felt it.

What began as a brief visit ended up lasting a week. In that time, we did several beautiful ceremonies in our backyard, sharing cultures and spirituality. One very special ceremony took place on the Navajo Reservation on Dennison's land at the edge of a small canyon, during a full moon. It ended in a beautiful and spontaneous "Give Away," where valued items were exchanged between everyone.

Another very special ceremony took place the day before they left. The Cree Elder, after meditating and praying, gave Dennison a Cree name, "Asinika Paminat," which means "Rock Protector" or "Earth Protector." It was a very great honor.

At last, it was time for them to return to Canada. It was hard to say good-bye after such a wonderful and spiritual week.

A Dream of Teachings from a Doctor
AUGUST 1991

DENNISON'S STRANGE AND VIVID DREAMS CONTINUED. On August 10, as we lay in bed listening to the early birds welcoming the dawn, he laughingly said, "I dreamed I was the student of a doctor whose name sounded something like Enfriend Enzuk. He was foreign and spoke with a thick accent of some sort. He called me Danielle.

"He was demonstrating on a patient. The room was lit by candlelight, and I watched it reflect off his instruments as he sterilized them with alcohol.

"He explained to me how he used his hands to send energy to his patients and to sense where problems were. He said he used crystals in some of his diagnosing, as well as in his healing work, and even to energize water. When diagnosing, he would place the crystals in a bowl of water, then wet his hands in the water and scan the patient with his wet hand while looking at the bowl of water. He claimed he could 'see' inside the patient when he did this. He told me his colleagues ridiculed him, but he had achieved impressive results by doing this.

"The doctor said he would treat patients with terminal illnesses and serious ailments by soaking them in energized baths and had achieved good results.

"He had some sort of a round device which he would strike, and the device would hummmmm. Then he would proceed to move it up and down the body.

"He told me he had been working with using hot and cold shocks in treating some patients, with moderate success. The process involved applying either heat or cold to the patient for awhile, then suddenly applying the opposite. The theory was that the metabolism would be shocked into a new course of action and hopefully get back on track."

Another Doctor Dream
AUGUST 1991

On August 20, Dennison had yet another doctor dream.

"I dreamed I was talking with three doctors. One was a psychologist, one treated the nervous system, and one worked with the eyes.

"The doctor who worked with the nerves was telling me about a lot of studies that showed what sound does to the nervous system, both good and bad. For example, if you live or work where there is a lot of noise, like machinery, it has a negative affect on the nervous system and is the cause of some illnesses. Also, in relationships where there is a lot of arguing and yelling, some people's nerves are very sensitive; just the sound of yelling affects them negatively, causing blockages in the signals that travel along the nerves.

"The doctor who worked with the eye explained how color affects the nervous system in certain ways and could actually create moods, soothe anger, etc. He said they were beginning to find how certain colors can actually speed up the healing process and how wave lengths of light, which is what color really is, affect the nervous system in different ways. They were finding ways of using sound and color in certain ways to affect the nerves to heal.

"They went on to explain that the medical profession was becoming interested in how medicine men worked on people, because they had always been treating illness both from the psychological standpoint as well as the physical. They somehow realized illness begins in the mind often before it manifests in the body. They said Native herbs were also of great interest now. For instance, there was a certain bird in Africa, which medicine men there used to create medicine to treat nervous disorders. It was found to show great promise in Western medicine to treat some kinds of diseases of the nervous system.

"I asked them why they wanted to talk with me. I don't really know anything like that. They told me I had been highly recommended."

The Presidential Race

AUGUST 1991

IT WAS NOW THE END OF AUGUST, and the presidential campaign was getting underway. During a meditation, Dennison was told, "Your Governmental system needs changing. There was a society before you who had a similar system, but it fell. The initial plan is correct; it's the people within the Government who are causing the problems now. The original planners were guided, but the plan isn't really followed now. The people who are running your system are in it for themselves.

"There's a group of people coming onto the scene soon who are going to try to change it back, but they will be resisted. There will be lots of conflict. Those now holding office will fight hard to resist this new influence. There will be a space of confusion before the new ideas take hold and things change.

"There's going to be more females holding high positions within the government. Don't be surprised if a woman runs for President again."

This was before Ross Perot began his campaign.

A Dream of Aliens at the South Pole
SEPTEMBER 1991

WE WERE ON OUR WAY TO SEDONA to sell some jewelry and show a visiting friend the sights. It was almost impossible to carry on a conversation with our passenger sitting in the back seat of the van. We rode in silence, each lost in our own thoughts. After a time, Dennison looked over at me, "I had a really weird dream last night. It seemed so real that even now thinking about it makes me feel like it actually happened." I leaned closer to hear him better.

"I dreamed I was at the South Pole. At least, in a sense I felt I was there, yet there was also a feeling I was observing, like through a TV screen. It was as if I was being allowed to see, but not be a part of it.

"I was talking to a strange being. He was about five feet tall, very slender built, but appearing to be human-like. His face was thin, with a kind of pointed chin, a thin mouth with no real lips, and a tiny sort of upturned nose. His eyes were pretty normal looking, and he smiled. His arms and legs were thin but not abnormal looking, except that there were three fingers and a thumb on each hand. He was wearing a tight-fitting, dull white coverall. It almost looked like skin because it fit so close; however, it had a high collar, so I knew it wasn't skin. He was wearing gloves that went up to his elbows. He was also wearing boots that reminded me of snow boots, you know, moon boots.

"Beyond him was like a flat plain that extended far into the distance. On the horizon were snow-covered mounds or low hills. It seemed like early morning or twilight.

"Scattered across the plain were flying discs of all different shapes. There were several beings engaged in different activities. These beings looked different from the one who was talking with me. (Actually, communication was taking place in my head. I would just think something, and he would answer in my mind.) The other beings were real, real thin, and their heads were shaped different, and they sort of moved strangely. They were unloading, carrying, and stacking materials from the discs. Some carried cylinders that reminded me of acetylene bottles. There were several stacks of these. They were also carrying sheets of thin material, maybe plastic. It reminded me of sheets of silver, except it was not shiny; there was no reflective quality to it. It had no color, but it was not transparent. There were several stacks of this material around. Off to one side, I could see part of a large building made of this material. It was hard to see; it seemed to mirror back the surroundings, and it just blended with everything. There was a diffused, bluish light, sort of like phosphorescent light, coming out of the building. There was no harsh quality to it, like normal lighting would have.

"My companion mentioned that they had to create their own atmosphere to live; they can't interact with our atmosphere for extended periods. I asked what they were doing there, and he explained they were relocating from their underground facilities, because some humans were getting closer and closer to finding them. He said that there were some people within our government who were aware of them and were working with them, but pressure from the public was beginning to cause some of them to release information, and it wasn't yet time for everyone to know about them. He said the current president wasn't fully working with them in a positive way.

"I asked what they were doing on earth, and he said they were mining certain minerals. I asked if it was things like gold or diamonds, and he told me they were after softer minerals like certain salts, sulfur, and substances deep within the earth, of which we were yet unaware. They were also mining some crystals, which they combine with certain minerals to achieve desired results. When I asked what they used them for, he said that was something we would have to discover for ourselves, since we nearly destroyed ourselves by the misuse of crystals in the past. Maybe by the time we discover this, we would know how to use them properly.

"He told me they were also here to watch over and guide mankind. He showed me what looked like a big TV screen. Nodding toward it, he said, *'We are working with many people like you. Even now, we are working with everyone in your household.'* I asked him if I was effective, doing what I was doing, trying to combine my healing work with making jewelry and doing art, or if it would be better to be working at a normal job.

"He told me, *'You can go either way, because you will be affecting those you come in contact with. We know you are having a difficult time. We are working to make things easier for you, arranging contacts with certain people who can help you in many ways. For now, you must continue as you are. Soon you will be doing a lot of traveling, speaking, healing, and working with people. Don't worry about what to say or what to do; you will be guided. We will work through you.'*

"He raised his eyebrows in mock surprise, and said, *'I notice you are healing with your hands and mind now. Does that surprise you? You were a powerful healer long ago in the past, using your hands and visualizing. You are just beginning to remember how. It will continue to come if you choose to work with it.'*

"I asked him how I could be more effective and he said, *'You are as effective as you can be within the present system. In order for things to change for the better, the present system must be broken down, completely destroyed. There will be a space of time while mankind finds new*

A Dream of Aliens at the South Pole

ways, more spiritual ways. You need to work toward becoming more self-sufficient over the next two years. Beginning in 1992, there will be many changes taking place; these will continue over the next several years. You must not fear or worry; we are always with you and watching over you. You have numerous helpers and guides. We haven't contacted you for awhile, because we've been very busy. There is much happening in the world. Much to be done.'"

A Dream of Banks in Trouble
SEPTEMBER 1991

ON SEPTEMBER 9, as we were eating breakfast, Dennison asked me what a private bank was. I thought about this for awhile, then replied, "I suppose it would be a hometown bank as opposed to a large interstate bank or international bank." He said, "Last night I dreamed 'they' were telling me to do business only with private banks, because the larger banks were in serious trouble. They have loaned large amounts of money to big corporations, and because of this the banks are in a sense owned by and supported by the interest paid from these loans and from the business from these large corporations. They have to act on behalf of the big corporations in order to protect themselves. Later, there's going to be serious problems in the financial world and many, many large corporations will be in financial trouble and can't repay their loans. The banks will then be in trouble, and many, many will fail. Only after this will the small private banks will be affected, but you can see it coming. The best thing to do is to invest in precious metals like gold and silver and precious stones and jewelry and things to barter with."

A Dream of an Assassination Attempt
NOVEMBER 1991

THINGS WERE QUIET FOR SEVERAL WEEKS, then on November 11, Dennison said, "Last night I dreamed there was an assassination attempt at the White House. There was an explosion, maybe a bomb. I think it was at a gathering of people. I think it's going to happen to some politician, but I don't think it was *in* the White House, but will affect the White House."

Special Teachings
NOVEMBER 1991

EARLY THE MORNING OF NOVEMBER 21, Dennison took his pipe and went into the woods to meditate and pray. As he sat in meditation, two beings came to him. One seemed to be his Grandfather; the other was a woman who at first he thought was his Grandmother, but later he realized it wasn't.

The pipe he carried was new; he had just finished putting the finishing touches on it the day before. The woman told him, "Bury your bowl in the earth, for it comes from the earth and represents the Mother and all female things." His Grandfather then told him, "Go put the stem in that cedar tree, for it was carved from the sacred cedar and represents the Male. Know these acts are a consecration, an initiation for the pipe. I must remind you that the pipe contains a living Spirit; it is a being, with its own powers and teachings. To carry the pipe, you must respect this and allow it always to lead you.

"You will be receiving many powerful teachings, and, as a result, many more people will be coming to you. Be aware also that there will come those who will challenge you or disagree with and oppose you openly. You must recognize they aren't opened up yet and are still living in fear. You must *never* raise your voice in anger to them; just quietly maintain your stand and know they are being taken care of already. Remember, you have the power to heal. Every power has an opposite side, so along with the healing power comes the power to destroy. Should you become angry, you could unleash that destructive power without intending to.

"You are here to act as a teacher, a messenger, and a leader. As time goes by, you will be shown more and more things. You must not ally yourself with anyone or any group. You must love all equally and show no favorites. You must learn to detach yourself from those who seek you out. Love them, be there for them, guide them; then let them go and apply what you have shown them. Open the door for them to walk their own path, but you don't need to help them walk it. There will be increasingly more and more who need you, and always many waiting for you. Take care to make yourself available, but don't allow yourself to be used up. You will know when it is getting to be too much.

"You must come back here as often as possible—at least two or three times a week, more when you can, and sit and meditate and be with Nature. There are a lot of teachings to give you, a lot of instruction, and guidance, for the energies are changing even now on a subtle level. This next year there will be a major change in the Oval Office. The current president is not supposed to be there right now; it was supposed to have been a woman, but somehow the people didn't get the message. The feminine energies a woman president would provide are essential and have been greatly needed even before now. The Mother Earth is in great distress, and her need of feminine energy is great, so now it is time for some major changes, in order to bring in the feminine energies into the presidency.

"There are beings coming in now who are still of light. They are here to teach and to guide. They aren't here to interfere, and they won't 'save' you. They will only teach and guide those who are open to them. With them are coming great gifts. Great powers, and healing. A new race is being born, being created."

At this point, Dennison was introduced to two beautiful people. They were both wearing white robes, and the man wore a blue stone around his neck. The woman had very long, golden hair. They said they would soon be working with him.

His Grandfather then told him, "They are two of the beings who will be seen within the next two years. They have manifested bodies out of organic materials. They have no Mother or Father. They are both male and female, though for the sake of understanding, one appears as male and the other as female. They are coming as teachers. Many will report seeing them, in many countries."

With this, the beings vanished, and Dennison got his pipe, put it together, smoked it in a prayer of thanks, and returned home full of excitement.

A Dream of Nostradamus
DECEMBER 1991

ON DECEMBER 3, Dennison woke me up early in the morning to say, "I was just dreaming about a man named Astrodamas." Sleepily, I asked if it could have been Nostradamus? Agreeably, he said, "Yeah, I guess so. Anyway, he was short and heavy set. Dark-complexioned with a gray beard, and his hair was mostly gray, mixed with a little black. His hair was to his shoulders and getting thin on top. He wore real thick glasses.

"He said that we are getting ready to enter the third phase. This will be a time where the people who are into spiritual things and the people who are focused in material things will begin separating more and more. People's values will become more and more clear. This will create conflicts between them, and the division will grow deeper and deeper.

"Corrupt politicians will begin to surface and be brought to public attention. Environmental issues will become political issues, and a major move to stop environmental programs will happen at top governmental levels. Man will be faced with a choice. Material or Spiritual. If he doesn't choose spiritual ways, he will self-destruct."

I reflected on what an interesting year it had been, and I eagerly looked forward to what the new year would bring. Dennison had grown and evolved and was much more confident. He was hardly the same man he had been three years ago.

Dream of a Stock Market Crash

FEBRUARY 1992

IT WAS FEBRUARY 9, 1992 before Dennison was to get any more information. Then, early one morning, Dennison got up and went to the bathroom. When he returned to bed, he said, "I was dreaming about what I would call an underground organization, kind of like a Mafia or something. There were a lot of different countries that were part of it. They were taking over cities by buying American businesses that were in serious financial trouble and gaining control of financial resources that way. They were moving their own people into the businesses and causing a lot of people to be unemployed. There were a lot of people fighting in the streets."

I remarked that it was an unusual dream and asked if he thought it might mean something. He replied he felt sure it did, but didn't know who or what the "underground" was. He was quiet for a few moments, then asked, "What does a stock market crash really mean?" I sort of explained it and reminded him of the one in the 1930s. He then told me he had another dream. "I dreamed I was in a very large room full of people. At first I thought of the Oval Office, you know, the President, because I associated it with the President for some reason. But someone told me it was the Stock Market.

"As I stood in this room, the walls began to crumble, and the ceiling was caving in. People began running everywhere in a panic. I felt myself getting panicked too, and I started to look for a way out, but every doorway would be blocked and sealed off before anyone could get out. People were fighting with each other and running over chairs and everything. I kept looking and looking for an opening and getting more and more afraid, when someone said, *'Just stay calm and look around; there is still a way out.'* So I just stood there and looked around. Pretty soon I could see a clearing, a break in the people and an open door, so I went out."

A Future Purpose
FEBRUARY 1992

ON FEBRUARY 12, Dennison again went out and meditated. He heard two voices, one that was deep and mature, and this he identified with his Grandfather. The other was softer, milder, almost feminine.

He asked what was in store for the future, and what he needed to be doing.

"You need to turn your thinking around and help others to do the same. Right now you are seeing what is happening with the economy and the environment. Look for the good, for there is a lot of good out there. There are a lot of people doing ceremonies and energy work for peace and healing the earth. You are not in a position to hear much about it, but it's there, and it's effective. Send out hope and positive feelings, and give this to others who come to you. That's what's needed right now.

"There will come a time in the future when you will meet with other spiritual leaders for healing the earth. You must remain neutral for now; that isn't your place yet. There are many who are searching and seeking spiritual and physical healing, and that is to be your focus for now.

"Keep working on becoming self-sufficient over the next two years."

A Return to the Valley
FEBRUARY 1992

SINCE DECEMBER, Dennison had been going out to a special power spot in the woods to meditate and pray as instructed.

On February 14, he received a special "valentine" when he went out to do his prayers. As he meditated, a voice said, *"Let's go on a journey and see how it goes."*

"I felt myself being drawn down a tunnel very, very fast. Suddenly, I was on the edge of a canyon overlooking a beautiful valley. It looked a lot like the valley I saw a long time ago when I had that first experience (April, 1988). From where I was, I could see a strange city below.

"There were beautiful curving walkways and strange-shaped buildings. I could see tiny beings far below, going about their daily routine. In the distance I could see a huge, metal—or maybe glass—'dish' standing on end, kind of like a TV satellite dish. I saw this pyramid-shaped building with a gray and white surface. There were star-shaped openings above the doorways. I saw a bright light beaming either from the windows or into the windows from somewhere else. There were other strange-shaped buildings with lots of light coming from inside them.

"There was a lake or pool at the edge of the city, like the city hugged the canyon walls at the edge of the water. I could see this huge dome, made of glass or metal, standing in the water; it was revolving, and a bright light was coming from it. There was a walkway over the water, but it was dark, and I couldn't see where it went. To one side of the walkway was a whirlpool, and I kind of felt like the dome was somehow mixing the water.

"What's really weird is that I felt like I was underground. When I looked way up, high above my head I could just make out what looked like grooves—kind of like what you would see in a culvert pipe. Like maybe a huge tunnel or something.

"That scene faded, and pretty soon I saw some strange writing or symbols on a wall. It was a huge, stone wall, maybe a canyon wall or mountainside. The wall was about thirty to fifty feet high. There was a sun with an eye in it and beams going across and below the writing. Above the writing was a smaller circle with "sides" and light coming from it, maybe like a meteor.

"The next scene I saw was a large stone, about eight inches in diameter. It was so beautiful, a kinda clear purple. As I looked at it, it turned blue, then green. The stone was faceted, and in the facets I could see these images moving, but I couldn't quite make out what they were. What was strange was the stone was sitting on a tree stump.

"A few minutes later, another scene came to me. A beautiful woman appeared; she seemed to be covered in a mist, like fog or smoke. She was wearing a beautiful, jeweled headband or crown, and she was carrying a large, flat dish; I guess you would call it a platter. There were several objects on the dish, maybe food or jewels, I don't know for sure what. There was a very bright light around the platter, and I couldn't make out what it was. The woman was standing in a garden, and I sensed she was like a goddess.

"After this, I saw myself going down this path. Ahead I could see that the path led between two cliffs. I wanted to go in, but a swarm of huge

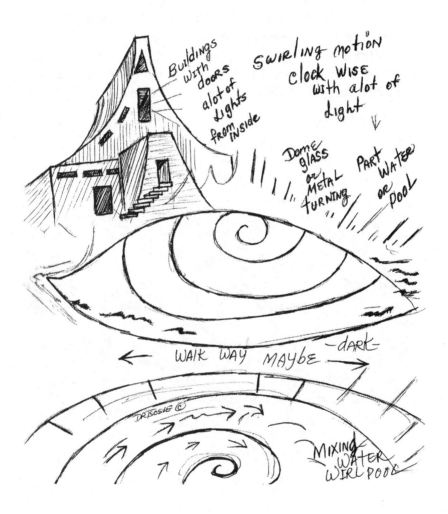

bees came out (or maybe I was very small). The bees were carrying beautiful stones, like diamonds, but many different colors. The bees dropped these stones along the path, and I thought maybe they were trying to get me to pay attention to the jewels instead of going on. But I didn't try to pick them up. Then this huge wasp came out with the bees, and he kept flying at me in a menacing way, picking at my hair and brushing against me like he was trying to keep me from going in any further. He even tried to pick me up and carry me. I could see his stinger, and I felt very intimidated. Then I decided I didn't know enough about what I was doing, so I decided to leave, but when I did, the wasp tried to

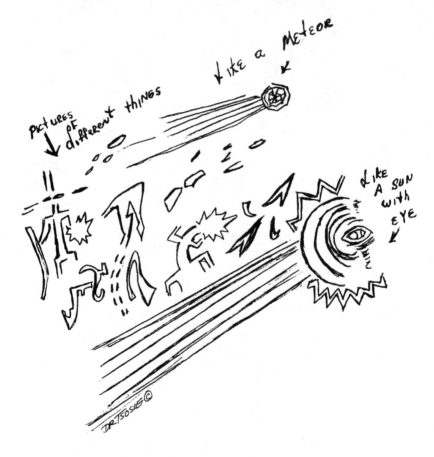

All on canyon wall, thirty or fifty feet high,
like picture writing or something similar

take my power. I had to struggle really hard to get back to ordinary reality. I felt like I was struggling through thick Jell-O or something. When I finally got back, I was told I needed to ground myself better. I was shocked to discover the sun was going down. Nearly four hours had passed!"

As Dennison described his visions, I felt at least part of it was possibly connected to the information he had gotten last year on the Holy Grail—in particular, the description of the stone wall with writing on it and the woman holding a large, flat dish or platter. In some stories, the Grail was a shallow dish or platter called a Graal. What this might mean was anybody's guess. The pictures are sketches of what he saw.

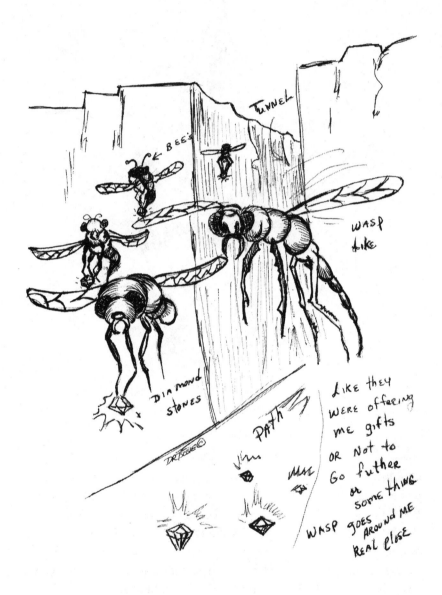

The Secret Government
FEBRUARY 1992

Two WEEKS LATER, ON THE 25TH, Dennison went out to his "spot" again, to meditate. When he returned, I asked him about what he experienced. He replied, "You know, I don't know anything about governmental and political stuff or the financial world. I never really understood that stuff. I just let it pass on by me and don't pay any attention to it. Now, for some reason, the Grandfathers keep showing me things that have to do with those people, and I don't really understand what they are talking about. They told me this time I need to make a booklet of some of the stuff they are showing me and give it to the people we come into contact with. They said a lot of people won't believe it or just ignore it, but I should tell them anyway.

"They said the earth changes and the cleansing has begun. Everyone is pretty well aware of some of the things, but along with the earth changes, there will also be major economic and political changes we need to be aware of and prepared for. We need to try to be self-sufficient within the next two years.

"They said our economy will seem to level out for awhile and even improve a little, but then it is going to get much worse. Many large corporations and industries will fail, and the unemployment will be much worse than now. The banks will fail, and the stock market will crash. The world economy will come to a standstill for a time. People will riot in the streets, and things will be pretty bad for awhile.

"Now this is the part I'm having trouble understanding, because they said our own government, as well as other governments in the world, are actually *creating* this economic crisis. That is why our government hasn't put up trade barriers and why it's allowing foreign countries like Japan to buy up our present financial resources. It's part of a plan to break down our present financial system.

"They said there is an Underground organization made up of very powerful and influential people with a lot of money and resources behind it. There are all the major powers involved, and their objective is to have a World Government and a world money system. This secret organization has been quietly manipulating world affairs for a long, long time to bring this about. On the surface, the world affairs are what we see in the news, but behind the scenes there is something else completely going on.

"The first step in the plan that we will be aware of is already taking place to some extent, with the people on welfare. As the economy gets worse and there are more unemployed and homeless and desperate people, our social services won't be able to handle it. Already there isn't enough money in the system, and there are a lot of cutbacks. A new plan will go into effect, where the government will issue these people a "credit" card. With this card, they can purchase food, clothing, shelter, etc. In return, the people will go to work for the government. They will be given jobs doing public service work. This is going to be on an international basis. Maybe there would be a need for our government to send some aid to a country where a disaster hit; they would call on people who were on the card system to go and do whatever work needed to be done. In return, they would get room and board, and their family would be taken care of with the card. Their wages would be applied toward their "loan" or debt incurred with the card. The card would never be paid off. If something happens to the person working and they can't continue to work, another family member will inherit the debt. An international work force would be created.

"Natural disasters will add to the economic problems. As the economy grows worse and worse, more and more people will be on the card system, and it will be viewed as a good thing, an acceptable alternative to a serious problem. Then the banks will fail, and the world will be thrown into an economic and political disaster. From this upheaval will emerge a plan to create a World Government, a body of people representing the major powers to pull the world out of the economic crisis. This is when the Underground organization will make itself known, with its financial resources. A new, cashless money system will be instituted, using a card in much the same manner as the one issued to the unemployed. An electronic debit and credit system. All buying and selling, all wages, all taxes, etc., will be negotiated with the card. Everything you do will be monitored through the card.

"The only way to avoid becoming a part of the card system is to be self-sufficient and self-supporting, creating barter systems and a net-work of services within our own people. We will have to grow our own food, make many of our own necessities, learn to help each other, and remain spiritual, creating a strong unit, an "underground" system of our own. As time goes by, many others will seek to escape the card system and join those who remained outside the system."

The Middle East
MARCH 1992

ON MARCH 1, Dennison returned from meditating. He was told many things which were for his own use; however, he related the following:

"They told me the Universe is changing; all the energies are changing. Some of these changing energies will be bringing more Earth awareness to the consciousness of Mankind. Environmental issues will become more and more important. There will be more and more ads concerning the environment appearing on TV. Environmentalists will appear on talk shows and in public debates. Movies, videos, and so forth dealing with environmental issues will become popular. Public figures will come forward and make a stand for the environment. We'll be surprised at who they are. There will be a strong division between those who are for the environment and those who aren't.

"Then they were telling me about the Middle East. There's going to be peace for awhile. There's even going to be peace between some of the Arabs and Israel. Then there's going to be a strong Arab leader who is going to unite all the Arab world. At first he will seem like he's going along with the rest of the world, but this man is a religious figure, and he will inspire a resurgence of religious feelings. Then he will call for a Holy War against the rest of the world in an attempt to take control of the world. The rest of the world will be caught unaware. I saw a map showing Israel, and then there was a nuclear explosion there. The Arabs will use nuclear weapons, chemical warfare, germ warfare, etc. The rest of the world will unite because of what is happening. There will be a great loss of life. Every able-bodied man and boy will be called on to fight in the war against the Arabs.

"Then I saw a symbol like a cross with another shorter line across it. I don't know what it represents."

Is it possible for two religions to unite to create a great force? (I thought about this for awhile, and after a few questions, I told Dennison that the Jews and Christians had the Old Testament in common. The Christian belief that Christ had come was the really major disagreement, so it was conceivable that they could.) He continued, "I strongly sense something significant concerning two religions uniting to create a strong force will be happening. I don't understand exactly what is going on yet. I keep hearing them say something about Jodea. Is there a People of Jodea? They keep saying 'The People of Jodea.'" (I asked if it could be The People of Judeah? He felt it was likely the name, and I told him it was an old Biblical name for the Jews.)

Symbol seen in connection with a war to come in the Middle East

Earthquakes and Droughts
APRIL 1992

THIS MORNING, APRIL 24, Dennison went out to pray and meditate, as had become his habit. He was told, "As you know, the Earth Changes that have been talked about for so long have begun. Your people need to become aware of these things. The energies are changing, the weather patterns are changing, animal behavior is changing. Speak to them of the reason they are being brought together—to build a love and trust between them, so you can all work together to help each other when it is needed, for such times are coming. You must not alarm anyone, for people are already afraid of the future. There is no need to panic.

"There will be several earthquakes coming up soon, in California. Many towns along the coast will be affected. You see, there is a fault (Dennison kept saying a vault) that extends down California. At this time, the earth is slipping back and forth because of pressure inside the earth. The quakes will be felt into San Diego and even into Mexico. The quakes will damage water lines, and there will be problems with the water becoming contaminated. Later, there will be a large, severe earthquake, again in California. It will be so strong you will feel it in Arizona. People are being warned, and those who are open will be guided to leave when it is time.

"There will be riots in the cities. Gang-related and racial problems. Many will leave the cities because of this.

"In the Northwest, where all the clear-cutting of the forest has taken place, there will be severe drought. It is already beginning. There will be landslides. Man will begin to reap what he has sown."

Dennison said he strongly sensed a volcano, but he didn't know where. Maybe in California or the Northwest.

A Dream of Mt. Shasta
APRIL 1992

THE NEXT MORNING, Dennison asked me, "Where is Mt. Shasta?" I told him it was in northern California. He said, "Last night I dreamed I was climbing up Mt. Shasta. I was going up the South side. There was a path that took you up where it wasn't too steep. Sort of a gentle slope at first. I noticed these small bushes; they looked sort of like fur. At first I thought it was sage, but it wasn't anything I was familiar with. I was climbing up, because someone had said there was a cave up there where the Light People lived, and I wanted to go see it, but all I could find were these holes in the side of the mountain that looked like mine shafts, like there had been some mining there at some time. Some were smaller, like vent holes. I could see a small town below and some dwellings in the surrounding areas. As I climbed, I put my hand on some rocks. They were very hot, like a stove. I don't know what that meant."

Premonition of a Tragedy
MAY 1992

ON FRIDAY, MAY 8, we went down to Phoenix to attend a ballet as the guests of a good friend who works for the ballet company there.

After the performance, we went backstage to wait for our friend. We had done this on several other occasions and had become acquainted with many of the dancers. Some of them had even come up to spend time with us in our home. This evening, as we waited, one of the dancers came up to Dennison and asked if he could have a few moments of his time. They moved a little ways away and talked for several minutes. He then embraced Dennison and turned to walk away. I couldn't help but notice the dancer had tears in his eyes as he turned to go. As we walked to the car a little later, Dennison said, "He asked me to pray for him. He just found out he is HIV positive, and he is very scared. He's just a baby, barely twenty-two." As we drove to my mom's for the night, Dennison remained quiet and withdrawn. I tried to engage him in conversation, asking what he thought of the performance, but he remained silent. Finally, I asked why he was feeling so down. He simply replied, "I don't really know, maybe it is the dancer. I just feel really sad inside."

Later that night, after we had gone to sleep, I was awakened by the sound of Dennison sniffling. As I lay there, I began to realize he was sobbing. Alarmed, I whispered, "Oh, Lovey, what's wrong?" He didn't answer me, so I put my arm over his shoulder and snuggled close and again asked, "Whatever is the matter?" He took a deep breath and seemed slightly confused, saying, "What?" "What's wrong?" I asked. "Are you okay? You sounded like you were crying or something." He turned over to face me, and said, "I was just dreaming about Elaine. It was really weird. I was dreaming a black Cadillac drove up into our driveway at home. I looked out the window and wondered who in the heck it could be. Then Elaine got out of the passenger side and walked up and knocked at the door. She was dressed up real nice, and I asked her where she was going so dressed up. She told me she was going away for awhile, and it would be a long time before she saw me again, and she just wanted to tell me good-bye before she left. I said, 'Where are you going?' But she just smiled and turned and walked away. I called after her and said, 'Wait, don't go!' but she turned and waved and got back into the Cadillac. Then I noticed that Rena was the driver." (Rena was one of Elaine's best friends. She had been killed in a tragic accident last year.)

He took a deep breath, almost a sob, as he finished telling the dream, "I don't know why, but I feel so sad now. Like she's really gone or something. Empty feeling inside." I tried to reassure him it was partly because of the young dancer and maybe the ballet itself. It had been a very moving interpretation of a young Navajo woman falling in love, bearing a daughter, watching her child grow up. Time passes, she grows old, dies, and her daughter, following in her foot steps, falls in love and has her own child. Endings and beginnings; the cycle of life. This was done to a beautiful piece of Native flute music by R. Carlos Nakai. It left us both feeling a little sad.

On Saturday, when we arrived back home, our answering machine was completely filled with calls. Friday evening, Elaine had come home from work feeling ill with an upset stomach. She died suddenly, later that same evening, about 11:00 p.m., of an aneurysm. She was a vital part of all our lives, always vibrant and happy and full of light. She had a way of nurturing you and making you feel so very special. It was such a shock and a great loss to everyone.

As I write this, another memory comes to my mind of an evening the previous summer, when several friends had gathered at our home, including Elaine and her family. The conversation had turned to meta-physical and spiritual subjects. Someone asked Dennison about crystals and wondered if he really believed they had mystical powers. He replied he personally felt they did and told of how some Navajo medicine men known as crystal gazers used them in diagnosing illnesses and personal problems, as well as for looking into the future. Someone asked if he personally had any experiences such as this. He acknowledged he had, but didn't elaborate.

Soon it was suggested it might be interesting to try to meditate with a crystal to see what we experienced. Before long, I was trying to find a crystal for everyone to use. A candle was lit and placed in the center of the group as we gathered to sit in a circle around it. All lights were turned off, and Dennison lit some sage and cedar and guided us into breathing and relaxing and then in going "inside" our crystal, becoming one with it. After a time, he again brought us back to the present, and the lights were turned on. One by one we went around the circle, and those wishing to, shared their experience.

I noticed Elaine had been crying a little and was searching her purse for a Kleenex. When her turn came she said, "I don't think I like this. I went into the crystal, like you said, and I saw myself in a large room, like a church. There was a coffin there, and the lid was open. I felt like I was supposed to look inside it, but I didn't want to, because I thought it was my mother, and I didn't want to have to let her go yet. But something was making me go closer and closer, and suddenly I was looking inside, and it was *me!* Now what does that mean? It has really upset me." Another person in the group said, "In the Tarot deck, the death card means the ending of something and the beginning of something new. I feel that is what this was. I really don't think it means you are going to die." Others agreed, but Elaine remained a little disturbed the remainder of the evening, saying, regardless of the meaning, it was very upsetting, and even though she had really wanted to do this in the beginning, she would be very reluctant to try such a thing again.

Mother Nature
MAY 1992

ON THE 16TH OF MAY, there was a full moon, and Dennison decided to go out to meditate and pray and to just be alone. He had had a lot of demands made on him, and since the loss of Elaine it seemed like he hadn't had a space of time alone to grieve. It seemed to be wearing on him a bit.

While meditating, he asked why so many people were coming to him and complained that he was tired and really didn't know how to help them.

He heard a woman's voice say, *"You are for the Mother. . . . In service to the Goddess. What you call Mother Earth, the Spirit of Nature. In ages past, you would be called a Witch, a Merlin, and many other things. You are here to help bring back the Nature religions, the Earth religions."*

At this point, Dennison said, "I am no Witch!" There was a laugh, and she said, *"Yes, you are a Witch. You thought you were something different, didn't you? A true Witch is a healer of the earth and is dedicated to the Goddess."*

Dennison asked, "Who are you?" She replied, *"I have many, many names. I am Ishtar and Isis. To you, I am White Shell Woman, Yolkai Estan, Estanatlehi. To the Christians, I am Eve and the Virgin Mary. I am the energy within Mother Nature; I am the Mother of Creation, and I have been the center of the Earth Religions for thousands of years, way before the time of the Egyptians. My symbol and my companion in mythology is the dragon or the snake. It symbolizes the kundalini, that force which rises up through the spine like a serpent and out through the top of the head and connects man with all creation.*

"My energies, my religions, have been forgotten for a time, put down and feared. But it is time to bring them back in a new way. There must be a balance. At the beginning of Christianity, a balance was attempted. The Catholic Church had much of the Nature Religions within it, and the Virgin Mary and Jesus the Christ were the balance of the male and female energies. Fear of the feminine energies and women in general put an end to much of the female energy, and the male energy grew and grew. It became a male-dominated world, and it is now out of balance to the point of destruction. Male energy is sexual, physical, technological, aggressive. Female energy is creative, nurturing, intuitive, loving.

"You have the balance of the energies in you—a lot of feminine energy, without being feminine. That is why women are drawn to you. All men have the feminine energies within them, but very often the balance

is not struck. Either they repress it greatly, or they go the other way and become homosexual. You remained balanced because of your Native religion, which is feminine, an Earth religion, and because of the influence of your Grandparents.

"If you had stayed in your old relationship, you would have self-destructed, for when you reached your mid-life, your Kundalini began to stir. It first manifested as sexual energy, for it lies in the base chakra, the sexual chakra. This brought a dissatisfaction and a longing, and you began to search for an outlet. Your old relationship left you no room expand with it. When the Kundalini rises to a certain point and there is no room to grow with it, no acceptance of it within a relationship, you will emotionally and/or physically self-destruct.

"When you got together with Teddi, she had already gone past the sexual and emotional openings with the rise of her Kundalini and was able to guide you and keep you balanced while you went on your spiritual path. Now you have opened all the way and are in communion with all Creation. You are called to serve the Goddess.

"You will be traveling lots more soon, doing seminars and healing and teaching others how to open up and achieve a balance."

A Dream of Nuclear Subs
MAY 1992

ON MAY 27, Dennison woke me up to say, "I was just dreaming of nuclear subs again." (He has had two or three similar dreams this past year.) "They had a red star on them, and I saw an underwater installation and frog men. I felt very strongly they were a threat, and no one was aware of their activities."

An Earthquake in California
JUNE 1992

YESTERDAY, JUNE 2, two strong earthquakes shook California. The first one was felt clear down into Mexico and into Arizona, as Dennison had described last April 25. He went out to meditate today, to see what was going on.

First he was told he needed to pray and send energy to California, because there was a lot of fear there, and they were in great need now. They went on to say, *"There will be some more quakes, some causing moderate to severe damage, but the big one everyone talks about will not happen for a few more years. These are just warnings."*

Dennison went on to say, "They showed me fault lines and how earthquakes happen. They said the most severe quakes are when two plates of the earth rub together back and forth. I could hear the deep rumbling sound of the quake as they rubbed together.

"There is going to be an earthquake in Phoenix; I don't know when. Maybe it will happen in connection with the *big* California quake. There is a fault line that extends southwest from Phoenix toward California, through some mountains. It also goes the other way toward Apache Junction. There is also a fault line near Kingman; it goes up toward where your sister lives in Fredonia, near Kanab, Utah. There will be a quake there, too." Sometime back, Dennison had had a dream about a dam breaking, because of an undetected weakness in the structure caused by an earthquake. The name of the dam in his dream was Glen Dam. Glen Canyon Dam is near Kanab, and I wondered if such a quake could indeed cause this to happen.

He went on, "I strongly sense a volcano, maybe two. I can't quite get where it is, but I feel like California, or maybe Washington or Oregon. I don't know why I keep getting volcanoes over and over."

New Energies and More Predictions
JUNE 1992

THE EVENING OF JUNE 5, Dennison went out to meditate. He was told, *"There are new energies that will start coming in within the next month. Many who are open and spiritual will feel them as they become more intense. These energies will start another resurgence or awakening to spirituality, such as was experienced in the '70s. Many who are now closed will begin to open and seek answers to their lives' meanings. There will also be a strengthening and gathering together of certain peoples already open and spiritual. Old ties and bonds between peoples will be strengthened, and new people will be drawn into these groups.*

"You will have many more people seeking you out. Many will take what they can use and continue on their path; your function is simply to open their minds. Others will stay in contact with you and become part of your network, drawing closer to you and to each other; spiritual family."

Dennison asked, "What am I really here for? What am I supposed to be doing?" The reply was, *"Just what you are doing, for the time being. We cannot tell you your overall purpose at this time. Simply trust you will be guided in what to do and where to go when it is time."*

They went on to tell him, *"There will be more riots in the cities in the future. These will be race and gang-related. This time they will involve taking over of neighborhoods. Many, many will move away from the cities. They will move to the rural areas."*

They continued, *"There is another race of people being created on another planet, which is being prepared for them. They have human genetic material, but they look a little different. They will be smaller, also. The souls that go into these beings will be more spiritually evolved."*

Dennison went on to say, "Somehow, I don't really understand how, a lot of souls or a lot of people who are very open and spiritual here on earth will be going there in the future."

People of the Light
JUNE 1992

DENNISON CONTINUED HIS FREQUENT MEDITATIONS out at his sacred place. On June 20, he received the following from the "Grandfathers," as he calls those who he communes with.

"There is a group of people in California who are highly-evolved, spiritually. The 'Star People,' or the so-called Aliens, are working with them now, and soon they will be taking these teachings out into the world. They will be doing a lot of healing with their hands and with light. The beings working with them are called People of the Light. They come from the Source and are very powerful beings, almost like the legends of the Gods of old. They look human, but they aren't; you can tell them by their

eyes. They have looked after Mankind since the beginning. You see, Mankind was created for a different purpose than what we are now. We were given a very powerful tool, our minds, and we misused it. It's like giving someone a shovel to be used for spiritual purposes, like fanning sage smoke. But it's been used to dig with instead. It is a good tool for digging, too, but you forget it was for a spiritual purpose, because you are too busy digging. Right now they are trying to get us to remember what the shovel was really supposed to be used for. We're not using our minds the right way, and we've nearly forgotten how, and now it's time to remember, before we destroy ourselves again.

"There are other beings who are working to try to clean our atmosphere. They have covered the earth with something to create moisture ... something about a ball ... freezing it by sending ice crystals. They are trying to find an antidote to our toxic chemicals.

"There is one religion that is getting strong; they are trying to get their people reunited. Watch for them; they are not for the good of Mankind.

"Don't put fear into people's minds by saying this is going to happen or that's going to happen. There is enough of that out there already. Teach them how to stay open spiritually, how to love. They are the ones who will be guided."

Upcoming Changes in the Energies
JUNE 1992

ON THE 23RD, during his meditation he was told, *"There is an alignment of planets coming up in July. . . . There's a lot of changes beginning the first part of July and growing stronger by the end of July, then decreasing by the end of August. Even the weather will reflect change. People who are in transitions will change. Those who are in upheavals will level out one way or the other. Others will find situations which force change.*

"It has something to do with the balancing of the energies on the earth and will strongly affect people and personal lives. It will affect politics as well, bringing forced changes. The economy and money system will be affected too."

The Red Sea and Questions about the Photon Belt
JULY 1992

ON JULY 1, Dennison related the following, after he had gone out and meditated. "I sense something is going on with the Soviets. Where is Africa from Russia?" I told him it was down below Saudi Arabia. He then asked, "Where is the Red Sea? I sense there's going to be something going on in that area. I don't know if they're going to close it off, or what." I told him I wasn't too sure about the location of the Red Sea, I only knew that Moses had crossed it. I found our Atlas (a wonderful and much used gift from a friend who has been following Dennison's information). I found that the Red Sea was between Saudi Arabia and Africa. Dennison showed me an area in the Red Sea and said, "I saw submarines through this area, and also in this area. I think this is where they're going to close off something." He was pointing to a narrow area between the Red Sea and the Mediterranean Sea, between Egypt and Israel. The name on the map was Suways. It didn't look like there was any water there. I looked in the index and found Suways was the Suez Canal. Now it made a little more sense. Dennison went on talking, "What's in Africa that they would want? Oil? I'm sure they're going to make a move on Africa." I told him I wasn't sure there was much oil, but Africa had gold, diamonds, and other valuable resources, and Russia was now in deep economic trouble. I could see why they might want to make such a move.

He said, "I sense an Arab leader is involved in some way, too. Maybe they're in cahoots with Sadam? I see a lot of people being pushed out of Africa. Russia is really having very hard times, and the people are looking for someone to lead them. Someone is going to come forward and lead them, and they will follow, like the Germans did Hitler. He's for the negative; he won't be a positive and peaceful leader."

A friend of ours had called the day before, asking what Dennison knew about the "Photon Belt" that we were supposed to be coming into. I had to admit we knew nothing about anything by that name, and I asked her to describe it. She said there was some sort of energy that was supposed to be coming to earth by the 26th of July that could cause severe electrical disturbances and even several days of darkness or, conversely, very bright, intense light, like an arc welder, which could damage the eyes. This energy could cause other things like tidal waves, volcanoes, or earthquakes. I knew Dennison had gotten many things about the energies changing and many things on earth changes, and even energy changes in July, but knew nothing of this. Curiously, that day I received a little Metaphysical newspaper in the mail that had a small paragraph on the "photon belt," which said something completely different. Then a friend from Sedona came by, and I asked her if she had ever heard of it, and she said, "Oh, yeah, it's all over Sedona. Everyone has their own ideas on what's happening."

This evening, while meditating, Dennison asked about the photon belt and was told, "At certain times, every so many thousands of years, the Universe disperses a new type of energy. It happens like a starburst and slowly goes out and expands. It lasts over several years and eventually affects our atmosphere, where it pushes particles through it and onto the earth. It will affect everything on earth, the clouds, the air, the sunlight, and the ocean currents, as well as the land areas. It will create disturbances like volcanoes, earthquakes, tidal waves, and drastic storms. It will create heat waves and droughts. When it first happens, we'll feel it strongly, but it will gradually diminish over the next three years, though its effects will continue on in many ways over the next ten years. The dispersing of the energies have already started." I asked if it could cause a bright light or darkness, or even an ice age, like many were saying, and he replied, "Anything can happen. Like I said, it is like a burst of energy. It could cause a bright flash or heat wave, or darkness and an ice age. It will affect all electrical energies, the lower parts of the range, whatever that means. There can be tidal waves; the polar ice caps could melt, floods, anything.

"All life will be affected—plants, trees, animals, birds. The Northern hemisphere will be greatly affected, especially the North Pole. It can actually create ice cold winds that will just suck up the moisture." I asked when this would happen, and he said, "In a way it is already starting to happen; the energy is going out." I asked what we could do to prepare for it, and he said, "Deal with it as it comes; there is no real way to prepare for it."

Dennison said, "They told me again—we need to try to be self-sufficient within the next two years. I told them, I can't even keep up with my normal living expenses. Should I look for a steady job? Should I move back to the Reservation? In order to be self-sufficient, I need to be somewhere where I have access to water and good soil. Some place warmer, with a decent growing season. . . ." They replied, *"Don't worry about that now. A way will be provided when it is time. There will be those who will come into your life, who will be guided to help you. You are needed to be right where you are, doing just what you are doing right now. You worry about too many things. Has your car quit running? Has your landlord told you to leave? Are you starving? All is being taken care of."*

Symbolic Visions
JULY 1992

ON JULY 29, Dennison told me, "While I was meditating, I saw this comet coming; it had a long, blue tail. As I watched, the tail became wavy, sort of like a snake, and the comet itself was red. As I watched, it took on the shape of a dragon. I felt strongly it was like a warning of something. Maybe a disaster.

"Then I saw a rainbow. It was huge, going from horizon to horizon. It was completely circular, the bottom half of the circle was inside of the earth. At the places where the rainbow entered the earth, people were emerging. On one side, the people looked like Natives, in traditional dress; on the other side, the people looked white, and they were wearing white shawls or robes. They all joined together in the center of the earth under the rainbow.

"After this, I saw a huge grapevine growing out of the center of the earth. It grew higher and higher, and branches began sprouting from the sides. At the ends of the branches grew beautiful flowers of different colors. When the flowers opened, butterflies and beautiful birds emerged.

"After this, I saw dried branches woven together like a lattice, forming an archway. Intertwined in the branches were long, thin green leaves and pink roses. Small bundles were hanging from the arch, like in a blessingway ceremony.

"Beneath the archway stood a man and a woman. Both were wearing shawls. Her hair was drawn up in a bun, and she wore a headband made of silver wire. He wore his hair cut straight, just below his ears.

"In one hand the woman held a palm leaf, and the man held a skin bag of water. Their other hands were joined, hers facing palm upward and his facing palm downward. Their eyes were strange . . . they were too large—much larger than normal human eyes, but otherwise they looked human.

"Suddenly I heard a lot of loud yelling, and I came back to ordinary reality with a start. At first I thought there was someone out there with me, yelling at me or calling me. After a moment, I realized I was alone and all was quiet."

Something Strange Happened
AUGUST 1992

On August 3, Dennison went out to meditate. We had had a very demanding week, and he was mentally and physically drained. When he returned, the first thing I noticed was that he looked very fresh and rested. To be sure, as I talked with him, I couldn't help but observe that he looked radiant, even younger. His skin looked smoother and "dewy" or moist. I had noticed this same look a couple of other times when he had gone out. During those times he had experiences which left him full of wonder and excited. This time was no exception.

"They worked on me tonight. They told me to take off my shoes, and I could feel them like pushing certain points of the bottoms of my feet, then on up my legs. They even worked on my shoulders and gave me some energy and relaxed me. I really feel *a lot* better.

"They were telling me we should quit worrying so much. Things will work out so I can concentrate more on my spiritual work. There will be people coming into our lives soon, who will be of great help to us.

"I think we're going to be moving in the future, maybe to a larger place, or at least a place more suited to what I'm doing. They said we need to make up our minds what we really want to do. We can stay home and concentrate on healing, like I'm doing now, or we can travel more and do gatherings and seminars, etc. Both are open to us; we just need to make up our minds what we want. There's people who will be there to work with us and back us up either way. I think I would rather just concentrate on letting people come to me, like I'm doing now.

"It's funny, they showed me I can have anything I want. It's all right there in front of me. All I have to do is be clear about what I want and make a move; put the thought into motion. Then comes the hardest part, *know* it will happen. Just not worry about *how* it will come; just know it will come, and it will.

"I felt like something or someone was watching me. I think I kind of felt it before, but not as strong as this time. This time, I knew it was there, but I couldn't ever see it. It felt like maybe an animal of some sort, maybe the size of a small bear. What's weird is that I couldn't tell if it was on this plane or not, because I felt it making some sort of contact with me. I could feel it send like electricity into me and around me.

"Another thing was I could smell this odor. Sort of like a burnt match or a candle just blown out . . . even a little like burning rubber, or maybe a wet animal or wet cardboard. It was there at first when I began to feel something was watching me, but then it faded away.

"They told me there was once an alien base up here. You can see some of the outlines of it from the air, but most of it has been covered and overgrown with time. The Aliens used to take energy from certain minerals inside the earth crust up here. I saw like a blue energy coming out of the earth. I also sensed maybe it was liquid, like maybe mercury or something."

A few minutes passed, then Dennison said, "Something really weird happened to me while I was out there. I keep thinking I remember something more. . . . I almost remember something more. . . . Something more happened to me. Like when I first got there, before I meditated, I walked around for a little while before it got dark and just enjoyed the evening. But when I was walking, I felt kind of funny, like I was real tall or up on stilts or something. . . .

"I keep seeing this thing in my mind. (Dennison drew a design on a note pad.) I remember seeing it on a door or something.

"I also remember a mirror without a back to it. I thought it was a mirror, but when I looked in it, I just kept going . . . like a doorway or something. . . . I remember a lot of buildings and lots of people. Activity. . . . There was this sound, a hummmmm of sorts, like a cylinder going up and down.

"I felt a lot of love and very, very nourished. I know this is how I'm supposed to feel about everyone. I need to love everyone the same.

"When I was finished meditating, I felt real funny, sort of like I wasn't all together. Like I was loose inside my body, not all connected. There was a funny taste in my mouth. Kind of salty. I was and still am really thirsty. Kind of like dehydrated, like I sweated out in the sun all day."

Dennison was quietly thoughtful for awhile, then went on to say, "It was strange, when I got in the van. I went to turn the key to start it, but it was already running. I don't really think I ever started it. And the engine was running real quiet, not at all like it normally sounds. Then, when I drove, it was like I wasn't in control of driving it. I'd push the gas pedal, but it wouldn't respond by going faster; it just kept going real slow and smooth. When I steered, it went its own way, really smooth. I couldn't feel the bumps and ruts in the road. It was like this until I was almost back on the pavement. All of a sudden, I could feel the bumps and hear the engine, and I was in control again. I still feel sort of strange. Sort of loose inside."

Design seen on a door during a possible abduction

A Possible Cover-up
AUGUST 1992

ONE EVENING, AFTER GOING OUT TO PRAY, Dennison said, "When I was meditating, I was told that our government is getting ready to cover up the existence of some Alien bodies that they have. There are too many people getting too close to the truth.

"However, there are two people who will have definite proof of their existence and what the government has done, and they will show it to the public. The world will be amazed."

Secret Government, Secret Military
AUGUST 1992

A FEW NIGHTS LATER, ON AUGUST 23, Dennison received the following during meditation. I have to say I had a hard time deciding whether to include it with the rest of his information or not. It is pretty incredible and not something I would normally believe. Then, as I thought about it, I had to laugh at myself and my personal prejudices, because this whole journal is pretty incredible and had I not been experiencing a lot of it, and had it not been Dennison receiving it, I would likely dismiss most of it.

"Our Government isn't what we thought it was; it isn't really what it was supposed to stand for. Money is going into places we aren't aware of. Great misuse of funds, major cover ups and mismanagement. We will be hearing more of what's really going on within our own system. They are in deep shit. There are things the President doesn't even know about. Our economy is in serious trouble; programs for the elderly, money for our school systems, libraries, etc. is no longer there, because our Government is putting it into Alien Research. They've developed technology they will never use. Our Government has sold us down the river.

"You see, there is a Military within the Military—the military we see, and another 'inside' military that makes its own rules, has it's own leaders.

"There are certain Aliens who work with our Government, our Military, on top secret research. There is the Military we see and relate to as protecting our country. Then there is an inner, Top Secret Military. This inner, top secret system became seduced by the thought of Power, Ultimate Secret Weapons, and they worked out an agreement with unscrupulous Aliens. For certain 'favors,' the Aliens gave the Government their technology.

"Secret underground facilities were created, and experiments using Alien technology were conducted there. Some top scientists were involved; even some Soviet scientists are here in this country, working with them. Humans were abducted and experimented with, animals too. Terrible things were done. Machines you can't even imagine were constructed. Things way, way beyond anything you ever even dreamed. Experiments with time, changing matter, genetic manipulation. Creating Frankenstein-like monsters. Building advanced weapons, things of power. They've even built a craft that looks like a flying saucer.

"There are some people within the Military that stay in these underground facilities and never return to society; they just stay there and work, donate their whole life to it, "for their country." Mostly these are people without families, without outside connections. There are also people who just "disappear." No one knows what really happened to them.

"There's lots and lots of money that's being taken from legitimate funds like for schools and being used for this research, and that's what is really hurting our economy.

"Now these Aliens, known as 'Grays,' have decided not to work with our Government any longer and aren't cooperating. Our Government has killed some of them and tortured some of them, trying to force them to keep working with them. Without the help of the Aliens, the Military can't continue what they are doing.

"There are other Aliens, who are here to benefit Mankind and to help us; they have interfered and have stopped the 'Grays' from working with the Government. They have even gone in with superior technology and destroyed some of the weapons created by these people. The 'Grays' are in conflict with our Government and are afraid of the 'good' Aliens. There is a danger of a war between our Government and the 'Grays.' If it happens, our regular military would become involved. They are *very* serious about keeping people out of those underground facilities."

Future Earthquakes

SEPTEMBER 1992

THE EVENING OF SEPTEMBER 3, after Dennison returned from meditating, he said, "They told me there's going to be a lot of earthquakes coming in the future. We'll even feel them here. They will cause a lot of damage, especially in the cities. They showed me a map of California, Arizona, and Colorado. There was a zigzag line which started out in the ocean by California and angled up toward Phoenix, continued upward near Flagstaff, past the Grand Canyon, up into Utah, angling toward the Four Corners area and into Colorado. There is a lot of heat under the earth's crust right now, and that's what's going to cause this area to move. They told me this was part of an ancient Ley line. The Grand Canyon and the Colorado River was partly created by this line shifting, long ago, and now it's being activated again.

"The way I understand it, the Ley lines are kind of like nerves or veins in the Earth. There have been a lot of minerals mined and a lot of underground nuclear testing done near this nerve—a lot of negative put into the earth here, and the Earth has to react.

"There's three of these Ley lines that run near here. They sort of begin out in the ocean off the coast of California. One line runs from there through Phoenix and up through the Four Corners area. Another runs across the border of Arizona and then down into Mexico. The third one runs out in the ocean along the California coast and down along the coast of Mexico. All of this area will be strongly affected by earthquakes in the future.

"There is also a lot of changes going on in the Earth's atmosphere, a lot of pressure building up. There are serious problems with the ozone layer and heat building up in certain places, which is affecting the atmosphere. This is caused from many things, like the burning of the rain forests, volcanic eruptions, and industrial pollution. These hot spots in the atmosphere are going to mix with the natural cold winter air over the United States, and that is going to create a real mess with the weather patterns. There will be very severe weather, like hurricanes and tornadoes. Drastic weather changes—tornadoes where none have ever been seen before, even around here. There will be severe freezing. Places like even Phoenix will be affected, and crops will be lost. Flooding, severe rain, deep snows. Severe cold and freezing winds. Severe winds. All hell is going to break loose, weatherwise."

An Invitation to Go to Canada
SEPTEMBER 1992

ON SEPTEMBER 4, our Cree friends called and invited us to come up to Canada to visit and to participate in some ceremonies with them in early October. The air fare and all accommodations were taken care of. It was hard for us to get away, because this was the time to make and sell jewelry for the Christmas season, but we felt we would be foolish to pass up an opportunity like this. We were very excited.

A New Crystal
SEPTEMBER 1992

ON SEPTEMBER 5, a close friend came to visit us on her way home from vacation. She mysteriously brought in an object wrapped in a sweatshirt and handed it to Dennison. He unwrapped the shirt and exposed a very large, smoky citrine crystal. With delight, she exclaimed, "It's yours! I found it in a shop in Colorado and knew it was yours, so here it is." He was overwhelmed, to say the least. Shortly after receiving the stone, Dennison excused himself and went out to his power spot to meditate with his new treasure. He was gone nearly four hours. He related the following experience when he returned.

"When I first began to meditate with the crystal, I saw tiny dancing lights coming out from the crystal and surrounding me. Then there was like a burst of air, which shot out from the crystal and went around my head. I heard a buzzing sound, like bees. After this, there was a ringing in my ears, followed by a warm feeling all over my body.

"Suddenly, I realized I was way up high, looking down at my body sitting below. I could see all around, even see the lights of town, everything.

"Everything was covered in blue light. Everything seemed to have a blue glow. I saw faces of animals and spirit-looking things. Then I was surrounded with a white light, and I saw these different colored bubbles drift by, one after another. After awhile, they began to disappear. It was as if I was going through layers, and as I became aware of them I moved on.

"Soon I saw a hole, and I went into it. It became a tunnel, and I was traveling along in it. It was lit, but I couldn't locate the source of the light. At this point, I could see that I was connected to my physical body by a shiny, silvery cord, and that I was blue, green, and white.

"After this, I saw tiny people. Sort of like fairies, with wings on their backs. Their feet were webbed. They began feeling my eyes and all over my body and actually through my body. Their heads were oblong, with pointed ears slanting toward the back. They looked to be about twelve inches tall and were holding long, thin wires in their hands.

"I began to notice a sound, kind of like a drum beat. Slowly, I realized it was a heart . . . *my* heart beat. Then there was an image of myself in front of me, and the next thing I knew, I was inside of it! I mean really inside. They were showing me firsthand what the human body looks like on the inside. I saw the organs, the lungs, the heart, the veins and arteries, and how blood circulates, everything. As we traveled along, they pointed out different things. They even showed me the stomach and how little fingerlike things inside it push the food through the digestive tract.

"After awhile, I could hear my heart beating faster, and the little 'people' began pushing me back, and I knew I needed to go back to my real body. The next thing I knew, I was above my body, and zip, I re-entered it just where my skull and spine connect, the base of my skull.

"I was told the crystal is connected with a larger crystal, really a giant crystal that's inside the Earth. This larger crystal was programmed by using a type of light that penetrates into the Earth. The light goes to the giant crystal and information is relayed to my crystal.

"After I got back into my body, I had a hard time getting myself reoriented. I actually couldn't even get up. I crawled around on my knees for awhile, just trying to get myself together. I finally grabbed my pipe and tried to light it and laughed out loud at myself and wondered what the heck I was doing.

"I found my crystal off to my left, and it seemed to be glowing sort of pink. I picked it up, and it felt light as a feather and hot, really hot.

"They said the crystal is programmed for healing, for when people really begin to use crystals for healing. There's a lot of experimenting being done by the Japanese, using stones and gems for healing, but American science isn't open to this yet.

"I felt a lot of love and warm light. Like I was being nurtured. I wanted to stay there forever. Man, it was hard for me to come back to this world. You go out of your body to a place of light, where you are soothed and nurtured, then come back here . . . ugh!"

Crystal Vision
SEPTEMBER 1992

WE RETURNED FROM A SELLING TRIP TO SEDONA the evening of the 7th. It was about 10:30 p.m. The moon was nearly full, and it was very light outside. Dennison decided to take his new crystal and go meditate for awhile. It was after 1:00 a.m. before he returned. He said there was a herd of elk nearby. Rutting season is beginning, and the shrill bugling of the males and the clash of their horns distracted him for awhile.

"Finally, I sat down and began meditating. I wanted to try to get back to where I was the other day and see what else I could experience. I saw some of the same things as before, but I just hurried on. I felt myself moving fast, and I looked down. Off in the distance I could see a large body of water, like an ocean, with a white sandy beach as far as the eye could see. It was nearly deserted, only a few people. They were wearing natural colored clothing, like white, tan and brown. No bright colors. Their hair was also white or blond. . . .

"Suddenly, I was in a room with walls made of dark gray stone. Above I could hear a sound of like church bells. It seemed to be some distance away. There were several staircases leading out of the room. I chose one and went down, down, down, down. After awhile, I came to a room. In it were some large disks, which seemed to be suspended in mid-air somehow. There seemed to be sort of an electrical or magnetic power in there, and I sensed these disks were charged so that they sort of floated, but never touched or bumped each other. It was as if they repelled each other. There was a glass globe of water in the center of the room; the water seemed to be churning inside of it. It gave off a sort of glowing light. The disks looked like drops of quicksilver.

"I decided to cross the room to another door, to see where it went. As I went across the room, I seemed to be weightless, because I just sort of floated across. The disks parted for me, as if I, too, repelled them. I entered the door and found myself in another room. There was an old man seated at a table in this room. He wore a robe and his hair was white, about shoulder length. He also had a white, neatly trimmed beard, not very long. Suspended in front of him was a stone, shaped like a pyramid with a rounded top. At first I thought he was holding the stone, but after looking closer, I realized he was holding his hands a little away from it. After a few moments, he reached over to a clear, glass, vase-like container containing a clear red liquid. He poured some of this on the stone, and as I watched, it began to glow with a greenish light, which slowly turned to purple, then other colors. Then the old man took a drink of the red liquid and turned and handed me the flask. Until this moment, I didn't know he was even aware of me. I took the flask and took a drink of it. It had no taste, more like water, but it warmed me inside like a drink of brandy would. It made me feel good, and I felt I was receiving a rare privilege.

"At this point, it crossed my mind to wonder where the heck I was and what I was supposed to be doing and why I was there. At the moment I wondered this, everything disappeared. This time, when I came back to this reality, I didn't have as hard a time getting oriented."

Predictions

SEPTEMBER 1992

ON SEPTEMBER 15, after returning from meditating, Dennison asked, "Where is New Zealand? They were telling me there's some highly evolved people living there. They are very close to the earth, very in tune with the earth. There's some very powerful healers there, too, and they have some powerful healing herbs.

"A time will come in the future when Shamans from these and other Native Tribes will gather together to share their knowledge and exchange information, in order to work together for Mother Earth and Mankind.

"We're eventually all going to have to go back to natural healing, and people like these, who are still in touch with the old ways, can still teach us all a lot of things.

"Also, I still saw there's going to be a lot more hurricanes and tornadoes and severe weather coming. We haven't seen nothing yet. There will also be a lot of hail—large, large hail stones. There will be freezing rain and ice storms in places that have never seen weather like that before. The coasts will especially be hit, both the East and West coasts. I saw big, huge waves wiping out towns along the beaches. Deep, deep snows in the mountains. . . .

"Over the next year we are going to be involved in several small wars all over the world.

"The banking system is in serious trouble. Many smaller banks will either fail or be taken over by a few large banks.

"The price of gold, silver, and precious stones will soar. Paper money will have little value. Whoever has the most gold and silver will be the ones in power. Prices will go sky high. Gasoline prices will soar."

Strange Visions

SEPTEMBER 1992

DENNISON WENT OUT TO MEDITATE as usual one afternoon. It was well after dark when he returned. He was excited when he got home, and I could see that "glow" about him, which he sometimes has after he's had a special experience.

"I really had a weird experience while I was out there. I did my prayers and sat down to meditate. Suddenly, I felt I was wrapped in some sort of soft gel . . . kind of cool and clammy. I also felt like I was riding on something flat. I had the sense of standing on something, and it moved to wherever 'they' wanted me to go.

"Remember that little stream near Sedona? You know that place . . . Montezuma's Well? I saw either that place or another place almost like it, except it was in a different time. There were these people, but they were real short; maybe five feet tall, at the most. They were dark, like Indians. There were several of them, maybe a small village. They were totally naked, and they were all carrying branches, or green leaves bunched together like a bouquet, in their hands. They were waving them and walking in a circle, doing a ceremony. There were these tall white stones in a circle, a lot like Stonehenge-type stones. They were dancing around a large carved stone in the center. This stone was transparent, like a crystal, but it was yellow. It appeared to be carved into some sort of a bird shape.

"Behind the people was a pool of water, and coming from this pool was a rainbow sort of light, arching over to the ceremony and entering the stone. The stone seemed to glow from the inside. A thought popped into my mind, 'These are the Water People.' I noticed they had little round mud huts where they lived nearby.

"Next, I was taken to a cave with a large stone over the entrance. As I got closer, the stone just moved aside, and I found myself going inside. The first thing I noticed were these stone slabs stacked against the wall. They were about 4 feet by 3 feet by 6 inches and seemed to be made of sandstone. Then I noticed that the floor seemed to be made of metal tiles. A little farther on was a long box made of stone, I think. It seemed to radiate a light. It was perhaps 6 feet long and 3 feet wide and 3 feet deep. There was some sort of writing or symbols on the side of it. On the top was like a staff with some sort of stone at either end. There were several people in there, maybe ten or twelve, and they were building a wall in front of the box. The wall was made of the large stone slabs I saw stacked against the wall. They were being mortared together. The people didn't look like the people I had just seen. These guys were wearing short tunics that were belted at the waist. They were lighter-skinned, with blond or brown hair. The hair was cropped in a square cut around their face. They wore sandals, and their legs were wrapped with cloth leggings.

"Next, I was taken toward a beautiful city; I could see it off in the distance. It was down within a place that looked like a volcanic crater. There were buildings built around the shores of a large lake. The buildings were white and beautiful, with arches and terraces everywhere. There were waterfalls coming down from the sides of the crater and onto different levels of the city and finally coming on down to the lake in the center. There was lots of vegetation growing near the waterfalls. It was a very beautiful city. There were people living there, but they weren't completely human. They looked sort of like lizards. They didn't stand completely upright, and their arms were short, and their heads looked reptilian, with large dark eyes. They wore long robes. There was a procession coming down a long flight of stairs, and the one in front was carrying a long staff with a ball on top.

"After this, I was taken to a canyon. The entrance to the canyon was blocked by a fence made of small branches. The sides of the canyon were covered with something like Anasazi cliff dwellings. I could see what I thought at first were large birds carrying bundles of sticks. Then I began to notice they looked more like humans, except they had bird wings. They were carrying things to work on their houses. I watched them for a long time, trying to figure out what they really were.

Ceremony

"Then I noticed I was traveling above a canal of water. It went on for miles. The sides were made of stone that sloped down to the water. At last I came to a large mountain; the water seemed to be coming from the side of this mountain. There was what appeared to be lightning in the air around the mountain, but there was no rain or coolness.

"All around were mounds of earth with holes in the center. I thought they once were dwellings, but they seemed deserted now. There were bits of trash and rubble littered around, things like bits of pottery and broken pots. Thick jungle surrounded this flat area.

"The last thing I was shown was what looked like a landslide off a mountainside. Heaps of rubble, stones, bricks, wood, debris, like from a demolished town. There was lots and lots of rain coming down. I felt there had just been an earthquake or something. There were little groups of people (modern-day, ordinary people) walking and carrying some

Long Box Being Hidden in a Cave

Reptilian People

Bird People

Abandoned Dwellings

Recent Disaster

belongings. They looked very dazed and frightened. I was overwhelmed with a feeling of sadness.

"You know, I also saw large sheets of maybe paper, except they seemed to be soft, like cotton. They were stacked on wooden racks, and there was no writing on them."

More Strange Visions
SEPTEMBER 1992

WHEN DENNISON RETURNED FROM MEDITATING the evening of the 25th, he expressed puzzlement over the strange things he had been getting in his meditations lately. He was feeling at a loss with what it might mean. Tonight only added to his confusion.

"I saw volcanoes erupting out in the ocean, the lava creating new land around them. The ocean was bubbling hot all around them, and steam and ash made it dark all around, with only bright red sparks coming out of the craters.

"I saw a stream of water, or more like a moat that created a circle. Around the moat were groves of fruit trees. Crossing the moat were four bridges at the four directions. Within the moat was a fence, creating a barrier. Within the fence were several small, pyramid-shaped houses or huts. I had the feeling they were used for meditating or something like that. Within the center of this area was another circular hole, reminding me of a Kiva. There were another four bridges leading to it, facing the four directions.

"On a hill overlooking this circular area was a structure that looked much like a castle; behind the hill was a large body of water. The horizon had a reddish glow, and there were three moons or planets in the sky. One was half yellow in color and half gray-blue; one was reddish, and one was orange. I have no idea if I was on earth or where.

"I saw another scene that looked much like Monument Valley, except the land seemed to have a bright glow to it, going from white to blue and green. I noticed five points of light in the sky; as I watched, they moved really close, and I could see five bright spheres of light; light was shining down from them and creating the glow on the land. I felt they were UFOs.

"The next thing I saw was a sphere, like a planet or a star. It had bands of different colors on it, and there were also rings of colors circling it, kind of like Jupiter. There was purple spiraling energy going down and red spiraling energy going up. There were faint rays of light going off in different directions from this planet or star. I felt as if earth is connected to this planet or star. The rays from it are blue as they touch the earth.

"I saw another planet or star; the outer half was glowing hot like a fire, and the other half was dark, like charcoal, only glowing a little. I felt it represented a sun that was burning out. It was traveling swiftly through space like an asteroid. It might have been a comet; I'm not really sure.

"I saw a white cloud; it was whiter than white. As I watched, it became a mushroom cloud, and white dust or ash was falling everywhere. I felt this was on earth and it could happen.

"Then I saw this huge bird, like an Eagle, in flames. In the center of the bird was a lighted candle, and there were circles of different colors radiating out from the bottom of the candle, like a rock thrown in a pond creates ripples. The bird was rising out of a body of water. In the bird's mouth was an olive branch of peace.

"I was told as its feet rise out of the water it will signal the increase of the earth changes. The bird represents the birth of a new awareness and life for us. The candle means there is still hope. The bird also represents a new race of people with greater awareness, psychic abilities, and wisdom, even as children. This includes the animals, too. There will be new plants. I saw one cactus-like plant with four-leaved flowers rising

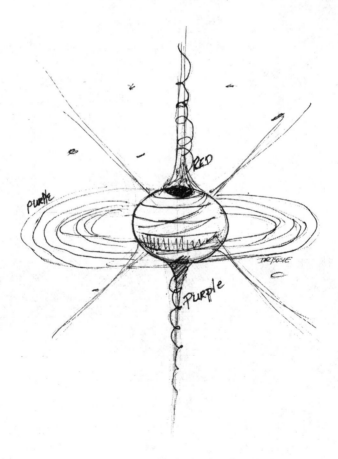

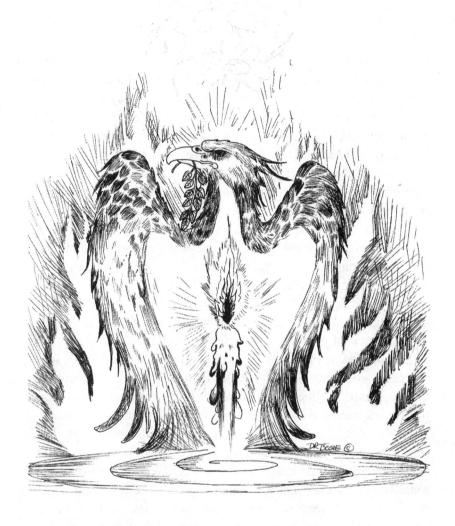

from it. We will eat the bud, and it will provide food, cure illness, provide vitamins and minerals, etc.

"We are each the bird, and collectively we are the bird. Like a snake shedding its skin, we must finish the process in order to grow. Like the bird, we must get our feet out of the water and fly. We all have the candle of hope burning within us."

A Possible Encounter

SEPTEMBER 1992

ON SEPTEMBER 30, after returning from his prayers and meditation, Dennison said, "There's new energy coming in, and it will be uniting spiritual people, and they are going to grow strong. They will be able to make a lot of changes. Then I sensed another type of energy and I felt like it was from the so-called Aliens; they are going to become a lot more known. More and more people will be in contact with them.

"I sensed the Watchers are coming back to contact me again. In fact, I felt like they were there tonight for a little while, and I'll be hearing from them some more. Hearing them and dreaming dreams, too.

"It was weird tonight. I felt like an invisible ball of energy surrounded me like a cocoon for awhile. I noticed the smoke from my sage was going straight up; no breeze, when a little before there had been. There was a hush, as if the world stopped for a few minutes. I couldn't hear *any* sounds, no birds, no insects, no rustle of the trees, no traffic out on the highway. I could hear a kind of buzzing sound in my left ear, like I used to get a lot. I sensed the Watchers. I felt just like I used to . . . this sensation, kind of like static electricity, all around me. Almost like a magnet or something. There was this tingling in my feet, and I could feel the muscles in my thighs twitching. I honestly expected them to show themselves, and it really sort of scared me. I wasn't sure I was ready to see them. I felt this warmth come over me, but nothing else happened. I strongly sense they will be back. They were just testing my reaction.

"I was just getting ready to send out my healing energies, when I sensed them, and then I got all fearful and couldn't do anything except sit there and wait. It seemed like about fifteen minutes, but I think it was more like an hour, maybe more, that I felt like this. Funny how it feels like you are walking on air after that. . . ."

Curiously, as Dennison was relating his feelings, our cat, Ubu, jumped up on the couch with us. She walked over to Dennison and immediately fuzzed up and hissed; her eyes were wide with fear. A low, wailing growl came from her, and she suddenly ran into the bedroom. She wouldn't let Dennison approach her the rest of the evening.

Star People
OCTOBER 1992

AFTER HIS LAST EXPERIENCE, Dennison felt a little apprehensive about going out to meditate, and yet at the same time curious and anxious to go. When he returned that evening, he said, "Everything was pretty normal; nothing weird happened.

"While I was meditating, they were telling me there is an atmosphere that surrounds the earth in layers. Because of our pollution, the burning of the rain forests, etc., the first layer is greatly affected, and the second layer is now being affected. When the third layer is affected, moisture will leave the earth, and there will be droughts, especially in the higher elevations.

"Where exactly is Australia? They were telling me that there is a tiny island out in the ocean off the coast of Australia. I don't think it is inhabited. There are certain Aliens calling themselves Star People who are setting up there. They were here in ancient times to help the people. Legends are told about them. They are coming back now. What's happening is that they've transformed some of their people into the Human life form, and they are going to start working in many parts of the world. They are bringing with them a new type of energy called "Nasperius," which is a type of healing by touch. They will be like the Great Teachers. What they do is move their hands over people, and these people will then be empowered to be healers. They will be very spiritual healers and will do great works in the world.

"These Star People have been working with some Natives already. Like some people in Peru; they are working with them right now.

"There is a new type of stone, other than Crystal, that will be coming out soon. It works with the stars and gives off energies that open the psychic centers in people. It is much stronger than stones being used now.

"There's some type of war 'they' are watching over in Africa. It can turn into something big if the wrong people get involved.

"Watch the Germans . . . and the Russians.

"There is some type of mineral in our area that's going to be found. It was used before, long ago, and will be used again as it is needed. People who are sensitive will be drawn to it. I also sense a lot of people in the cities being drawn to this area and also to New Mexico. There will be like a land boom here by next summer.

"'They' have also been working with some Oriental people, I think some monks. People will be seeking them out, because they are *very* spiritual. We will be meeting at least one of them.

"Have you ever thought seriously about writing a book? They said you are to write a book. In fact, you are to write two books. One is written on what they term intuitive-based guidance. You will be guided, and they will just come together. They said when you come to an understanding of why things happened in a certain way, you will know what to do.

"There's going to be lots of unexpected things happening in our lives. Things that will just suddenly come up. People are even now being guided to us for certain reasons.

"There's going to be a serious drought that will hit here in three years. For the next couple of years there will be lots of moisture; then the drought will come."

Our Trip to Canada
OCTOBER 1992

LITTLE DID WE DREAM LAST YEAR when Dennison heard a voice say, "Get ready to go Canadian," that we would be going to Canada!

Our Cree friends, whom we met last year, arranged for an all-expense-paid trip to visit them, and while we were there, Dennison would be part of a panel discussion on Native Spirituality and Traditions. We would also participate in several ceremonies in connection with the 500-year anniversary of Columbus' discovery of America.

We were received as honored guests and lavished with food and gifts. October 10 was their Thanksgiving day, and in celebration, we drove out to their reserve the day before, to participate in a Sweat Lodge. It was to be my first experience, and I was a bit nervous.

It was dusk before everything was ready. A very cold mist was rising, and we huddled around the fire as the medicine man finished his final preparations. At last, we all crowded inside the sweat lodge and heated stones were brought in and placed in a pit prepared for them in the center.

Water mixed with special herbs was sprinkled lavishly over the stones, and a fragrant hot steam arose. At first, the heat felt good after the damp chill outside. Soon, though, I was faced with unknown fears of claustro-phobia. I pushed the feeling to the back of my mind and concentrated on the men as they took turns doing chants and drumming. The heat from the stones and the energy created by the prayers and singing were almost unbearable. At last, we emerged for a short break; then we again entered for another round. Then again, and again, and again, we sang and prayed and sweated, round after round. Darkness fell, and at last the women were given one last round for ourselves. Led by a powerful medicine woman, we shared the pipe and prayed for Mother Earth, sending Her our love and prayers. It was a very powerful round, and when it was finished and the flap covering the doorway was opened, I indeed felt I was being reborn. As I crawled out, I was greeted with a breath-taking full moon, just rising through the mist; tall fir trees stood stark against its golden light.

Later, we gathered for a meal, and afterward several young men drummed and sang, while everyone else softly visited and children ran around playing.

Some tipis had been set up for sleeping, and a large fire had been built outside. I lay there in my cold, clammy sleeping bag long into the night, as the chants, drumming, prayers, and the smells of sage and sweet grass kept replaying themselves in my mind. At last I fell into a semi-sleep. I awoke around 4:00 a.m., stiff and chilled to the marrow of my bones. I finally got up and went outside where the camp fire still flickered and added some more wood. My groggy consciousness finally noticed the sky was dancing with a mysterious and wondrous light. I was beholding a display of the Northern Lights!

At sunrise, we all gathered to greet the sun as Dennison and the medicine man gave prayers of thanksgiving with their pipes. A huge feast was being prepared, and all the women were busily chopping, baking, frying, and keeping kids out of trouble. Some people from a local TV station came to do an interview. They were seeking the Native viewpoints on the Columbus Day 500-year celebration. Several of us gathered in one of the tipis and invited them to join us in a talking circle. Sage and sweet grass were lit, and we all smudged ourselves. An eagle feather was passed, and each of us took a turn to speak our hearts. Instead of the expected anger and outrage over the past and present outrages brought to the Natives by the Europeans, there was talk of our connect-edness to each other and all things. There was talk of our love of Mother Earth and of a hope of reuniting all peoples and of recognition that we are all brothers and sisters who came from the same Father and nourish from the same Mother. There was talk of laying down of anger and hate and the desire of finding ways to work together to heal ourselves and the Earth, and there was talk of our thankfulness for all the gifts we are given each day from the Creator. Finally, the feather was passed to the person doing the interview. In surprise, she at first protested, then, with encourage-ment from the group, she spoke. As she spoke, her voice became choked with emotion, and tears filled her eyes. She told us how touched she was by our circle. She said that all over the country were demonstrations and protests and anger by the Natives. Here, in this circle, she felt the other side, the spiritual side of the Natives, and it deeply touched her.

That night, we all gathered for the 10:00 p.m. news and watched as speeches and protests by Natives around the country indeed did reflect anger and bitterness. The end of the news showed the spiritual side of the Natives; our little circle.

The rest of our stay was hectic. Dennison was involved in many, many other events. Speaking to young Native men in prison for drug and alcohol-related crimes, participating in a weekly gathering of the Mother Earth Healing Society, counseling many seeking guidance, and just sight-seeing. The time came to leave, and reluctantly we returned home, feeling filled with spirit and laden with wonderful gifts.

Signs and Predictions
OCTOBER 1992

ON THE 21ST, Dennison went out as usual to pray and send healing. Later, he said, "They told me to watch for strange lights to show in the sky, like the Northern lights. It will be a sign that severe changes are eminent." Dennison went on to ask me, "Where is The Holy Place?" I pondered this for a moment and told him, "Probably either Jerusalem or maybe the Vatican." "They said something is going to happen soon at the Holy Place, and it will also be a sign."

Next he asked me, "When does the comet come?" I was puzzled by the way he put it, "the comet," like it was something everyone was expecting. I told him I didn't know of any coming soon, but that didn't mean there wasn't one coming. He told me, "They said there is a comet coming soon. It is large and has a long blue and white tail. It, too, will be a warning sign. There's actually two, but no one knows about the other one yet. It will be the largest ever seen, and it will have a big effect on the earth."

Next, he asked me, "Who controls most of the world's oil?" I told him I thought OPEC. He said, "Something is going to happen soon to cause the price of oil to go way up. We'll have to go elsewhere to buy our oil."

He continued, "There's also going to be dangerous gases coming up out of the earth in California after the earthquakes. There will be a bad smell, a strange smell. People should get away from it; it will be dangerous."

More Predictions
OCTOBER 1992

AFTER MEDITATING ON OCTOBER 28, Dennison said, "There's going to be a very large volcano that's going to erupt somewhere . . . on an island, I think maybe in the Pacific. Soon, within the next month or two. It's going to cover the whole area with ash. A big ash cloud will be created. There will be some other volcanoes in that area that will become active later on. Some out in the ocean too. I saw lots of volcanoes erupting all over the world.

"There's going to be something happening in Utah. I don't know exactly what it is. I saw a large explosion of some kind, maybe an atomic explosion.

"They said there's another war brewing in the Middle East. The U.S. is going to be involved in it.

"Remember, I told you about the Light People? Well, they are making themselves known now. There will be reports of contacts with beings surrounded by a blue light. They will be healing the Earth and will be giving warnings such as, 'Get to higher ground.'

"There's going to be lots of sightings of that Lady I saw. Some will see her as the Virgin Mary. She will be appearing in different places, bringing back the feminine energy.

"There's going to be lots of weird things in connection with migrating animals. Unexplained, abnormal behavior. Some will be seen where they've never been seen before. It would be like seeing a herd of elk on a golf course in Phoenix, or a flock of parrots in our front yard. They are going to be confused and behaving very strangely.

"They had me send energy into the Earth by taking hold of a young tree and sending my energy down through its roots. Boy, it was very powerful for me. I felt really connected with the tree, like it was a helpless human baby. I don't think I can ever cut a living tree after that. Man! I swear I could feel its vital, living spirit connected to mine. Think how powerful it would be if lots of people would do this.

"I saw something I don't understand . . .I saw a hole open up, like a cave. Just a black opening. I understood that when the earth changes get real, real bad in certain places, some people will be directed to this hole, and they will go inside and will be transformed instantly to the Other Side—actually leaving their physical bodies behind and their spirit crossing into another vibration. When it's all over, they will come back into the physical world again. They said this was done when the Earth was cleansed in the past."

A Science Lesson and Curious Symbols
OCTOBER1992

THE NEXT AFTERNOON, Dennison returned from meditating and praying, and I asked him if he had gotten any new information in his meditation. He replied, "I don't know . . . I don't think I got much of anything, really. I just prayed mostly and sent energy; then I walked around for awhile. It was really weird, though; while I was walking around, I kept seeing some numbers and letters and stuff that didn't really make any sense. Maybe I'm spending too much time meditating . . . it's hard to get back sometimes. Maybe I'm going weird or something."

I asked him what exactly he saw, and he said, "Things like mathematical formulas or something." He picked up a notepad by the phone and wrote down some things which did indeed look like mathematical equations, but nothing I was familiar with. He went on to say, "It's funny, but it's like I know what I'm doing, but I don't remember what it means. Someone was trying to explain some scientific sounding stuff to me too. Things like Fire vs. Water and Air vs. Earth. And anything that overpowers one another, creates a third thing. When two opposing forces come together, they create a third dynamic. They were talking about hydrogen molecules and the molecular structure of trees, and the hardness of stone and how it is not really hard. They explained about vibrations and sound. How you can have three of the same kinds of stone, and if you were to tap two of them together until a certain tone or vibration is created, it can shatter the third stone with the vibration created by the other two stones.

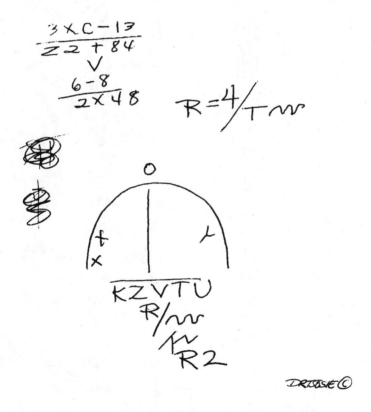

An Alchemical or Symbolic Equation

"They said that everything on earth is a reflection of what's in the universe. Our universe is like a cell in a body. Our atmosphere is also like a cell wall, and everything inside is a living thing. They went on to say that when a seemingly solid stone is heated to a certain temperature, it will melt, or become what is called molten. When this is exposed to air and gravity, it begins a heat exchange with the air and begins to form a thin crust. In a vacuum, the molten rock would remain liquid. The air pressure and gravity acts to eventually put a cap on a volcanic eruption.

Two Staffs of Great Importance

*Large Carved Stone
Overlooking a Valley*

"I think maybe there was some other things in there that they were explaining to me, but I can't quite remember them now.

"I saw two long staffs. One was topped with like an eagle's head, and the other was topped with like a dove's head. They stand for something very important . . .were carried for something very important . . . I can't remember what.

"I saw a large stone with a snake carved in it, but the top was sort of diamond-shaped. . . . I think there were two heads on it. A two-headed snake. I think maybe it was a cobra, with two heads. One was a snake head, the other a bird, I think a vulture. The snake was carved out of a rock on a cliff, you know, like a sculpture, sort of. It was overlooking a valley below.

"I saw something like a large sundial with symbols all around it. The pointer on the dial was casting a shadow on a symbol that looked like a sun. You know, a circle with squiggly lines all around it.

A Few More Predictions

OCTOBER 1992

ON OCTOBER 31, Dennison received the following, "I still sense something in a big city, like New York City. I saw fires; huge fires.

"I saw that dark cloud over California like I've been seeing, and I saw the explosion in Utah again.

"I also sense an upheaval in the White House. A scandal or negative information comes out. I also sense an assassination attempt is still going to happen.

"I also saw a curious thing, like I saw a couple of days ago. There was this huge rock with some symbols on it, and there were two people standing beside it, one on each side. One was wearing a white cloth

Symbols on a Huge Rock—in Greece?

headdress, with a headband holding it on. The other had a metal helmet. This rock seemed to be inside a room, and it was lit by a torch or firelight.

"What's in Greece? I saw some mountains, a mountain range that formed a sort of U-shape, with sort of hilly plains below. I knew this was in Greece. The funny thing was, I saw red and yellow, maybe energy patterns, on these mountains."

An Unusual History Lesson
NOVEMBER 1992

ON NOVEMBER 2, Dennison came home from his meditations saying, "When I meditated this afternoon, I wanted to try and find out more about those strange symbols I've been getting.

"The first thing I saw was an hourglass. It was a little different-looking, in that the two containers of sand was connected by a long tube in the middle. The next thing I saw was sundials. Several different sundials.

(It is curious to note that after Dennison finished meditating, he walked around a little. As he walked near a fallen tree, he found a wrist watch someone had lost. It was in fairly good condition but no longer worked. He felt it was some how symbolic.)

Watch Found after Meditating
It was stopped at fifteen minutes
before nine with the second hand
about three seconds before the
twelve. The date is the 19th.

"The next thing, I felt I was flying down a long tunnel. I was standing on a flat, triangular device. Out of the corner of my eye I could see a being that looked sort of human and sort of bird or reptile-like, sitting on one side. He paid no attention to me, sort of like a cab driver. I sensed he was a guardian of some sort. As I flew down this tunnel, I saw symbols flying past me, like strange writing, squares and triangles, etc. I felt maybe I was traveling through time.

A Guardian of Some Sort

"Then I saw a symbol that reminded me of a tree with a central trunk and branches coming out on either side. There was writing and symbols along each of the branches. Each branch ended in a circle of symbols. Someone was speaking to me in a strange language. I felt like I should know it, but I couldn't quite understand. I felt they were explaining things to me. Strangely, now I feel like I understand what they were saying.

"First, I think I was shown a brief history of the earth. I saw what I think was the earth, but it was elliptical instead of round. The land masses were not at all like they are now. More lined up and different shaped.

"Then I saw two moons, and one moon crashed into the earth.

"Then I saw earth, but it was tropical and lots of volcanoes. Dinosaurs living on it.

"Next seemed to be different stages of Man, or maybe forms of Man. The first was like a lizard-looking being, then bird-looking, then on into

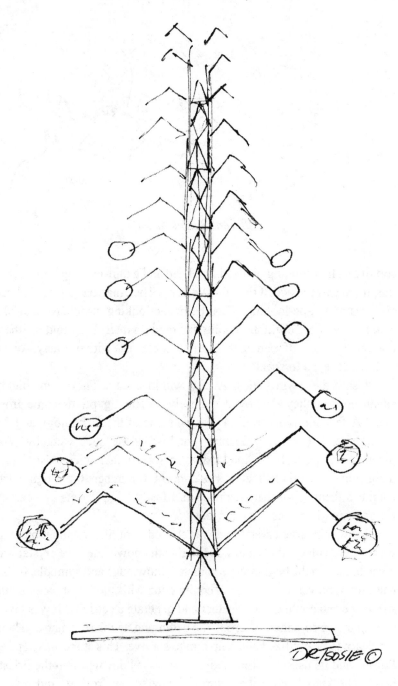

A Tree of Symbols

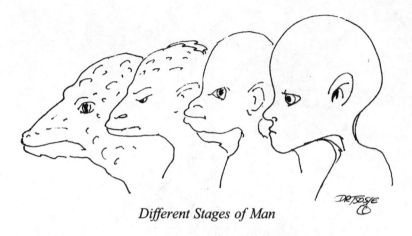

Different Stages of Man

sort of an alien-looking, with a large head and a thin-looking body. After this, there was a space of time that went by. Then man had a smaller head and was more ape-looking. Then he began looking more caveman-like and, finally, more upright, looking like modern man. They told me there is another species of man on this earth that coexists with us today. A race within a race, so to speak.

"I saw the Twin Cities. A city within a city. They were highly advanced, but they destroyed themselves. The Egyptians came from them. A few survivors tried to pass on some of the technology and the knowledge, but its true meaning got lost as the ages went by. The pyramid was part of this knowledge; so was mathematics. Also something called Sacred Geometry. The concept of numbers 0 through 9 was taught to them as all that was needed. Mostly High Priests and certain Kings were given this knowledge.

"I saw this large crystal that was shaped a lot like a human brain. It was etched with symbols and was filled with knowledge. The crystal was given to man in the beginning. It radiated knowledge and symbols. It also had a lot of power. It was used in conjunction with another stone or metal substance and could create weather and generate electricity. It was given to Man by the so-called Aliens in the beginning, to instruct man and help him learn to be civilized and help him to survive. This stone was kept by Priests, and its uses and knowledge was passed down within the Priesthood. The knowledge it held simply radiated out from it, and people would get new ideas and concepts. It gave the people in possession of it certain advantages and powers, so it was fought over, creating many wars.

"Because of this, it was hidden away, maybe not even on the earth plane. I think it will be brought back again, after the earth changes, to help rebuild and teach mankind again. Only the very spiritual will be back to rebuild the earth.

"The last thing I saw was like a glass window. Inside was like an arrow on the floor pointing down a long corridor. The corridor extended as far as I could see. There were symbols over the entrance to the corridor. There appeared to be a series of rooms extending down this corridor as far as I could see. At the end was a black 'hole'."

Looking Through a Window Down a Long Corridor

Vision of an Ancient Ceremony
NOVEMBER 1992

ON NOVEMBER 6, Dennison went out to meditate and pray as usual. While praying, he heard a clear voice say, *"Can you hear me."* The same voice came several times while he prayed, but he could make no contact. After getting home, he felt disturbed that someone might need him, so before retiring for the night we both meditated again, to see if either of us could get anything. Thirty minutes or more passed with no results.

Suddenly, Dennison asked, "Is there such a person as I-Zack?" I thought a bit and said, "Maybe. There was an ancient biblical name of Isaac. Could that be the name?" Firmly, he replied, "I-Zack."

After a few moments, he said, "He lived around 1600 BC." A few more moments passed and he said, "I see a group of people, like tribesmen. They call themselves Ishlam; it's the name of a small group There's a man showing me a stone. It's a purplish stone, and there's like tin foil; yellow tin foil or maybe real thin gold around it. This stone is sort of pyramid-shaped in the middle and four points around it at the corners . . . it's that way naturally. . . . It's in a stone box, about 5 inches square, and it's covered with a cloth draped over it. A very thin cloth . . . what's cheese cloth? . . . The stone is glowing. There are other stones around it, but I mostly see it.

"There are four people in a room. Their faces are covered with cloth. Everyone's dressed real fancy, in silks and gold jewelry. There is a large stone head of a lion or maybe a dragon, with its mouth open. The purple stone is sitting in its lower jaw, and it's glowing. The inside of the jaw is like a pit. There's cobras coming out of a hole in the back of the mouth and moving around the stone. Their heads have like a figure eight on them and are kind of diamond-shape. There's one that's very large, and he has a ruby glued between his eyes and he's rearing up. A man steps forward and points his finger at the big cobra. He's wearing a large ring with a reddish stone on his first finger, and he is pointing at the cobra with it. I can smell sulfur. The cobra is quieting down now. He's going back into his hole. Now everyone is holding out both hands toward the glowing stone, either sending energy or receiving it. Now they've started bowing and backing out of the room. The man with the ring takes it off and places it in a secret hole in the wall and turns something, and the jaws of the lion begin to close.

"Everyone is leaving, and I hear the sound of stones moving. Stones are being moved. (Dennison begins to breathe harder.) The air is getting tight in here. (Dennison breathes faster and harder.) The light went out and it's dark in here. I can't breathe! . . . It's time to get out of here!"

A Lesson in Numerology
NOVEMBER 1992

A FEW DAYS LATER, ON THE 10TH, we were eating supper when Dennison reached for a piece of scratch paper and a pen. He asked me when my birthday was and wrote down the numbers and began adding them up. He then did the same for his own. I smiled and asked if he knew he was doing a step in Numerology. He explained to me, "I've been seeing lots and lots of numbers, like 888 and 666. Did you know 8 stands for balance? 'They' told me the whole universe is made up of numbers. Numbers all have certain vibrations, all mean something other than just a quantity. Combinations of numbers mean things, and used in the right way can be very powerful. There is a lot of information in numbers. Learning about numbers can give you the keys to how the universe works.

Odd numbers are male, and even numbers are female. For example, the numbers 12 and 13. There were 12 Apostles plus Jesus, the 13th one. There were 12 Knights to the Round Table, and the King was the 13th one. The 13 is an odd number, but it is balanced by the 12, an even number, so it is a powerful combination.

You can learn a lot about the 1990s by adding up each year.

1990 $1+9+9+0=19$, $1+9=10$, $1+0=1$, so 1990 adds up to one. One stands for the individual, the "me" generation.

1991 adds up to 20, $2+0=2$ Two represents duality. Male vs. female.

1992 adds up to 21, $2+1=3$ Three is the triad, the divine expression of love. Two forces joined together to create a third and greater force. Return to family values.

1993 adds up to 22, 2+2=4
Four is the square. The building block. The foundation is created to build a new relationship between male and female forces.

1994 adds up to 23, 2+3=5
Five is the number of Man. It is the midpoint between 0 and 10. It represents the point where Man connects with the Creator. The midpoint between Heaven and Earth. The joining of Spirit and Matter.

1995 adds up to 24, 2+4=6
Six is the number of Creation. The union of Male and Female energies.

1996 adds up to 25, 2+5=7
Seven is the magic number. It is perfection. The four-sided square, the foundation, is topped by the triad. It creates a home for the new family of Man. Everything begins to smooth out then.

1997 adds up to 26, 2+6=8
Eight is the number of balance. Paradise regained. Gateway to the spiritual.

1998 adds up to 27, 2+7=9
Nine is completion. The end of a cycle.

1999 adds up to 28 2+8=10
Ten symbolizes perfection. 1 is Man and 0 is God. It represents love and peace.

2000 adds up to 2 followed by three zeros. 2 is Male and Female 0 represents potential, nothing and all things. Very, very powerful. The balance of the male and female.

Each number is related to the next, and each number is built on the last, so 5 has 4 in it plus one more. It contains elements of the number of four in it. Six is built of two triads, and nine is built of three triads.

MAN = △

SPIRIT OR GOD = +

Man is like this = ▽   He should be like this = (symbols)

I was amazed at this, since I knew next to nothing about Numerology and had very little interest in it. "They" seem to be teaching him about Numerology! I planned to purchase a good beginning book on Numerology at the first opportunity that presented itself.

More Predictions

NOVEMBER 1992

On NOVEMBER 14, Dennison related, "Today when I meditated, I just got a series of different scenes and impressions. For instance, I saw Washington state, the name Washington was printed on it. I strongly sensed something is going to happen there. I sensed a vibration there, maybe a rumbling.

"I was once again shown the Red Sea, and I saw submarines in there again. I saw Egypt, Africa, Saudi Arabia, and Israel was involved too.

"Our economy will get worse. We're at a point where it could begin to grow again, but I sense it is going to get lots worse later. They showed me lots of people out of work. Lots of industries laying off people, lots of businesses failing. Problems in the auto industry.

"There are going to be some problems in the White House. Something connected with the government. Perhaps a fight between politicians. I saw lots of fighting, almost a riot. I saw a big building and people outside really in an uproar, throwing things and yelling. I sensed it had something to do with politics, but strangely it felt like religion, too.

"There's a new energy coming in soon. It is an energy for change, change of systems, relationships, everything.

"I saw small groups of people; they were connected with each other, you know people with similar beliefs. They were fighting each other, each thinking they were right, that they had the TRUTH. They could be of benefit to each other, but they wouldn't help each other.

"There have been a lot of religious wars fought since the beginning of time. I sense there will be another religious war, maybe World War III. It will be the last religious war."

More Symbols
NOVEMBER 1992

ON NOVEMBER 22, Dennison was given some more information about symbols when he meditated. "They were telling me that the universe is made up of symbols. Everything can be understood through symbols and numbers. If you can understand the symbols, you can understand how everything works.

"There are four basic shapes, the circle, the cross, the triangle, and the square. Each shape has a number that it vibrates to. Symbols and numbers and words all affect us and our reality.

"Our life is like a triangle. The peak at the top is our spiritual self. From there you can divide the bottom into three smaller triangles (see drawing). One represents our emotional growth, one represents our physical growth and one represents out spiritual growth. You will notice that in the beginning the emotional and physical triangles are wider. We are usually more involved in physical and emotional issues when we are younger. At this same time, the spiritual triangle is small. As we grow older, the spiritual triangle becomes wider, and the physical and emotional triangles grow smaller. If these aren't kept in balance, we could 'fail' and have to start over again and rebuild. It's kind of like having your own business. Maybe you can sell like crazy and you are bringing money in hand over fist. If you just spend the money on high living and fancy cars, but don't pay your bills or buy more supplies, the business becomes out of balance, and sooner or later everything falls apart, even your marriage, and you have to begin again. If you gain wisdom from this, then you grow a little, and that's the middle triangle. The thing is that you have to stay open in order to grow.

"As you grow and learn to keep these things in balance, you will reach spiritual enlightenment. You will be in harmony with all that is.

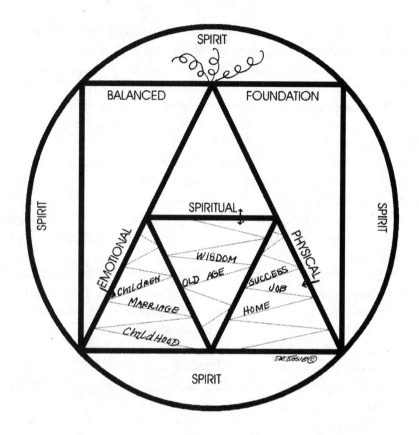

That is the square. Your balance and your foundation. Eventually, you will learn to let go of all fear and let the Universe sustain you, and you will be one with the Spirit. That's the circle, The All Knowing which surrounds us.

Do Not Fear

NOVEMBER 1992

ON THE 24TH, Dennison was told, "There are going to be more and more spiritual people who feel the end times are almost here, and one day they will just quit their jobs. All of a sudden quit, even without anything else to go to. They will sell their houses, leave families and friends, and just move. A lot of them will come up here, and some will go other places, away from the negativity of the cities. Those who can, will retire early, others will just give up everything and leave. We will get a lot of them through here, looking for a direction to go in, wondering what to do next. Wanting to grow spiritually as much as possible.

"The cities are going to get worse. People who are reasonable and normal will become more and more afraid. They buy into the fear around them, and the media helps feed that fear. They buy guns to protect themselves, so that they too become killers, victims of their fears. In awhile, cities will create their own armies, enforce martial law. There will be strict curfews; if you are on the streets after certain hours, you had better have a good reason, like going to work. Even that won't be enough for some people. They will become so fearful that they won't leave their homes at all.

"This will cause many, many people to move to the rural areas. They will follow behind the spiritual people who were the first wave. These will become the second wave. It won't be earthquakes or disasters that make people move. It will be the violence that makes them leave; they can cope with the disasters as needed, but not the violence.

"Businesses and industries will follow, and the rural areas will turn into new cities. It's already starting, and we'll see more of it by this summer.

"There is going to be a move to stop violence in the movies, on the TV, in computer games, and in children's toys.

"We must be careful not to buy into the fear. We must not become part of any particular way of thinking or following. Fear is the worst thing, and it blocks everything positive. We must keep teaching love and spreading love. Try to calm others down and show them how not to fear. Being One with the Creator is simply living without fear. Don't even worry about bills or your kids and how they are going to make it. Every time you worry or fear, you add to that fear energy, and you block the positive energies from coming in. Just *know* everything is in harmony with God's plan and that everything is perfect. Just *Be Love.*"

The Ozone Layer and the Weather
NOVEMBER 1992

THE NEXT DAY he said, "They were telling me about the layers of the atmosphere again. We worry about the holes in the ozone layer causing global warming, but it is actually causing an effect that's a little different. The way I understand it, hot spots are created in different places, and through a complicated series of events, hot air and cold air currents are stirred up. This causes a spinning motion, creating tornadoes in places where they have never been seen before. Not just one or two, but lots and lots, over and over again. Out over the oceans a slightly different thing happens, because its a different kind of moisture; terrible storms are created, like hurricanes and typhoons. Certain types of clouds are created; I can't remember what they called them.

"There are going to be strange weather happenings everywhere, because the normal weather patterns are unbalanced as a result of the hot spots in the atmosphere. There will be terrible storms, like dry electrical storms where lightning causes lots of fires and damage. There will be hot spells in the middle of winter and severe cold in the middle of summer. Cold enough to freeze and ruin crops, right in the middle of the growing season. There will be severe droughts where none have ever been, and floods where it is normally dry. Deep snows. Crazy weather. This is beginning already and will be increasing over the next two years.

"They told me again that there is a war coming. There will be several small wars, then one big one. I still feel like it will be like a religious war.

"I also sense there will be like religious wars within the United States as well, maybe somehow connected to the big war. I think it will involve some of the fundamental or conservative Christian religions against people like us who believe and practice Native Spirituality, as well as the New Age peoples. They fear us and they will go after us like they did the Witches and the Earth Religions during the middle ages. They will call us the Anti-Christ. There will be a lot of fear on both sides. We must NOT fear."

1993

1993 BEGAN COLD AND WET and continued to be so for most of January and February. This made it nearly impossible for Dennison to spend the time meditating and praying that he would normally spend. He does go out for short periods to be in Nature and to pray.

On February 20, we were watching a movie on TV when Dennison said, "I keep sensing there's going to be some strong winds, really severe winds, like a hurricane or something. I also keep sensing tornadoes. I keep thinking the whole East Coast is going to be hit with winds and tornadoes. Some real severe weather. Snow where it doesn't usually snow, like Florida, maybe."

Abduction?

FEBRUARY 1993

THERE IS AN ELDERLY COUPLE WHO LIVE BEHIND US. They are in their 90s; she is a bit senile, and he is crippled. We have been helping them since last fall and daily keeping an eye on them. The evening of February 26, the Mrs. called and asked Dennison to come over. Her husband had fallen in the bathroom and couldn't get up. Dennison arrived to find he had hit his nose in the fall; it was bleeding a little and quite swollen. Other than that, he seemed to be okay. He said he had tripped on the bath mat. Dennison cleaned him up and helped him to bed, then applied some herbs to help the swelling. He stacked more wood on their porch and a few other things, then once again checked on the old man before returning home. By this time, it was nearly 10:30 p.m. Oddly enough, upon arriving home he felt strongly that he needed to go out and meditate, even though it was late and very cold out. I protested, but he insisted he had to go. It was after 1:00 a.m. before he returned. I got up and made some tea to help warm him up; he was chilled to the bone. As we sat in the kitchen, he said, "It's kind of funny, but there was a lot of static electricity out there."

I asked what exactly he meant by static electricity. He replied, "When I got out of the Jeep, it felt kind of like when you take off a sweater or something that's been dried in a dryer without any softener." I noted that he was wearing only cotton. Cotton jeans, sweat shirt, long johns, levi coat, leather boots. Nothing that would create static electricity. It seemed a curious thing to have happen.

He continued, "I got out my pipe, and as I put it together, I could see and feel the static electricity all around me. It was even on my pipe. Those little static sparks crackling. I went ahead and smudged myself and began to do my prayers, when I noticed it became real dark, like the moon was behind a cloud. About this same time, I saw a blue light about the size of a baseball, off in the distance a little ways. It was a real intense blue. It was up in the air, higher than a human could reach, but not way up. I watched it as it moved, trying to figure what the heck it could be. It moved quickly in one direction, then suddenly zipped back, then it dropped toward the ground. Suddenly it shot upward and looped around and then, *pouf,* it went out. I started to feel sort of strange, like I was in a vacuum or something.

"Then I noticed a little ways from me, behind some bushes and trees, there was a soft, blue glow. It lit up the branches of the tree and the ground and rocks nearby, but it was a soft light, sort of diffused. It would grow larger and then smaller, like a campfire flickering, and I noticed little sparks of light coming up out of the glow and kind of moving around, a lot like fireflies. I thought to get up and go see what it was, but somehow I couldn't go over. My mind wanted to go, but my body wouldn't cooperate.

"I could hear this odd sound, kind of like air escaping, sort of a high-pitched whistle. I could feel a vibration under me and all around me. There was sort of a sound and pressure in my ears, too. You know how it sounds and feels when you put your fingertips in your ears? A little like that . . . and there was an odd smell, sort of a sulfur smell. I've smelled it before . . . a little like wet cardboard.

"I just sat there for a few minutes and waited to see what would happen; then the glow went out, and everything returned to normal. The moon was shining, and the night sounds were normal again. I got up then and got my pipe and things and got in the Jeep. Funny, my pipe was taken apart and back in the pipe bag when I got it, and I don't remember putting it back at all. I just headed out, but I kept looking back to see if I could see any more lights."

At this point, I asked him if he thought to again try to go over to where he saw the blue glow or drive around the area? He replied, "No, I don't know why I didn't do that, but I just left, like I saw that every day. I felt a little like I was in a daze."

I asked if he had started to meditate before he saw the light, if maybe he was in an altered state of consciousness. He replied, "Not at all. I was in a fully conscious state. I just got out of the Jeep, and the electricity started to happen, and it was just right after that, that I saw the blue light. . . . You know, it's funny, but the way the light moved reminded me of something I saw before . . . something about the way it moved means something to me . . . makes me remember something, something. . . . It made me feel weird. Still does when I think about it. . . .The way it moved, it was like a symbol or something. It went across and back and then across and a loop, then up and over." His hand described the movement of the light. He again described the size of the light and how it couldn't be a flashlight or a person holding a light. He went on to say, "It like went into my mind, like a symbol of something I'm familiar with." He got up and found a piece of paper and drew how he remembered the light moving. This reminded me somewhat of a design he had seen during an unusual experience the previous August (1992). I looked it up and showed it to him, and he said, "Yeah, that's it, but I didn't do it exactly right. . . . When I look at it, I get a strange feeling in my mind.

"You know, there was something else weird. When I sat down to do my ceremony, I was sitting cross-legged, and I thought I just sat there watching all of this, but later it was as if I just came to my senses, and my feet were stretched out in front of me and crossed at the ankle, and I was leaning back like I was in a recliner, and my arms were up in the air and out to my sides, like they were resting on the arms of the chair. That's how I felt, like I was sitting in a recliner, but there was nothing I was leaning against, nothing to support me, and I felt a little foolish sitting there like that.

"Now, as I'm thinking about everything, I wonder if there was something *above* me? It never occurred to me to look up, even though I usually do when I go out at night. I was too busy looking at the blue light. Could that sound and the electricity have been coming from above?"

I sat there writing my notes and wondering about the implications of Dennison's descriptions. As I was writing, Dennison for some reason took off his sweat shirt and began to examine his forearms. He got close to the lamp and continued to look at his arms. He walked over to me and said, "A long time ago, when I had that other weird experience (August, 1992), I noticed some marks on my arms the next day, but I didn't say anything, because I didn't really know how they got there. I was just looking to see if there were any more, and there are." He showed me a puncture mark on each wrist. They were on the inside of the wrist, not on the top, and about three inches above the hand on the wrist. The punctures were perfectly round and about the size of a typewritten period. I could see they went deep into the skin; though no blood was coming from the hole, I could see blood down inside.

I can't think of any logical explanation for two such perfectly round puncture marks, so perfectly placed on each wrist.

Symbol seen during
possible abduction

Fire in the Sky, Aliens, and the Secret Government
MARCH 1993

THE AFTERNOON OF MARCH 2 was warm, and Dennison took advantage of the weather and went out to meditate, the first time since his strange experience with the blue light. He wanted to go to the spot where he saw the blue glow and see what he could sense.

He returned saying he found nothing unusual. He sat under a tree and went into his meditation.

"They were telling me this new movie about Travis Walton that is getting ready to come out *(Fire in the Sky)* is pretty fear-based, and it presents the so-called aliens in a negative and fearful way. Somehow, I guess, the Government had some influence over what was presented to the public. They want aliens to be seen as something fearful and evil." I wondered why the Government would want the aliens presented in a negative light, to make people afraid? Dennison explained, "It isn't just the Government, it is the Government within the Government, the Secret Government, who want to create fear. There are what you would call negative aliens working within this Secret Government. They aren't for the benefit of Mankind. They and this Government are creating vehicles, so-called saucers, which look like ours and in many ways function like ours, but aren't ours; they belong to the Government and Military, and they are being used to create fear. They will be used to convince the general populace that there is the threat of an alien invasion. They are to create a lot of fear, and that fear will be associated with us. We are going to have to come in and somehow destroy these machines before this happens."

I interrupted at this point and asked, "You just said, saucers like *ours,* and the fear will be associated with *us,* and *we* have to come in and destroy . . . do you mean the Aliens?" "I mean Light Beings; they don't like to be called Aliens. They told me, 'We are Light Beings, we are energy. We are here for the benefit of Mankind, to bring light energy back to the Earth.' Anyway, saucers like those of the Light Beings are being created by our Government, and the Light Beings are going to have to destroy these Saucers."

I was still a little confused, so I asked him to explain from the beginning, as if I knew nothing about Aliens and Secret Governments.

"The way I understand it, there were some Beings from elsewhere who made contact with the U.S. Government several years ago. Now these Beings aren't actually evil, they just aren't as spiritually evolved as some other Beings. Actually they are kind of like children, in that they are easily manipulated. They don't understand human thinking well enough to see ulterior motives. Another thing is that these beings don't look human.

"Now, forget about the Beings for awhile. Like I said before, there's a Government within the Government, made up of VERY powerful people, with unlimited resources. It is made up of people from all over the world. There are Russians, Red Chinese, Japanese, Europeans, Americans, etc. It is their aim to one day control the whole world. Right now they manipulate wars by supplying arms to both sides of a conflict, ruin economies of small countries, put their people into key political positions, deal in drugs, anything to further their long term goals.

"There is also a Military within the Military, who answer to this higher authority. Most of the people in our regular Government and regular Military aren't really aware of this Secret Government and Military, though they see glimpses of it sometimes. This Higher Authority insulate themselves with other people under them and use these people for their own purposes. They have people in certain positions working for them, like scientists, politicians, military leaders, etc., and these people have people working for them, and so on.

"The ultimate goal is to break the world's economy and kill off much of the world's population, so they can re-create the world their own way. The survivors will be under their control.

"Now, back to the Beings. When they first made contact with the U.S. President, he turned them over to the Secret Military and through them, the Secret Government. This was done in order to create an insulation between the Presidency and what they were doing with the Beings. That way, if they were ever discovered, the President wouldn't appear to be involved. Since then, most Presidents have known at least partly about what's going on, but they stay pretty much out of it.

"These Beings were manipulated by the Secret Government and the Secret Military, and ended up giving them very advanced technology and machines—machines that can go forward and backward in time, machines that can dematerialize matter, create holograms, alter a persons thinking and behavior, and much, much more. One thing led to another, and one experiment led to another, until there were horrible machines and horrible experiments beyond belief. They, together with the Beings, created and are still creating Alien and Human mixed beings, using human genetic material and eggs and sperm and human embryos. These beings are Alien in their mind, but have an acceptable Human look. They are completely under control of the Secret Government and work for them. They have machines that look like UFOs, and they even fly like UFOs. They are far beyond what the public thinks technology can do.

"The purpose of this is that the Secret Government wants to create an Alien War in order to break the world economies and to reduce the Earth's population. They will also be releasing unknown viruses, biological warfare, to reduce the population. It will appear this was all caused by Aliens.

"They have created resources for industrialization, which has severely depleted the earth's resources and increased environmental pollution, thus creating a global crisis and causing many earth changes.

"I was shown where they have built these elaborate underground facilities where they will go when things get too bad. These are large cities. Incredible underground cities.

"Now the Light Beings must go in there and destroy these machines and this technology, and there is a danger this could cause an Alien war, just like what the Secret Government is trying to create.

"We have our own Human-Alien crossbreeds who are entering the Earth Plane now, who are of the Light. They are to help Mankind. You will know them, for they won't be spreading fear."

I remarked to Dennison, "Do you realize you keep saying *we* every so often, instead of *they,* like you are one of them?" He said, "I *am* one of them. They told me I am one of them. They said I am one of many who chose to incarnate in a human body, to help the Earth at this time. There are a lot who haven't awakened to their true purpose yet. They are still searching, allying themselves to one group or one way of thinking, then another. When they can stand upright, they will know who they are. It is like a triangle with a line sticking up through the center and surrounded by a circle. They keep going up one side or the other, then sliding back down. I did the same for a long time. Seeking here and there for answers. Having many trials to overcome. They said when I slid back, they were harder and harder on me, until I learned to stand alone in the Light. That's what the center line is. Myself standing alone in the Light, seeking the Spiritual. That is the circle, the All Knowing. I am in a human form and have to live as a human, so I have to feel love, anger, hurt, frustration, sadness and pain, grief and loss, but under it all I am neutral. I must love everyone the same, but ally myself to no group or way of thinking. When my body dies, I will go back to the Light People.

"That design I was shown the other night that was so familiar, is *me*. It is my vibration, my signal, and my name. It is activating my memory."

We Are Like Plants
MARCH 1993

THERE ARE TIMES WHEN DENNISON COMES BACK FROM MEDITATING and I really regret not having a tape recorder set up. This was one of those times, where information simply poured out of him.

"They were telling me we are like plants. We are rooted in Mother Earth. As we grow, our life energy rises, much like sap that nourishes a plant. Different energies at different stages of life. There are times when the energy becomes stuck at one point; this is usually caused by a physical or an emotional trauma. You can tell what's wrong emotionally by how it manifests. Shocks can change the flow of life energy, sometimes drastically, where you become a totally different person. Like grooves in a record, the shock skips you to another part.

"Ideally, life energy *should* flow up through the body and out the top of the head, connect with the Source and then come back down around the body and back into the Earth, to rise up again through the roots and nourish us. Like the ebb and flow of the tides and the rising and falling of the sap in a plant, so flows our life energy.

"Most of us are actually depriving ourselves of our nourishment from Mother Earth. One thing that does this is rubber soles on our shoes. We have a natural electrical energy around us. We draw energy from the Earth through our feet, and the rubber soles block the energy. In the old days we wore leather, wooden, and plant fiber soles or went barefoot. Now we walk on concrete, carpet, etc., in insulating shoes. The electrical energy from lights and appliances interrupts and affects our energy flow.

Our circuit is not complete, and it blocks contact with Spiritual guidance. The Source is interfered with. The same is true with synthetic clothing, bedding, all synthetics. This results in many illnesses for which we go to a medical doctor. He can't resolve the problem, only try to treat the symptom. Sunlight, Air, Earth, and Water, all are necessary for nourishment of the body. Think how much we are really cut off from these simple things, especially in a city.

"Energy flows in a circular pattern. Medicine wheels focus energy within. Round homes, like hogans, tipis, etc., do the same. The Native Peoples knew this. Dirt floors to keep contact with the Earth, so energy flows completely around us. Blocked energy creates problems in us, just the same as a plant with a bent stem.

"In old age, we reach a crisis point, when we realize we are nearing the time of completion and death. If this is not dealt with properly, if there is no spiritual connection to hold on to, you will just give up on life and be dead in a living body. If you are spiritually connected, you will face the fear of death, and your life energy will split into two parts, the male (physical) and the female (spiritual). These two energies will again become one—female, like Mother Earth. You will surrender the male, physical-oriented self and replace it with the female self, whose place is to nourish, love, and give, and finally surrender the body to the Earth Mother, like a plant does when it dies.

"Our roots are our beginnings. How they are nourished when we are small determines how our plant grows. Lack of nourishment, physical or emotional, damages our plant, our *self*. This later creates weaknesses and blockages in the life energy, and we become stunted or illness manifests. Shock and trauma, both physical and emotional, changes us. It is like when you transplant a plant and its roots are deprived of their nourishment for a time, the plant goes into shock. The same is true of us when we are deprived of physical or spiritual nourishment. Herbs and natural whole foods provide vitamins and minerals needed to keep our bodies alive; things of the Spirit are just as necessary to nourish our soul. Take one thing away and the plant suffers, and so do we.

"Plants pollinate or spread seeds to reproduce. We too reproduce. A new plant is an individual plant, separate from its parent and it finds its own nourishment. We should see our children in much the same way. They come from us, but they are not ours. As our children grow, we should not let them live off us emotionally or physically, or eventually they will take our nourishment and we will starve. Instead we must make sure they have strong roots, so they can find their own nourishment. The same is true of our mates. We are two individual pillars holding up the same roof.

"Too often money or other things becomes the support we hold on to. Take that away and we fall. That is what these hard times coming up are going to teach us; how to be individual and yet be *one*. One in color, one in Spirit. We are a community, working together to replace those other things as a support system. The day will come when the last drop of water will be shared equally by Black and White with no prejudice, so both might live. Money will be replaced by helping one who needs, and in return you will be helped when you are in need. That's the only way we will be able to survive. We help ourselves by helping each other. Thus we learn unconditional love and giving.

"The new world will be where we live naturally with the Earth as we were supposed to in the beginning. There will be no money and no greed. Our bodies are so designed and so is our Spirit. Native ways of old taught this; that's why it is coming back now, to save those who will listen."

We'll Be Traveling More
MARCH 1993

ON MARCH 11, after returning from praying and meditating, Dennison said, "They were telling me we will be traveling a lot more in the future because of our book. We will be working to open people's minds.

"I was also sensing a lot of tornadoes somewhere. There's something getting ready to happen, I feel like it is back East."

A Large Storm in the East
MARCH 1993

ON THE 13TH, we were returning from a trip to Phoenix when Dennison turned on the radio. We tuned into the news and heard of a severe storm hitting the East coast. Snow in places where it doesn't snow, high winds, tornadoes. . . . I assume this is the severe weather Dennison saw last February and again a couple of days ago.

Alternative Building Materials
APRIL 1993

THE FIRST OF APRIL, Dennison returned from meditating and said, "They were telling me that those who are working to save the environment will really have to be strong. The public is focusing more on the environment, and President Clinton is somewhat supportive of environmental issues. This is going to cause the businesses who make a living off the environment and producing products that are harmful to the environment to fight for their livelihood. They are really going to put the pressure on the President. They also told me, ours is the first civilization who has focused so much on using wood for building, and because of that, we have really upset the natural balance of the earth. We *must not* allow any more of the old growth forests to be cut down. There is very little left, and if it's all destroyed, we are doomed. They were telling me about some other alternatives we could be using instead of trees. I was shown a vine, kind of like a grape vine, which grows like a weed where it is moist. It has a woody stem that could be harvested and processed for many things, pressed into wood, made into pulp, etc. There is also a fiber that can be made into cloth, like canvas, and it can also be made into board that is very strong and has many other uses besides. They showed me those reed-like things they used to make fishing poles out of a long time ago (bamboo) that could be used for a lot of things. Even straw can be used for building. Trees are used because they are so easy to get and cut up into boards. Greed is at the bottom of it all.

"It was stressed that we all need to send lots of energy to Mother Earth now. Form groups and do group meditations to send her energy. We need to concentrate on the ley lines and the power spots; they are going to be more sensitive now.

"Remember the Kogi Indians in South America? (from the PBS special, "The Elder Brother's Warning") Their priests as well as some others are going to be withdrawing for a year, in order to work intensely with sending energy to the Earth. She is going to be very sensitive for awhile.

"In two or three months from now there's going to be a lot of changes happening, serious weather, floods, etc. Have you noticed there's lots of babies being born now? Not only humans, but every living thing? The energies are for replenishing. Abundance. That's because after the changes really get started, there will be great loss of life. During these times it will mostly be the children who survive. They will be the ones to inherit the new world; only a few others will survive to get them through it all. There's also going to be a lot of twins born.

"Earth changes from July onward will be getting more intense. The negativity in the cities is increasing. There will be more gang wars and drug wars. Things that aren't needed on earth will be pushed to the surface, brought to everyone's attention so they can be dealt with; that's part of the cleansing process. People will be pushed more and more, in order to make them grow. Old garbage, emotional issues, relationship problems, things like that will surface in peoples lives. It's time to resolve them, clean up the mental and emotional issues that are getting in the way of spiritual growth. They stressed that people need to begin cleansing themselves. Not only emotional cleansing, but cleansing of the body. Fasting, sweats, better diets, more exercise. You see, the energies will be increasing, and our bodies and minds need to be ready to receive it. People need to purify their water too, especially at the lower elevations. The water table is being polluted. Everyone should begin to meditate lots more, too. That is *very important.*

"I don't really understand this; they were saying something about different kinds of electricity in the air which will somehow affect the body energy. More and more body work will be needed. People will have to be balanced at least every week. Body energy will be increasing, and people will need help in adjusting to it.

"The sun's rays will be devastating over the next few years. People should avoid sun bathing and unnecessary exposure to it. Wear hats and long sleeves.

"There needs to be more use of herbs in healing. Learn more and more about their uses, how to grow them, where to find them, how to harvest them, and how to prepare them. Get away from commercial medications. Healers and body workers need to begin teaching as many others as possible how to do what they are doing. Money should not be an issue. It will be urgently needed later. Things like herbs, sage, cedar, etc., are plentiful right now; they are being put there for later use. Even though it is plentiful for the time being, they should be respected and harvested properly, with concern for the environment and in a sacred manner. They should be shared and not used for monetary gain.

"They especially stressed the need to start networks across the country; really stay in touch, sharing, trading, and supporting each other emotionally. *Work toward self-sufficiency.* People who have gardens should begin sharing food with their community, within their networking system. They should plant for more than just their family. Learn efficient farming methods and how to plant and grow, using natural resources. Soft vegetables like tomatoes will soon need to be grown in green houses in order to protect them from the sun's rays. Learn canning and other methods of storing food that you grow.

"We all need to begin trading and bartering as much as possible. Start getting away from the money system. Share with others. Make it possible for everyone to have enough.

Symbols of Whales and Dolphins
APRIL 1993

THE WIND HAD BEEN BLOWING A LOT, and the air was hazy with pollen and dust. Dennison's allergies were so bad that he didn't go out to meditate for awhile. It was April 13 before the wind was calm enough to go out.

Upon returning he asked, "What do whales symbolize?" I was a little surprised by his question, because while he was out, a friend and I had been discussing whales and dolphins. She was wondering what symbolism, if any, the Native Americans attached to them. I had said, "I know they aren't in Dennison's normal reality, in that from a traditional sense he wouldn't relate to them in a spiritual way, as say an eagle or a hawk. But I am sure there are Native Tribes, like maybe the Hawaiians, who traditionally live closer to the ocean, who would."

I now tried to think of what they might symbolize. "I'm not sure what they would represent, but I know a lot of people really relate to them.

Funny, I was just talking about them awhile ago. You must have picked up on our conversation."

He told me he had been shown a puzzling vision, and he could make no sense of it. "I saw several whales swimming around in a circle, nose to tail, so that the nose of one was near the tail of the one in front. As they swam, the circle got larger and larger, and the movement created great waves. Then, in the center of the circle of whales, four dolphins leaped up into the air, each one going in a different direction, so that as they landed, they swam off in the four directions. (This brought to my mind's eye, the symbol of a medicine wheel.)

"There was one whale, the largest, who left the others and began swimming toward a sandy beach. I noticed on the beach were a lot of whales lying there with their bellies up, like they were dead. Huge waves of foam washed over them from the sea. There were palm trees along the beach, and they were bending way over, like a great wind was blowing. The whale approaching the shore was odd-looking, in that he had a white stripe across his eyes, kind of like a mask. He was making a loud sound, and I could see sound waves coming out from his head. I felt like he was trying to warn me about something. Then some of the whales on the beach began coming back to life and rolled back into the ocean, where they joined the other whales. Then all of them swam off toward the West.

"Next, I saw a very large, bright star with small clusters of light, like pinpoints of light in each cluster around the large star. There was a rainbow in a clear sky, with one end on the land and the other end in the ocean.

"Next, I saw like globs of ash coming out of the sky. It was mixed with rain or something. Just large drops of this dark gray stuff coming down and hanging on everything.

"I asked what it all meant, and I was shown the whole vision all over again, and they showed it to me a third time. I feel it is very important."

Earthquake near Grand Canyon

APRIL 1993

EARLY THE MORNING OF THE 27TH, there was an earthquake near the Grand Canyon registering 5.5 on the Richter scale, the second in two days.

While meditating, Dennison asked what was going on. "They were explaining how deep within the earth things are heating up. This causes pressures and steam to rise up to the surface through natural vents and holes in the earth. This creates movement.

"There's going to be lots more small quakes happening all over. Nevada's going to have some too, and also up in Utah. There may even be some down near Phoenix and even Yuma.

"There's changes taking place in the electrical currents, the electro-magnetic energies. This will affect the weather patterns and even affect behavior.

"There will be problems with electrical systems. Power outages for long periods of time.

"There's going to be sink holes appearing for no apparent reason—because the earth is shifting deep within. Parts of roadways will give way. Houses will be swallowed up. Whole areas will sink. Problems will arise with water, power, and food supplies."

Another Encounter with the Blue Light

MAY 1993

LAST NIGHT, THE 4TH OF MAY, Dennison returned from his meditations saying he had once again encountered the blue light, though this time nothing really happened. He had finished praying with his pipe and had closed his eyes to meditate; suddenly he felt and heard a hummmmmmm and immediately recognized the feeling he had felt previously. He opened his eyes and saw a fairly large blue glow behind some trees. This time he was able to get up and walk. He tried to go over to the tree, but the light would move farther away as he approached it. He said he felt waves of love and comfort coming from the light, but no communication.

I examined him for any unusual marks, but found nothing.

Severe Weather in 1995

MAY 1993

ON MAY 5, the evenings meditation brought the following: "We're going to be getting more heavy rain here later this year. Very, very heavy for days. Probably worse than this spring. (We had some severe flooding in parts of Arizona this spring.) I saw bridges washed out, that were weakened from the floods this spring. It is going to be drier than normal this summer; we won't get our rains until late, I think around August. Then the heavy rains will come after that time. It is to fill up the water table. The Earth is still calling for water.

"After this, there will be a drought that will last a couple of years beginning in 1995. At the same time, in other places there will be severe weather, lots and lots of cold, along with rain and snow. Worse than people have seen for a long time. It will be very, very cold, and there will be a short growing season. There's going to be lots of deep snow all over the country. They showed me snow with a bluish cast to it, I think from volcanic ash or impurities being cleansed from the air. After 1995, the weather all over will be so erratic it can no longer be predicted accurately.

"They were also telling me healers need to teach each other their skills. They need to form support groups. Many fundamentalist religions will label these alternative healing practices Satanic. Overall, there will be a strong move against such practices, as well as the use of herbs and vitamins. The same will go for sweats, group meditations, etc. Many will call them Satanic and even go so far as 'busting' them.

"People need to start food banks. Grow extra food and donate it to the 'bank' for the good of all. This should begin by 1995.

"The U.S. will be going to war in the future. The draft will eventually be reinstated. Tell everyone to send prayers for peace. Have gatherings and group prayers for peace. This war will not be like the Gulf War.

"The CARD is coming very fast, and cash will soon be a thing of the past.

"There will be some kind of script issued for awhile; they showed me different money that's going to be coming. It will have certain fibers or something in it that can be scanned to be sure it is not counterfeit. Then they will replace our old money with it. People who have lots of cash on hand will have to turn it in to the banks to get this new money, and then they will be reported to the IRS, and they'll be investigated to be sure they reported the money on their taxes. After this there will be nothing but The CARD. Everything that you buy or sell, every move you make financially will be able to be traced with the card. If you are stocking up on food, say, they will know it and can say you are hoarding food and have to stop or be penalized. Things like that."

The evening of the 12th, Dennison returned from meditating and said, "Man, they filled my mind with so much information tonight that my head is spinning. Some of the main things I remember is that they were saying we need to make up our minds where we want to live. Where we want to make our base. If we choose to stay here, this house will be made available to us. If it doesn't suit our needs, we need to be looking for some place that does. Soon we will be traveling a lot, and we'll need a base to work out of.

"They stressed strongly again that people need to start food banks for the future. We need to organize our friends in some way and begin storing food. Even if nobody wants to go along, we need to do it for ourselves. People need to store up herbs and things for natural healing and health care. Learn to prepare them and to use them. Soon they are going to stop the sale of many vitamins and herbs, or make them available by prescription only. We all need to store at a least one year's supply of all these things if we can. Also, things needed to plant and grow our own food—things like water purifiers, tents, camping equipment, blankets, sleeping bags, clothing, etc. Just get started storing, and you will find out what you need most and use most. Get rid of stuff we don't need or use. Replace it with things we might need.

"As things begin to happen, outlets for a lot of this kind of stuff will be bought out and controlled by special interest groups.

"I saw two volcanoes out in the ocean; they will be responsible for some big quakes which will hit California. There were people coming over here by the thousands, even a million or two. They weren't heading so much for the cities, as they were heading for the mountains and the small rural towns. You know the Mormons have a reputation for storing extra food and for being self-sufficient. These Mormon towns are where people will head first. There won't be shelter enough or jobs enough.

"During this time, the Underground will begin to make their move. Right now the big banks are buying up smaller banks who seem to be in financial difficulties. It appears these small banks have made bad loans and things to get them in trouble financially, but really a lot of money has been siphoned off and hidden in secret accounts by the Underground. The economy will get worse and worse, and the disasters will increase. Businesses will lay off more and restructure, and other businesses will fail. Insurance companies will go broke. As the banks fail, there won't be enough money to back up the people's losses. That's when the cash will be done away with and the Card will come into complete use. The plan is to have only *one* bank, and a World Banking System. When everyone is using the Card, they will use it to monitor everything we do."

Fasting and a Vision
MAY 1993

ON THE 15TH, Dennison had been fasting in preparation for an upcoming trip to Canada where we were to participate in some special ceremonies with our Cree friends.

He had just returned from his meditation and prayers. I was folding laundry, and I noticed immediately he had that radiant look he gets when something special has happened.

He was barely in the door when he began excitedly to tell me what happened. "I should fast more often! The Grandfathers came to me, and I sat with them in a ceremony. There were twelve of them, and I made the thirteenth. Four came from the East, four from the South, four from the North; I represented the West. They all sat in front of me in a semicircle. The Grandfathers in the East were wearing white skin shawls with fringe and beading in the front. Their hair was loose, with two eagle feathers tied in it. The Grandfathers in the South wore natural brown skin shawls, and their hair was also loose and tied with two turkey feathers in it. Those in the North wore bear skin robes, their hair loose, with no feathers. All had their faces painted and all wore moccasins. I too was wearing a shawl, but I noticed I was wearing regular shoes. (I wondered if this meant Dennison walks in the modern world?)

"One of the Grandfathers from the East approached me and placed a wooden hoop with four eagle feathers hanging off it, over my head.

"A second Grandfather from the East brought a bowl filled with herbs and placed it in front of me. It smelled like sunflowers. The outside edge of the bowl was lined with yellow petals, forming a circle. Next was a ring of small baby pine cones. In the center was a mound of leaves of some sort.

"The third Grandfather came to me, and in his hands he held a skin bag. He opened the bag and inside was some clay. He took the clay and marked my forehead, my cheeks, my chin, and each of my shoulders and the bottoms of my feet.

"The fourth Grandfather from the East approached with a small stone pipe, about twelve inches long. It had a crystal tied to the stem of it. He placed it in front of me, West to East.

"A Grandfather from the South spoke and said, 'The long boats landed and brought death for our people. Many, many times they came, until our people and our ways were nearly gone.'

"A Grandfather from the North said, 'It was foretold we would grow strong again. That time is at hand.'

"A Grandfather from the East said, 'Prophecy has told all the tribes will come together again as one, before the purification. Now is the time to gather the tribes together, to renew their spirituality. Most of the old spiritual leaders are gone. There are only a few of the new generation, your generation, to take their place. There needs to be a gathering, and a renewal of Spirit among the People. It should begin in the East, for that is where life began. Spiritual leaders from all tribes should come together; all tribes, all colors. They should gather every year as long as possible. There may only be a few at first, but it will grow.'

"I noticed at this time each Grandfather was wearing a stone neck-lace, each one of a different color, for the different races.

"Then each Grandfather began praying, each in a different language. I knew one was praying for the trees, another for the rocks, another for the birds, another for the animals, and so on. I heard myself praying for mankind. I didn't consciously intend to pray for man, but I was doing it. Then the hoop around my neck lifted off my head and went up over my head and became a rainbow. As I sat there, a gentle rain fell from the rainbow. I looked up and the rainbow became a white light that settled down on the ground. As I watched, it turned into a fire bird like I saw that other time (a Phoenix). It was wearing something around its neck. As I looked closer, I saw it was an ammunition belt, like soldiers wear. There were some other things around its neck, too, but I couldn't tell what they were, except for one thing that looked like roots, tree roots. The bird lifted all the way up; this time I saw its feet and every part of it. The earth trembled, and I could hear its wings beating and could feel a burning heat coming from it as it rose up into the sky. The sound of the wings became a roar and then a shrill whistle, sort of like the sound of a jet taking off."

Another Trip to Canada
MAY 1993

THE END OF MAY we again returned to Canada as the guests of our Cree friends. This trip was to participate in some ceremonies to honor their ancestors and to pray for the return of their Band's ancestral land. The trip was both wonderful and exhausting. While we were there, we shared some of Dennison's visions and experiences. It was very interesting to find how many of the Elders there had been getting very similar messages. They too felt 1995 would be a year of change, though many things were already beginning to happen.

Another Encounter with the Blue Light
JUNE, 1993

UPON RETURNING HOME, Dennison began either to meditate or simply pray and spend time in the forest on a daily basis. His symbolic visions continued, as did his experiences with the strange blue light.

On June 7, Dennison returned from his meditation saying, "I saw that light again, except this time it was like a column of light.

"I had started meditating when all of a sudden I could hear a woman singing. Not words, just a vocal sound. It was so beautiful; I've never heard anything so beautiful. As I was listening to her, I could also just make out a hummmmm sound, just at the edge of my hearing. It was sort of like an electrical hum.

"I opened my eyes and looked around and saw some electrical sparks again; then it was like a hole opened up in the sky about fifty feet in front of me. Light streamed down like a waterfall; a waterfall of light. There was movement within it, like a waterfall does, or sort of like how dust looks in a movie projector light. It came all the way to the ground and sort of flowed toward me like a mist. I tried to walk over to it, but I couldn't get any closer to it. It was always in front of me. It was like seeing into another dimension or something. I could sort of make out a figure in the light. You know, sort of materialized, but not quite. I was really scared; I could feel my heart beating so hard that my shirt was moving.

"Funny, but the first thing that came to my mind was how people see Saints and stuff; I wondered for a minute if this was something like that.

"As I watched this figure, I could see it was moving around, and I could see its arms and legs were real long and thin. I couldn't ever clearly see the face.

"I felt something pulling at my chest, like a magnetic force pulling on the inside of me.

"This went on for five minutes, maybe more; then the beam began to shrink up until it became a ball of light and then, pouf, it was suddenly gone.

"It seemed to last just a few minutes, but when I became aware of my surroundings, it was cold, and when I looked at the time, it was after 10:00 p.m. It was just barely dark when I first saw the light, about 8:00 p.m., because it was about 7:30 when I got out there."

Earth's Natural Cooling System Screwed Up
JUNE 1993

DENNISON CAME BACK FROM HIS MEDITATIONS and told me, "They were showing me that there is a lot of volcanic movement going on deep within the earth. I saw ancient tunnels that are inside the earth; some are natural, some were created by ancient civilizations, and some were created by Aliens. Some of them are *huge,* they said, as much as half a mile in diameter. They were saying the molten core of the earth is heating up, because we've screwed up the Earth's natural cooling system. The deforestation, pollution, burning of the rain forests, etc.—the things that are causing global warming—have screwed up the weather patterns. The Earth isn't cooling and heating in a balanced way any more. This is making the interior of the earth heat up more, and molten lava is rising up into these tunnels and vents. This heats up water in the Earth, which creates steam, and this creates tremendous pressure. Whole water tables can vaporize, and this will create problems, like huge sink holes opening up. Roadways, houses, and whole areas will just cave in and be swallowed up.

"Another thing will be water sources that supply water to cities will suddenly become hot. Coastal areas like New York and California will be affected most."

More Symbolic Visions
JUNE 1993

On the 17th, he said, "Tonight I saw some things that were like symbolic. I don't really know what they mean.

"First, I saw the White House. Above it appeared a roll of barbed wire, like you see around the top of a fence at a prison. On the roll of barbed wire was perched a bird with two heads, one was black and one was white.

"Next I saw a thin root; it grew up into a plant. As I watched it grow, it became a grapevine spreading out in all directions. It sprouted large green leaves and then flowers appeared. Out of the flowers flew lots and lots of small black birds. The flowers turned into grapes.

"Then I saw a skyline. The bottom was black, and this turned a deep blue as I looked upward. A glow appeared, like the sun coming up, but as the sky grew brighter, the moon appeared, very, very bright. It was weird, because it had a face. Just its eyes appeared above the horizon. It looked around, like a cartoon figure, and then it went back down. Later it came up again, this time all the way up to the nose, and again it went back down. Later it again came up, this time all the way to the mouth and looked around, then ducked back down again. A fourth time it came up; this time it came all the way up, and there was no face, only a *very* bright light.

(For some reason as Dennison described this, an old Credence Clearwater Revival song came to my mind, "Bad Moon Rising." This song describes these times we are entering into now.)

"Last, I saw a tree branch or a plant with a black bug crawling on it. As it crawled, it became a worm. As I watched the worm crawl, it became a butterfly, and it flew off. The butterfly was black, yellow, red, and white."

The Blue Light Again
JUNE 1993

On June 19, Dennison again saw the blue light. He returned home saying, "I saw that light again. It came down like a waterfall again, except this time I could see like a cave or an arched doorway behind it. It was like looking through a waterfall of light into another world. I could see beings moving around, going about their business. I tried to approach it again, but like the other time, it always was in front of me. Then, all of a sudden, I felt a warm beam of light hit my forehead, right between my eyes, and I couldn't move anymore. It felt like something was going into my mind. I don't know, maybe the whole scene was somehow being beamed into my mind."

We Find an Interesting Book
JULY 1993

WE WENT TO FLAGSTAFF TO CELEBRATE MY BIRTHDAY and also to try to sell some jewelry. We ended up going on down to Sedona in our attempts to sell. While there, we stopped at a metaphysical bookstore and I found a very interesting book, entitled *The Sign and the Seal: The Quest for the Lost Ark of the Covenant,* by Graham Hancock. We ended up purchasing it for my birthday gift. It turned out to be extremely interesting and informative. I was hardly able to put it down.

The author is *not* a metaphysical writer, but a correspondent for *The Economist,* as well as the author of several books on Africa. While in

Ethiopia, writing a commissioned work on Africa, he heard of a Christian Church in Axum that claimed to possess the Ark of the Covenant, as well as an ancient Ethiopian tradition of how they came to have it. This was later to lead him on his own quest as to the truth of this claim and to discover what had indeed happened to the Ark of the Covenant.

As I read, I discovered he interpreted the Knights Templar and their legend of the Holy Grail to be an esoteric symbol for the Ark of the Covenant and observes the similarities in their alleged powers.

He later speculates that the first resting place of the Ark, after it was taken from Jerusalem, was an island in Lake Tana. This brought to my mind way back in February of 1990, when we were watching the Indiana Jones movie, *The Last Crusade,* and Dennison had asked if there was a mountain named Tana or something like that in Greece.

I learned many other bits of interesting information, such as the Ark's last resting place being Solomon's Temple. The Ark was a prominent part of the Old Testament stories and the most sacred object of the Israelites, until sometime around 640 BC, after which it simply was mentioned no more. No one really knows what happened to it, though there are many theories and legends. The book also mentioned that the Ark was said to contain two stone tablets on which the Ten Commandments were written. Most serious Biblical scholars feel the stone tablets were in reality two pieces of meteorite. Since ancient times, the Children of Israel were known to venerate such stones. Also, pre-Islamic tribes of Arabs carried pairs of sacred stones known as betyls, with which they were said to communicate. Betyls were called "stones with a soul," and they were believed to be aerolites, a type of meteorite—stones fallen from the sky. Of course this brought to my mind Dennison's experiences with the Moldavite, which is a tektite, also related to meteorites.

In 587 BC, Solomon's Temple was destroyed by the Babylonians, and most of the population of Jerusalem was taken into exile to Babylon. There is no evidence that the Ark was taken, but many scholars believe it was carried away by the conquerors.

Jewish legend says moments before the Babylonians burst into the Holy of Holies, where the Ark was kept, it was hidden away in a secret cavern, directly beneath the large stone on which it rested in the temple.

There are many, many more interesting things in the book; many seem to verify or at least add substance to the information Dennison has been getting on the Holy Grail. I highly recommend reading the book.

More Predictions
JULY 1993

DENNISON CONTINUED HIS DAILY MEDITATIONS. On July 12, he related, "There is something going to happen out in the Pacific Ocean, like a large volcano building. It will affect California. I saw the West Coast being hit by a tidal wave as a result of this.

"I also saw Japan having a severe earthquake; I think it's going to happen in the near future.

"The people in the Midwest who are being hit by the floods will be having more. There will be more flooding again this fall, too. Serious problems will come up after the floods, like toxic waste getting into the water and affecting large areas, getting into the drinking water and the soil. The extent of the problem won't be known for a long time. I saw problems with sewage getting into the water systems and disease spreading to some extent. There will be great losses, much more than now; some places won't be able to rebuild. I saw flooding in other parts of the country; the Earth is calling for moisture. Low areas, such as desert areas, will be affected most, with bridges washing out. I still see a dam breaking. Higher areas will be cut off as a result—no fuel, no food for awhile, and water will be contaminated. Arizona will be affected.

"There will be serious hurricanes and much damage. Tornadoes where none have ever been before. High winds, large hailstones. Lots of lightning, dry storms, and lightning-caused fires. Other areas will have droughts."

I wondered if he had any time frame on any of these events, but he said they were only like scenes before his eyes, like a TV news program with the sound turned off. Along with it came "feelings" of things, but no specific dates, only "soon," whatever that may mean.

Prediction of an Earthquake
AUGUST 1993

ON AUGUST 7, we were driving, when Dennison said, "I sense there is going to be a large earthquake somewhere. I heard the earth rumbling, and I feel strongly something is going to happen soon."

The next day I turned on the radio for the morning news. There was a severe earthquake, 8.4 on the Richter scale, which had hit Guam.

A Gathering of Spiritual Elders to Come
AUGUST 1993

ON AUGUST 9, Dennison received the following, "They were telling me that there are other very spiritual people who, like myself, are working for mankind as a whole and not just for their own people. They aren't just Native American, but many different cultures and nationalities. They don't really fit into their own cultural systems and beliefs, but they see the larger scope of things. In the future, we will all be brought together, and we'll be able to share many things, from secret healing traditions to herbal preparations. We will each recognize each other when we meet. We are all being guided and worked with on another level, for the benefit of mankind as a whole.

"They also told me that while I am meditating, I'm being taught a lot of things, which will come out later as it is needed."

Symbolic Vision of Four Horses
AUGUST 1993

THE FOLLOWING EVENING he came home and said, "I was shown another one of those symbolic visions tonight while I was out there.

"I saw four horses running. One was black, one was white, one was red, and one was yellow. They were all running in a circle around a small hut or lodge, built of cedar. As they ran around it, they began to blend into the hut, which slowly became a large, gnarled, old cedar tree. It was gray and nearly dead. I could still partially see the shapes of the horses within the tree, their manes and tails becoming branches. Then a large number of birds came out of the branches. All different colors. They all flew straight upward until they disappeared. The tree, which had been nearly dead, became green again."

Feminine Energy Coming In
AUGUST 1993

ON THE 11TH, he explained to me, "They were telling me that people whose energies have been raised enough to become psychic, will begin noticing they are in conscious communication with each other. At first it will just be incidents, but as the energies increase, this will grow stronger and stronger, until it will be like picking up a phone and calling each other. The ultimate result will be their becoming one mind. The energy and thought force created by this unified mind can be called on and directed to where it is needed. There will be great need of this in the future.

"Another thing, as the energies increase, women will begin to feel more and more unsettled and unsure of their direction in life. This is because their feminine energy is linked with the Earth's energies. As more feminine energy is brought in, women will begin to assert themselves more. They will use their united strength to reclaim their power. Children and animals will also be affected by these energies to some degree, feeling more unsettled and running around without purpose.

"Women are who make men strong, families strong, and the Earth strong, for, like the Earth, they are the nourishers. Often, nowadays, women have so many demands placed upon them, the nourishing part of themselves is pushed aside or it is unappreciated. Without this nourishing, a part of us is weakened. A part of our Spirit dies."

One Family in Spirit
AUGUST 1993

ON AUGUST 13, as we were driving, Dennison asked, "Do you understand what *reuniting a bloodline through different cultures* could mean?" I thought about it and had a few guesses in mind, when he continued, "We are people of different cultures, different colors, and different creeds, who are of the same mind and belief. These beliefs don't necessarily reflect those of our own cultures or peoples. However, we are all of one family in the Spirit, but were separated into different shells when we came into the physical form. We are soon to come together to help unite our different cultures, to become one family of Man, that we might all drink from the same cup."

Crop Circles
AUGUST 1993

SOME FRIENDS OF OURS HAD GONE TO ENGLAND with a tour to see the Crop Circles. When they returned, they brought Dennison some stalks of wheat from a crop formation. On the 18th, he took them out to meditate with, to see if he could get any impressions. Instead of getting information on the particular circle, he received the following:

"The key to beginning to understand the Circles in England, is to understand how wheat and life were once connected; what it represented to the people.

"Wheat represents Life. *It was highly valued since before Egyptian times and was considered a sacred plant, in much the same way corn is sacred to the Navajo and Hopi Indians. Symbolically, to break a stalk of wheat represented the breaking of the spirit. To step over a wheat plant without breaking it showed the respect for life. The seed of the plant represents the seed of Mankind; the stem is the backbone or spine, through which the vital energy of life runs. The root is where the Creator and the Earth are connected, for the wheat is the offspring of the sacred union of the Creator with the Earth Mother. It symbolizes the fertility of the Earth, abundance, new life, and rebirth. Even when it looks dry and dead, the root is still alive. Life springing from death; resurrection. The wheat holds more energy than any other plant. To look at it another way, the root of the plant is actually connected to the heart of Mother Earth. The stalk is connected to the Creator and energized by the sun. If stored properly, it will still germinate, no matter how long it has been stored. It is an energy source like none other.*

"Wheat was never supposed to be sold for monetary gain. It was never meant to be tainted with chemicals or pesticides. It is Sacred.

"In looking at what is going on with the crop circles, the wheat itself needs to be considered, and why the circles are showing up in it.

"The shape and angles of the circles themselves create certain vibrations; they are Sounds. Their purpose is to balance the mind, body,

and soul of Man with the Earth and the Universe. They are actually changing the molecular structure of the human body, the Earth, and the atmosphere surrounding the Earth—actually changing the molecular structure of the Universe. Great changes are coming.

"They showed me lots and lots of symbols. They told me these were Crop Circles or would become crop circles later. They showed me the meanings of some of these symbols; these are a few of the ones I saw."

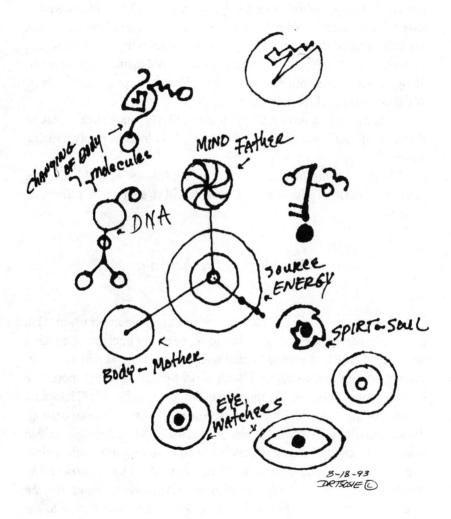

Crop Circle Designs

Blue Moon Energies
AUGUST 1993

AUGUST 31 WAS A BLUE MOON. After returning from his prayers and meditations, Dennison said, "They were telling me once again that we need to stock up on vitamins and herbs. It looks like the Government is going to try to force a lot of them off the market by this next year.

"They were also telling me this moon is a very powerful moon; very powerful energy. Babies born during this moon will be very powerful, have a lot of feminine energy. In fact all the babies that have been born since the first of the year are very special. Many will be very spiritual. There will be a lot of powerful teachers come from them. There are a pair of twins who were born this year that will be very powerful teachers. We'll be hearing of them in the future.

"This moon is affecting all land water, like springs, streams, lakes. Water in the earth is being pulled upward. It is to help purify existing waters.

"Women having their moon time during this moon will be having their blood purified, changed somehow. It will strengthen their immune systems."

Teaching of the Buffalo
OCTOBER 1993

IT WAS OCTOBER 3 before Dennison received any more information. That evening he came back saying, "They gave me a very interesting teaching tonight. When I first started to meditate, I heard what at first I thought was thunder in the distance. After a short time, it sounded more like hooves, running hooves. My immediate thought was *Buffalo!* The sound continued, and I soon realized it had become the sound of a heart beating, da-dum, da-dum, da-dum. A voice said to me, *'Do you recognize that sound?'* I listened a little longer and was surprised to hear myself saying, 'Yeah, it is the sound of a drum!' They replied, *'That's correct. The Buffalo heart used to represent a drum beat; it was synonymous with the heartbeat of the Earth. For this reason, the Buffalo was sacred to the Native Peoples. It was considered food for the Spirit as well as the body.*

There used to be a teaching called The Sacred Teaching of the Buffalo, which the spiritual elders of the tribes knew.

"'The Buffalo ate certain herbs and grasses, which made its meat nourishing and beneficial for The People. Its meat no longer holds this nutritive value, because it doesn't have access to these same herbs and grasses. When it was first killed, some of the blood and part of the heart was given back to the Earth, to honor the spirit of the animal and as an offering to the Earth Mother who provided it. The heart was sacred, because, like the drum, it represented the heartbeat of the Earth. Every part of the animal was used. It provided hide for robes, clothing, and sinew and bone for tools and wrapping; even the horn was ground up for medicine. When the Buffalo was killed off by the White men, it broke the spirit of The People. The source of their spiritual life, as well as their physical existence, was gone.

"'There is one thing, though, which was given to all Native peoples, which was not taken away, and it is still the key to regaining access to the Spirit. In every Native, there is like a drum located at the base of the spine, which vibrates to the beat of a drum when it is played. This vibration travels up the spine, and if there are no blockages, it synchronizes the vibration of the human body with that of the Earth and harmonizes it with the whole universe.

"'You see, all things in the universe vibrate, and these vibrations together create a harmony. Our Earth's vibration is the same frequency as the human heart.

"'The Earth's vibration or heartbeat is absorbed by the roots of plants and trees, and signals, or information, are transmitted up through the stem or trunk and out into the atmosphere, much like the drumbeat vibrating up our spine. For instance, if there is a need for moisture, the trees and plants actually send out this information and call for the clouds and the moisture.

"'When there are blockages in the human body, the drum's vibrations can't fully travel through the body, and the same is true with the Earth. The Earth has nerves, which you call Ley Lines, that contain certain minerals that are sensitive to the Earth's vibrations. They transmit these energies throughout the Earth as well as the Universe. This keeps the Earth in harmony with all that is on it, as well as with the Universe. If there are any blockages along these lines, it interrupts these

natural vibrations. For this reason, in the past there were certain structures built on some of these lines. The shapes of the structures created certain energies and helped keep a balance.

"'Now we have disrupted this energy balance with cement, pavement, mining, deforestation, underground nuclear testing, etc. These same things affect our own body's vibrations, as does the food we eat and the fabric we wear. It is worse in the cities, because the human body can't vibrate properly, and the Earth's energies are also blocked. Sooner or later, negative things happen. Like the human body, if energy is blocked in an area, eventually a cancer or some other disease will manifest.

"'People are naturally drawn to places where the Earth's natural energies are still strong, like Sedona, but as more and more people settle there and build, the Earth's energies will diminish.

"'The very words we use affect our bodies' energies. The words carry vibrations. You can raise your body's vibrations by speaking and living in harmony. You actually create a power spot where you are and others will be drawn to it.

"'In the old days, people would make offerings to the Earth. Many times, blood was used, for blood is very powerful; it carries life's energies. For instance, when killing an animal for food, the Earth and the animal were honored and thanked with the blood offering. In certain ceremonies and when seeking certain favors, Natives would cut their hand or arm or chest or leg, to allow their blood to go to the Earth. It was a purification for the person and an offering to the Earth. This was often done before a battle, to release fear and offer a prayer for protection.

"'You no longer recognize the power of blood. Even a small cut is immediately wrapped up in a Band-Aid. Even a woman's moon blood is very powerful, but it is not offered to the Earth any more.

"'You take and take and offer nothing in return. The imbalance within the whole system is very great. It should not be underestimated.'"

Strange Information
OCTOBER 1993

ON OCTOBER 27, Dennison had just returned from meditating and asked, "What is that planet that's out now?" I shot him a puzzled look. He added helpfully, "It's the second largest planet in our solar system." I sat on the couch trying to figure out what he could possibly mean. Finally, I asked, "When you say, 'out now,' do you mean visible now?" He shrugged and replied, "I guess so. I think it's just out now . . . they said that to me; they said, 'It's the second largest planet in your solar system, and it's just out now.' I think it is Saturn, does that sound right? Maybe it's Jupiter, I don't know, but I think they said Saturn."

I had no idea which planet it was, so I urged him to get on with what they were saying. He continued, "The Aliens are building something there, so they can keep an eye on the movement of the Earth's plates. They have a base here on Earth, but they are getting ready to leave because some real drastic things are going to happen soon. They are leaving for now, because they will be of more benefit to us later on if they leave. They will be contacting lots and lots of people on Earth, to guide them, and then they will return after it's all over, to help rebuild.

"There are two plates of the Earth's crust that come together. One is sort of sliding under the other, but for some reason, the one that's under the other is buckling. It is kind of twisting and will end up breaking apart under the other one, but first it will heave up underneath. This is happening because the Earth is heating up inside. Molten lava is making its way to the surface. Mexico will be the hardest hit, at first. Especially along the coastal areas. It will have several very devastating earth-quakes. Many more will continue up the West Coast, all the way up to Alaska.

"They showed me a map with a line that went up through the middle of Mexico, veered out into the ocean a little way, just missing San Diego, and then angled back in, continuing up through most of California and on up the coast all the way through Alaska. The first quakes will be most severe in Mexico. These will be followed sometime later with California being the most affected. A crack will form, and eventually a part will sink into the sea, for the underneath plate will heave up, then settle back down, causing the fracture to break off. When these quakes happen, Arizona will be strongly affected, especially down around Yuma and Tucson. Even Apache Junction and Scottsdale, all the way up to Payson. Sedona, Flagstaff, and the Grand Canyon will have real problems. Glen Canyon Dam will go. We'll be pretty badly shaken up here, too, and it will be pretty bad all over for awhile.

"They said there will be a lot of warnings given ahead of time. Many, many people in Mexico will be communicated with and warned in lots of different ways. There will be a lot of UFO sightings made in Mexico before it happens. Many of the Native Indians there will be warned, and they will bring their people up to safety before it happens. Later, some of their Spiritual teachings, the teachings of the Mayan and Inca, will be shared with the Natives up here. They said there's going to be a new generation of Native Elders, Native Teachers, come forth. They will be combining old Native Teachings with the New Teachings, or what we call New Age teachings. Some of the Mayan and Inca teachings will combine with this, too. It will create a new religion, one that is tied to the Earth, but it will have a lot more love and a lot less fear. This won't come about until after the Great Quakes; then the people will be much more receptive.

"Somehow, I'm a part of this, but I don't know just how yet. I feel like I'm being trained for something, but I don't quite remember the training. When the time is right, it will come out. I keep feeling an expectation, but I don't quite know what it is.

"There is going to be a severe drought in the desert areas. Arizona will be a part of it. It will be the worst in our history, with severe shortages of water. The earth is heating up, and the winds and weather patterns are changing. Remember the teachers they talked about before that will be coming to the Earth Plane? They will be coming in now and will soon be making themselves known to many."

Old Knowledge Has Been Lost
NOVEMBER 1993

ON NOVEMBER 6, Dennison said, "Tonight they were showing me a bunch of crystals. I think at least some of them will be coming to me in the future. There is one in particular that I know I am connected to. It was pretty large, maybe 18 inches high and 4 to 5 inches wide. It was kind of a light smoky color. It has some information in it about a lost city, an ancient Lemurian city."

He was quiet for a few moments, then he asked, "Do you know about some place called something like Lou Ginnee?" I could only think of

New Guinea and suggested that might be what he meant. He answered, "Yeah, probably so. Is it an island somewhere off the coast of Australia? That's where this lost Lemurian city was. There is or was a tribe of natives there that called themselves something that sounded like Selease. I was told this tribe was descended from the Lemurians. They had some Shamans who were very powerful and very knowledgeable people. When missionaries came, most of the tribe was wiped out. Some escaped, and through them, some of their knowledge was preserved.

"They showed me some kind of a tree that is very small, but it has a long, long root on it. This tree can be tied into a hoop that, when passed over a person, will balance his energies. It has small, brown, nutlike things growing on it, which can be made into a very nourishing tea.

"They said most of the old and powerful medicine men were gone now, and their knowledge is dying with them. It was the ancient Natives of many cultures who have kept the Earth in balance with their ceremonies and prayers, offerings, and dances. The Old Shamans knew the names of the winds and the clouds. They could call the rain or calm violent storms. They knew the Spirit names of the herbs and could call on the plants' powers to heal. In order to have a medicine be truly powerful, you must be able to communicate with the spirit of the plant, pay respect to it with an offering, and ask its assistance in healing. As this kind of knowledge dies out, the Earth becomes more and more out of balance.

"They were also telling me about a bird that is sacred to the Natives in Mexico. It is called a water bird, and it has a real long, beautiful tail. This bird is going to disappear for awhile, and when it does, it is a sign that the catastrophic changes are about to happen. The Natives will know it is a sign. Another sign is the Water Buffalo will disappear. Corn Pollen that has been properly gathered will disappear, and so will Native Corn, like the Blue corn and the White Corn. Natives everywhere will be praying and doing ceremonies for the return of these things and for the return of the rain.

"So much of the old knowledge has been lost. We will soon realize how little we know, when the Earth reacts. There will be no one left who will know the proper prayers, the proper ceremonies, or the correct names needed to bring balance back to the elements of the Earth."

More Information on the Holy Grail
NOVEMBER 1993

On November 28, Dennison once again received information on the Holy Grail.

"They were showing me about the Holy Grail again tonight. In the beginning, a physical object was created as a focus for the people. Something they could see, to believe in.

"This object was made from water and air. The minerals in the water settled and formed a sediment. From the sediment was made a clay. The clay was then formed around the air and water and shaped into a bowl to contain the Spirit. You see, the clay bowl represents matter, or the physical world. Inside the bowl was water, which represents the Spirit, life.

"The clay bowl also represents the womb, which holds the seed of life and the Spirit of the Creator. It is the combining of Spirit and Matter. Even the clay bowl of my pipe actually represents the same thing. It is made from Mother Earth and represents the womb of Creation. When I light it, the fire represents the spark of the Creator, which is in all life. I smoke to show my respect to all life.

"The Earth is also the Grail. It is the clay bowl, the womb of Creation, matter formed around air and water. The Oceans are the waters that held the seeds of life, and the sunlight that warms the Earth brought the Spark of Life of the Creator. Mankind is a part of each, a product of the joining of Spirit and Matter. WE are a part of the Grail. When we pass the dipper of water during a ceremony, we are representing this. The dipper, or bowl, is the Womb of our Mother Earth; the water is the Spirit, the essence of life. Again, the joining of Spirit and Matter, the creation of LIFE. We drink from the dipper to partake of the Spirit; we are joining in Creation, are a part of it. This is a most ancient of teachings, and only some of the Native Peoples still respect it in their ceremonies; it has been forgotten by all others. Now Natives are being called upon to help bring this back.

"Like I said before, the physical Grail was a clay bowl, and it had a handle on either side. It sat on four pillars, and these pillars sat on a clay tablet as a base. There was writing on the four pillars and on both sides of the tablet. There were twelve stones of different colors set around the outside rim of the bowl. I saw a thing like a wooden root surrounding the bowl. It looked sort of like the crown of thorns you see on figures of Christ.

"The clay bowl contained water that was activated by placing three certain stones in it. It also used energy from the Sun combined with the air.

"In the beginning, there were twelve angels who were the Guardians of the Grail. It was later passed into the keeping of twelve High Priests. It was used for the benefit of Mankind. It gave teachings, was used for healing, for miracles, and for prophesying, but after a time it was misused. It was used for greed and for destroying. So, in order to keep the principle of the Grail pure, it was taken apart, dismantled. Part of it was taken to another dimension; the parts remaining on this plane were hidden away.

"The teachings of the Grail were kept for a long time, and that is where the concept of the twelve apostles was derived from, as well as the twelve knights of the round table. But, as time has passed, most of it has been lost.

"When the Grail was taken away, its teachings were also put into the Universe to become part of the collective consciousness, a part of the universal knowledge. It can be accessed only by a sacrifice. The sacrifice is of the ego. The things which keep us from the Grail are Fear, Anger, and Greed—our egos. When we let go of these, we will find the Grail within ourselves.

"The Grail is also the Earth and its Waters. By our polluting of the Earth and her Waters, with our chemical waste, with our underground nuclear testing, and by our mining and our wanton stripping of her abundance for our greed, we are upsetting the perfect balance. We are destroying the Grail and thus are destroying ourselves.

"It was put inside all of us to search for the Grail. The Grail is in us and in the Earth, for we and the Earth are ONE.

"The Grail will be brought back when we again unite and realize we are all ONE. When we all drink the water of the Spirit from the same cup. When we are again one with the Earth and one with the Creator. There must be no more separations between us. We must let go of fear, anger, and greed. Let go of ego.

"The physical Grail will be returned to Earth after the Changes, to help rebuild Mankind."

Symbol of the Holy Grail

New Energies Coming in with the New Year
DECEMBER 1993

ON DECEMBER 28, Dennison was told, "You will begin to notice a new energy coming in; it will bring a time of testing. Relationships will be challenged. Couples who are not working together will have very difficult times. They will either have to find a way to work together or they will split apart. Relationships within families will also be tested. This will extend to spiritual families as well. There may be times when a family member will need assistance, and others will have to come up with money or food or time. So much so that it becomes a strain. You all need to re-evaluate your resources.

"Friendships will also be tested and tried. You will find if it is a true and selfless friendship, or if it is being maintained for what can be gained from it.

"Goal-setting and self-discipline will be extremely important. You must look within yourself and decide what you really want most, and that should become your goal. This will be needed, because these energies can bring a sort of depression to many. You may feel unsure of your direction and a lack of purpose and, with it, frustration. To get through this, focus on your goal.

"This is a time of deep personal introspection and self-evaluation, even to the point of stepping outside of oneself to observe. A time of having your teachings and spiritual values put to a test. Your beliefs will be challenged, and doubts, fears, and personal problems may over-shadow what you profess to believe. Will your spiritual strength serve you or fail you?

"This is a time of testing, self-evaluation, and growth. Those who waiver and fall will be tested even more, until they find their own inner strength. It will be greatly needed when the changes come.

"Earth's energy sources, like gas and electricity, will soon be in trouble. You will have to look at your dependency on them.

"The warnings of Earth Changes have been given over and over in order to give mankind a chance to change his thinking, change his ways. Instead, everyone stands back and waits for the catastrophes to bring the cleansing and FORCE man into changing. By taking personal responsibility and personal action, much could be done to diminish the need of changes. Are you sure you're ready for what is to come?"

Energy Entering the Earth
DECEMBER 1993

AFTER RETURNING FROM MEDITATING ON DECEMBER 30, Dennison asked, "What is it called when a Universe is created?" I simply gave him a look and shrugged, waiting for him to continue. "Tonight they were showing me what looked like a huge explosion, where matter and energy created outward, where debris, like dust and huge chunks of stone, were hurled through space to create a Universe. This happened eons ago, but some of this energy and debris is still traveling. It has now entered our solar system, and some of it is going to hit the earth. Somehow the energy will affect the gravity of the earth in such a way as to create a stress at the poles, and in effect compress the earth, so it goes into a shape kind of like an oval. It will be an uneven pull, and this will exaggerate the wobble that already exists. Large bodies of water and areas near these large bodies of water, like coastal areas, will be greatly affected. Some of the debris will enter the atmosphere and cause like a dusty haze. The color of the skies will look dull, and the color of the sun and moon will be affected. Weather changes will happen because of this dust. Some of this debris will be large, like meteors, and can cause great devastation. I sense a large comet coming in connection with this, but I don't think it will hit the earth.

"It will affect electricity and all things electrical. This will be starting after the next two years and actually has already happened a little bit. The energy that has reached the earth causes like a pressure in the head and ringing in the ears. This energy is actually going to raise our vibrations."

"Funny, I also sense Clinton might step down from office for some reason. Maybe he'll be forced out, what do they call it? Impeached. Gore will have to finish out his time in office."

1994

Hard Times Again

JANUARY 1994

JANUARY 1994 FOUND US ONCE AGAIN worrying about finances. Our slow season was in full swing, and as usual, we asked ourselves if this lifestyle was worth the stress. Dennison was restless and a little discouraged. Winter blues had set in. He toyed with thoughts of moving to another location, finding a home more suited to our needs—meaning a home with a workshop and more light. We even searched the want ads for another place to rent and spent several days looking, but nothing seemed suitable and, to be honest, we really didn't have the money to move. . . . Perhaps what we needed was a steady job for both of us and to try to live like "normal people." He said he was tired of worrying about how to pay bills and eat, never knowing from one day to the next if we would sell something or not.

At this point, my youngest son, who lives in Oregon, was involved in an automobile accident. He was hit from behind while stopped at a red light. The other car was traveling in excess of 55 mph! He received injuries to his back and shoulder, and severe whiplash; his car was totaled, but he was alive. He had been working for a janitorial service, cleaning office buildings. Now he would be unable to work for the next several months. This, of course, resulted in the loss of his job, and he was in need of financial assistance. I recalled the information Dennison received on Dec. 28; boy, did it hit home!

By the 15th, Dennison was filling out a few job applications for maintenance work with the National Park Service. By the end of the month, we were on our way to Farmington, New Mexico, for a job interview.

The next few days we waited to hear if he was hired. He had settled down a little, anticipating a move and a change in our lives. Then, one evening, he went out to meditate and was told that he was free to choose what was best for himself, but if he closed the door to his spiritual work, it would be very difficult to open again. He was reminded that there was a lot of work to do spiritually, and indeed we were being taken care of. There was much more said of a personal nature. By the time he returned, he had decided he wanted to continue as we had been, and to turn down any jobs offered.

A Teaching About Mazes
JANUARY 1994

A FRIEND IN PHOENIX INVITED US DOWN FOR A WEEKEND to visit and to show some of her friends our jewelry. Early Sunday morning, Dennison woke me and said,

"Weird, I dreamed about mazes last night. They were showing me all kinds of mazes. Did you know the medicine wheel is a kind of maze? So is the spiral.

"Going through a maze balances you and helps you get in touch with your innermost self. The true Self. Just the shapes of mazes create certain energies and open doorways to let energies in. They create vibrations, much like the crop circles do. A maze represents Mother Earth and the opening into the womb.

"Mazes symbolize our journey through life. You enter, and as you travel, you run into obstacles and dead ends. Sometimes you feel you are trapped, with no way out, but always there is a way, although you may have to retrace your steps. If you persevere until you come to the center, you will find your innermost being; your true self. You will find spiritual enlightenment.

"A person's hand is like a maze. The four fingers are the four races of man; the thumb is the Creator. The lines in the palm are your journey through life. There are three main lines that intersect or cross each other. In some people they form an "M." These people are very spiritually evolved. In other people, they (the lines in the palm) simply come together. These people are still searching and growing or, in some cases, just closed completely. The longest finger on the hand connects directly to the heart chakra. This finger is used to sense with, to receive and send energy with. What you are sensing travels through your arm to the heart chakra, where it is 'felt' or intuited. Below this finger, in the palm of the hand, is a point where you also receive energy the same way, through the heart chakra. The center of the palm is the same as the center of the maze.

"At one time, every culture was given a maze symbol. They would put this symbol on their pottery, their baskets, their jewelry, etc. They inscribed the symbol on canyon walls, in caves, and built large representations of it out of stones or earthen mounds. By doing this, certain energies were created, certain doorways to let energies in were created. People need to be doing this now, to help balance the energies coming at this time and also to balance themselves."

Teaching on the Growth of Our Souls
FEBRUARY 1994

ON FEBRUARY 24, after returning from meditating, Dennison said, "They were telling me that at the present time, mankind goes through a five-stage process in life to allow growth for the soul.

"First, there is the infant, who depends completely on his mom for all his needs. At this point he enters the second stage, where he learns about SELF and acquires his beliefs, but he is still under the protection of his family. He begins the third stage when he leaves home and the protection of his family, to establish his own life. The fourth stage begins after his children leave and he has time to grow spiritually. If a couple do not both seek spiritual growth together, a great separation may come between them, and they will grow apart, for with the children gone, there is nothing to keep the union together. The next stage is old age and spiritual fulfillment, then surrender and becoming one with the Creator.

"When we die, we go through similar stages. You first see your whole life as you lived it, all the good and the bad. You then evaluate it and see the lessons you set up for yourself and whether you learned them or not. Next, you choose if you want to return or not. You can stay there on "the other side" and like go to school, or choose to be a guide, while remaining there. That way you can experience both sides. Like a mother might choose to remain as a guide to her son or daughter. Or you might choose to go back and be born into another body. You can choose to go back into the same family, or you can choose to go into a completely different situation or another nationality. You decide what you need most to learn, then you set up circumstances or situations which will give you an opportunity to evolve your soul. When you are born again, you forget all of this.

"Sometimes, when one of these situations that you set up for yourself on the 'other side' happens on this side, you stay stuck there and don't progress, until it makes you ill or destroys your life. If you can resolve the situation, you will grow. For example, a small child suddenly loses his mom. She dies. His dad can't cope, and he becomes an alcoholic. The kid goes to one family member and then another, and in between he is with his dad. He feels abandoned. Later in life, when he has his own family, he still carries that old feeling of abandonment and anger toward his mom for leaving him. He feels hatred and disgust for his father. He is still stuck back in that stage of his life. His energy keeps going back there. Sooner or later, he develops heart trouble, because he hurts inside his "heart" center, or he gets cancer, because he has so much anger and hatred. It can affect his relationship with his wife, because he fears he'll be abandoned by her, so he is unreasonably jealous and possessive. If he can realize he himself set up this situation on the 'other side,' to give himself an opportunity to grow and learn, then he can open up and forgive and love, and move forward and even heal his illness.

"When a soul has done this enough times, it evolves spiritually. At this time, some may choose to come back to the Earth plane as teachers.

"Now, this system is about to end on Earth. The changes are already beginning, and much more is to come. It is like a great push of energy for the final evolvement of the soul. Many highly-evolved souls have reincarnated at this time, to help get the people through it. The new babies being born now are actually highly-evolved souls, who are coming in to help rebuild.

"Our world, as we know it, will be destroyed, in order to bring in a new world. The return of the Garden of Eden. The Golden Age. Not only the earth will change, but so will mankind. He will return to his original purpose, as a spiritual being living in harmony with the planet. The earth will become a totally spiritual planet. There will be no more illness, no war, no greed.

"Many will open up spiritually as the changes in the system, the wars, the natural disasters, etc., become worse and worse. They will have to change in order to survive. There is another place being prepared for those who do not evolve and open up spiritually. As these other souls who have not evolved spiritually reach their spiritual selves, they too, will come to Earth."

Another New Crystal
FEBRUARY 1994

EARLY IN THE MONTH, we went to a gem and mineral show. While we were there, Dennison found a fairly large crystal, about twelve inches long and three inches wide. The outside seemed covered with a thin, frost-like film. Its most striking feature was a large, diamond-shaped window on its face. He felt very attracted to it, and we ended up purchasing it. On February 26, he took it out to meditate with for the first time. When he returned home, he related the following:

"Funny, when I first got into the crystal, I saw this large lake or large body of water. The next thing I knew, I was in the water, going down, down, down really deep. I could see these three Dolphins swimming around the opening of a tunnel, and I could see a faint light, deep inside of it. I was wondering if I should go in there or if the Dolphins were like guardians or something, when suddenly one of them came up between my legs, and I was sitting on its back. The other two came up and swam on either side of me, like they were escorting me. We entered into the tunnel, and I was suddenly surrounded by this bright light. As I floated within this light, I was told a lot of information.

"I was told that I will be getting another stone pretty soon. It is to be put together with a different stone, and the energies of the two combined will create a third vibration. This stone will be giving me information or teachings that were encoded into it by someone like a high priestess or goddess called a water goddess. The information will be about some people who existed before Lemuria. They were called the Water People, or something like that. Their cities were beneath the Earth, beneath the ocean. These people were of a different vibration than we are. They communicated telepathically and had many, many other remarkable powers. They were like gods—way, way beyond what we are now. These people somehow mixed with humans at some time in the past and created a whole different race.

"There was a Book of Laws that they put together, like a book of knowledge. There were these Tablets, and there were also these Keys created to get into the information in the Tablets. The Keys were stones that were of certain vibrations, and when they were put together, they created another vibration.

"If a person who has knowledge took the stones and put them together with another thing, like water, and then put himself into a deep meditation, he could harmonize with the energies created. He would then actually see pictures and get information and knowledge from the tablets.

"Eventually, the information was misused by certain individuals; used for power and used to enslave and control people. The Tablets had to be taken apart and separated. I think part went into another dimension and part of them were buried, hidden away.

"Parts of this information have been brought back from time to time through the ages, like channeled to certain people; but then it was lost again. Soon the energies are going to be right to bring this knowledge back again.

"It scares me to think about it, but somehow I'm part of it. I feel like some of this is going to be brought back through me, and there's some others I don't even know about who are getting part of it, too. Later on, when the time is right, it will all be brought together to be a true teaching. It will change the way things are now.

"When the Earth was first formed, there was like dirt—minerals and dust and stuff that was attracted to each other and formed a ball around water. This was later covered with water, so there was water above and below the Earth. As lots of time went by, there were changes in temperature, pressure, and things, and the minerals inside the water in the Earth began to solidify, until it formed a huge rock that is like a crystal. This crystal is like a huge dome-shape on top, like a huge crystal cluster, and it tapers down to a sort of point. Kind of the shape of a snow cone. There were roots, veins of water, which ran from the central ball throughout the Earth. This huge, crystal structure within the Earth has a negative and a positive pole and gives off an electrical charge, which affects the whole Earth in like a grid. During the Earth changes, this huge crystal structure will be thrust up to the surface. It will rise and look like a big piece of land, a big island, but inside is this huge crystal. There is a beam of energy from the Source that is now coming to the Earth. This beam of energy will be attracted to this crystal and enter it and radiate out and surround the Earth. It will also travel inside the Earth along the roots of the crystal and will create a very high vibration, which will change all mankind. Our DNA will be changed. So will that of all the animals, every living thing.

"Right now the energy is moving. This energy is both negative and positive. People are being affected by both, so one day they feel clear and positive. Then, as negative energy comes in, they become unclear and feel doubtful and depressed. As they are able to raise their own vibration, their own energies, the negative energies won't affect them as much. The ones most seriously affected will be those who aren't open spiritually. They will feel like they are going crazy. Some will even become suicidal."

The Perfect Home Comes to Us
MARCH 1994

ON MARCH 1, a friend called and asked if we were still interested in finding another home to rent. I told her we had sort of backed off that idea, but if the right thing came up, we might consider it. She said she had a friend who was a teacher. This friend had a large, 3200 sq. ft. home in the mountains that had a large greenhouse as well as a large workshop and many other neat things. They were looking for someone reliable to rent it and would rent it at a very reasonable rate to the right people. As the conversation progressed, it began to sound too good to be true, and I sort of dismissed it as being some dump that someone was glorifying in order to get someone to look at it. It was nearly a three-hour drive to go there, so I made some excuse not to go look at it and forgot about it.

The next evening, the people trying to rent the house called us and asked if we would be interested in looking at it, that they wanted to rent it to us. They offered the same rent as we were then paying. Still we drug our feet. It seemed pretty remote, cold winters, deep snows, etc., so we said we weren't really interested.

A few days later they called again and begged us just to take a drive up and look at the home before we said "no." We finally agreed and made arrangements to go up and meet them at the house that weekend.

Of course, the house was ideal, everything we had said we wanted in a home. The scenery was beyond belief, fir and aspen trees, meadows, mountains, elk in our front yard. Without hesitation, we made the decision to move to paradise. We returned home and called our landlord and gave him a month's notice. He was sorry to see us leave, but he said he was glad in a way, because he wanted to put the place up for sale, and he hated to do so as long as we were living there.

Our lives were beginning to take a new direction.

More Earth Changes Coming
MARCH 1994

ON MARCH 9, Dennison was told, "Some really big earth changes are about to get going. Many sense it. The energies are really coming in strong. There is like a force, a vibration covering Mexico and the California coast; it is really strong out in the ocean. I saw huge storms, like hurricanes, that seemed to eat up the land on the coast. Lots of land erosion and mud slides. This was the west coast of Mexico and California.

"UFOs are making contacts more and more. There were ancient prophecies about this long ago among the Mayan. They were in touch with the Mayan in the past. Mayan priests are warning their people to prepare for hard times. People in Mexico are being warned. Even 'normal' people will begin to become aware the changes are really happening.

"There's a huge, huge storm, a hurricane, which will devastate much of the East Coast. I saw another one off the coast of Mexico traveling up into the Gulf of Mexico and the Gulf States. The Gulf States will be devastated. A bright light will be seen in the east. It will appear as a light or a rainbow. It will be seen at night, before the big storm. It will be a warning. There's also a very large earthquake which will hit Mexico before the year is over. It will begin out in the ocean and hit the land. Birds will suddenly disappear, and even fish will move out into the ocean; fishermen will notice the change right away. Bunches of dolphins will come up to the shore. All these will be given as signs of the coming disasters.

"There will be four or five Mayan Priests who are going to come forward to warn people that the earth changes are here; there are some Hopi Elders also."

More Symbolic Visions
MARCH 1994

ON THE 21ST, Dennison said, "I saw a series of scenes while I was out meditating, but there was no explanation of what they really meant.

"First I saw that red star I've seen before; you know like the Soviet emblem on their tanks? Anyway, I saw a red star go across the sky, like a shooting star. Not a real star, but an emblem of a red star.

"Next I saw some men in tan uniforms, like military uniforms of some sort. They were standing around a group of children, like they were either guarding them, or holding them hostage.

"Then I saw the White House, and there was a flag pole, with a U.S. flag flying at half mast. There were also lots and lots of yellow ribbons tied around the pole. There was a large crowd gathered there, and they looked like they were angry. They seemed to be yelling. Almost like a riot or something.

"The last thing I saw was a city in flames. Huge flames were leaping into the air. It looked like the whole city was burning.

"I tried to get something on what it all might mean or when it might happen, but I couldn't get anything."

An Invitation to Japan
APRIL 1994

ON APRIL 17, we were invited to go to Japan in late summer, to help in doing a seminar dealing with working on the inner self to achieve self-esteem and inner growth. Our part was to help put these people in touch with their spiritual selves and to help create an awareness of Spirit. We felt this could be done by sharing Native American concepts and spirituality, since the very roots of their religious teachings are similar.

The trip was to be for ten to fourteen days—all expenses paid.

We were both more than a little amazed. We wondered, why us? Why were we offered this? It was so unexpected, so out of left field— was there a greater purpose at work here?

How We've Misused Technology

MAY 1994

WE SPENT SEVERAL WEEKS packing, moving, and getting settled in our new home. May 4 was the first time Dennison had taken the time to truly meditate. When he returned home that evening, he said "I'm not sure I really understand what they were telling me. They talk in kind of like poetry, you know, kind of like how the Bible is written.

"They were telling me we are coming to the end of the age of technology; we've gone about as far as we can with it, without destroying ourselves. We were given the knowledge and the tools. We could have used technology to create such bounty for everyone; instead we have used it to create greed. If we had taken our technology and developed it in another direction, combined it with spiritual ways of living, and developed our spiritual selves more highly, think where we could be. If we had worked with the earth in a spiritual way while using our technology, think where we'd be. The earth's population has greatly increased in the last few years. This has never happened before. Soon there will be so many people, the earth cannot sustain them. It's like the farmer who has a cow that produces two gallons of milk a day. His family increases and increases, but they all nourish off the same cow. So the farmer uses his technology to get more and more milk out of the cow so he can feed his growing family. Still his family increases, and all of a sudden the poor cow gives up and dies. They used up all her resources and all the technology in the world couldn't put them back .

"We have tried to use our technology to contact other intelligence. We send radio signals out to try to make contact, but that is exactly the opposite of what we need to do. If our technology had been combined with spirituality, contact and interaction with other beings would have already happened.

"There are a lot of spiritual people who, instead of working to help raise the consciousness of others, are simply sitting back and waiting for the changes to come and take care of everything. It's like they've already left their bodies—they've withdrawn from everyday life. They forgot they are still in the physical world, and they chose to come here to experience that. They are waiting for the changes to provide them with something to do. Right now, there are many, many lost ones who need to be guided and shown the way to their spiritual selves, and these 'spiritual' people just write them off as lost.

"Mankind's contact with the earth, the elements, the seasons, the land, the animals, and all things of which he is a part, as well as his contact with the Creator, has been almost completely cut off with technology. He has forgotten he is a God. He gives away his power of self, to let the government take care of him. These are the ones who must be reached, for they are like babies with loaded guns. Their minds create. They have such powers, which they do not even recognize, and they are destroying themselves with it.

"Something is going to happen soon. Something which will shake up all the organized religions. I mean *really* shake them, just turn them upside down.

"There are new energies coming in that will end up bringing the 'spiritual' people who are 'way out there' and the people who are still really grounded in the physical world, together, because both of their belief systems will be destroyed. Earthquakes will shake up the physical world, but that is nothing compared to what happens to man when the very foundations of his religious beliefs are shaken. Even the spiritual people who think they are so aware and enlightened, will be shaken, because things won't be the way they think they will be. Power structures, financial institutions, political leaders, will all have their beliefs shaken, their foundations rocked, their foundations destroyed. They will turn inward and eventually seek out spiritual ways, because all these structures are actually built on spiritual beliefs. When that goes, what they stand for will mean nothing. Eventually, there will be a coming together spiritually of all people.

"Also, this summer something is going to happen which will affect Los Angeles and Phoenix—southern California and southern Arizona. Somehow something is going to happen to the water table underground. The water will suddenly become lots lower. There will be a serious water shortage, and there will be a drought. The places that have been cold, with severe storms, and the places that have had severe floods, will also have much more of the same things. Man has created these things himself.

"I also clearly, clearly saw a nuclear explosion. I don't know why it was, or where, or when.

"These things are going to be coming to help man back to his connection with the Source and with Nature. He was given technology to help him find God; instead he made technology his God, and in the process lost his spirituality. I asked what I needed to do, and they told me to send prayers for the opening of people's minds."

A Series of Visions
MAY 1994

ON MAY 20, Dennison received another symbolic vision of Dolphins. "When I first was getting into meditation, I saw these groups of dolphins out in the ocean. You know, like maybe ten in one group, and a little ways away another group of five or six, and another group a ways off. Then the ocean opened up, parted, so there was a large space of dry land. In this space, there was a ball of light which glowed reddish, with other colors of light that seemed to radiate out from it in all directions. As I watched, the center of the light began to grow very bright, until it turned into a very intense, reddish-white light, sort of like a white-hot piece of metal. This intense light shot up into the sky and then sort of exploded like fireworks. As these sparks fell, they turned into a thick swarm of small insects, like mosquitoes, and headed for shore, dispersing out over the land.

"Next, I saw lines of people, like they were waiting in line for something. Most of them were carrying large envelopes or something. Some had been there quite awhile, because they had bottles of water and stuff with them.

"Then I saw a huge warehouse filled with stacks of guns everywhere. There were piles of every kind of gun you can imagine. There were large wooden crates and guns stacked inside and even guns hanging on the walls.

"The next scene was a nuclear explosion like I've been seeing before. Then it all just shut off.

"Then they were telling me, people especially in the cities, will be suddenly quitting good jobs and just picking up and moving to the mountains. They're going to feel very claustrophobic in the cities and feel pressed to move. Even people who aren't open are going to feel it and move. We'll be seeing and hearing a lot of it real soon.

"There's going to be a lot of reports of people who are getting messages from angels or spirit beings from 'the other side' about things that are getting ready to happen. Maybe they'll see a loved one who has died and be given a message. Others will meet and talk to someone, a stranger, who will give them a message, and then suddenly disappear. These are warnings.

"Funny, when I began to come out of the meditation, I felt like it was raining. Really raining hard, and I was getting soaked. I thought to myself, 'I should have brought my coat with me out of the car or my rain serape. But I didn't know it was going to rain.' I opened my eyes, ready to make a run for the Jeep, and I realized it wasn't raining, and the sky was clear and everything, and I was dry. It was weird!"

(I wondered if this might represent cleansing?)

Watch North Korea

JUNE 1994

ON JUNE 2, Dennison came home and reported, "Tonight 'they' were telling me we should be keeping an eye on North Korea. It seems like things have calmed down a little, but the North Koreans are only stalling for time. They have something up their sleeves that will catch everyone unaware. Like a surprise attack where no one expects it. I strongly felt someone else was going to back them up, like China or even Iraq. They are building a nuclear bomb, and I keep feeling like it's being built out of the country, or somehow it is connected with another country.

"The big earthquake and volcano in Mexico is still on the horizon, and I was sensing another at Mt. Shasta. I want to say Mt. Rainier, but I keep getting Mt. Shasta.

"Also there's about to be something happening in India that will cause a huge loss of life. Maybe a plague or something; I couldn't really tune in on it.

"We are to send our prayers and energy to Haiti. Things there are heating up. It will be critical until after the first of July."

A Move to the Rural Areas
JUNE 1994

ON JUNE 8, he said, "They were telling me there's going to be a lot more people coming up here from the cities, especially from California. Utah, Colorado, and New Mexico will see lots of it, too. What's really bad is that they'll bring their big city ways with them. Their politics, greed, selfishness, and disregard for others and for the earth, too. They're going to turn whole rural areas into a city unless all the people there stand up and fight it. They showed me large corporations, and factories buying up land and building manufacturing plants, land developers buying up all available acreage and building homes, subdivisions, apartments, etc. I saw gangs getting started up in the schools, and drugs.

"The Apaches here are going to start logging their forests real heavy and open up another sawmill. I saw another casino going up near Show Low and a lodge or motel near Sunrise. In some now pristine areas, I saw a big factory going up. Big business is going to come in with the promise of lots of dollars, and greed will take over. It won't benefit the Apache people in the long run. I saw two more manufacturing plants of some sort going in close by Springerville, causing rapid growth there. Even here it will grow by leaps, and there won't be any acreage or homes left for sale, unless the local people refuse to let it happen. You see, this area is being looked at for its water resources, both for manufacturing and for drinking. Towns will be divided with those who want economic growth and those who want to keep things as they are. Flagstaff won't even be recognizable; neither will Payson and on up the Rim.

"There's going to be another earthquake or two in California—not the big one, but enough that people will leave by the thousands. They will overrun rural areas, buying up every available place to live, even small trailers to put on a piece of land. Then I saw something happening in Oregon or somewhere up there that will cause a bunch of those people to move, too. Utah will be overrun, the same way Arizona and Colorado are.

"Something is getting ready to happen in Mexico. A lot of people will be lost. It will trigger off a lot of other things.

"I also think 'alien' contact will be made soon—they will make themselves known all over the world."

A Shake-Up Coming in Top Government Offices
JUNE 1994

AFTER MEDITATING ON THE 23RD, Dennison explained, " Mother Earth is a living, feeling being, and she is going into a sort of depression, like she's going inside herself. Women will be going through much the same feelings, because their energies are closely connected with the earth. A lot of the hurt and resentment they feel will begin to surface. Many relationships will be in upheaval as a result.

"There will be shake-ups in top offices of the government—top positions in an upheaval. I also feel like we're being set up for war.

"Our gasoline reserves and our oil reserves are going to be depleted. There will be shortages, and prices will go sky high.

"I was told we need to be getting our household in order, whatever that means.

"They were also telling me that Russia and the U.S. have been testing some sort of device for the past one-and-a-half years. It's affecting the upper atmosphere, and we'll be finding out about it soon. I don't really understand what they meant, but I feel like it might be part of their secret military stuff, Starwars stuff, and we're being affected by it, and it won't be for the good. I don't think anyone will know for awhile what's really causing the problems."

A Dream of a UFO

JULY 1994

THE MORNING OF JULY 14, Dennison woke up saying, "I had a really weird dream last night. I dreamed I was hiking along this canyon. Then way in the bottom I saw something metallic, like the sun was glinting off of it. I wondered what on earth it could be and thought maybe an airplane had crashed and figured I'd better hike down on in and investigate.

"As I got closer, I could see it was a UFO. At first I was a little unsure if I should go closer, but then I decided to hike on over to it. When I got to the bottom of the canyon, there was this stream. On the other side was an old man with a long beard, fishing. I started to wade across the water, when he told me, 'Stop! You better not go any farther; there's a UFO over there.' So I told him, 'It's okay, I've been on one before.' So he said, 'Go ahead then.' And he let me come across.

"I got up to the UFO, and I could see a ramp coming down out of it, so I walked up on it. It was sort of like a conveyer belt, but it didn't move, so I walked up it and went inside. I was in a large room that was lit by a reddish-greenish light. I noticed two chairs, like captain's chairs, in front of a large screen, and there was a wall panel of knobs and buttons; some were lit. I could hear a faint hummmm-like sound, like some kind of a generator far away. There were some couch-like places to sit, too. I noticed a second floor and some stairs going up to it. I got on the first step, and it was rounded. When I stood on it, it started going up, like an escalator. On top was another large room, with some more couch-like places, all in a circle. In the center of the circle were several glass or crystal rods with pointed tips. They were of different lengths and were all clustered together in a circle. I wondered if this was its power source.

"Up above was a transparent dome, and I could see outside. There seemed to be no one around, and I wondered where everyone was. Then I noticed everything was sort of dusty, and I realized there hadn't been anyone in here for a long time. There were a lot of drawers along one wall, so I went over and thought about whether I should look inside. One drawer was larger than the others and had a latch on it, so I decided to open it. It slid open so very easily that I almost couldn't feel it open. Inside was a book, and I thought it might be a log book, so I opened it.

Inside it was written a date, 1995. I thought, that's impossible; it's only 1994.

"Then I went back downstairs and decided to see if I could turn on the big screen and see anything. I found a control that looked like a VCR control, with a red light and a green light on it. I pushed the green light, and the screen came on. The first scene I saw was of an explosion and a lot of smoke. As the smoke cleared a little, I could see a man in a blue uniform on a large white horse and men in red or blue uniforms fighting each other all around him.

"The next scene was of like the Civil War. There were some men hanging a black man and his son. There were some more blacks in wagons. Some were being whipped, some were in chains. There was more fighting going on between soldiers in blue uniforms and soldiers in gray uniforms. Lots of smoke and noise.

"Then there was another scene of the Mexicans in white clothes trying to get into this building—like an old adobe fort. They were trying to climb the walls and to break down the doors. There were soldiers on the other side fighting the Mexicans.

"The next thing I saw was German soldiers, except they were wearing funny helmets with points on top, and they were fighting other soldiers in greenish uniforms. Their helmets were funny too—sort of flat.

"Then I saw the Germans again, but this time they were Nazis, and they were fighting American soldiers, and then there were Japanese soldiers fighting the Americans, too.

"There were three more scenes in more modern-day type of war. I think one was maybe Korea and the next was Vietnam, because they were fighting Asian-looking soldiers, and the third was when they were in Saudi Arabia.

"Then the last scene was of a great white explosion, and the screen went off. No matter how hard I tried or how many buttons I pushed, I couldn't turn it back on."

Will the Comet That Hit Jupiter Affect Us??
JULY 1994

THE END OF JULY, Dennison asked during his meditation if the recent comet that hit Jupiter would have any effects on earth, as so many psychics had predicted.

He was told: *"All is part of the whole. When one thing is affected, it affects all things in the long run. Electromagnetic energies from the impacts are indeed affecting the earth, but the results won't begin to be seen for awhile. About five or six months from now, we'll begin to have severe weather in some parts of the world. Coastal areas especially will have great storms and floods. It will get worse into 1995 and 1996. There will also be earthquakes and volcanoes beginning about that time."*

Why We Are Going to Japan
AUGUST 1994

OUR JAPAN TRIP WAS DRAWING MUCH CLOSER and still we were wondering why we were going. On August 6, Dennison returned from meditating and said, "I asked the Grandfathers why we are going to Japan and what do I need to do there.

"They told me I need to take that crystal I got at the Gem and Mineral Show—you know, that big one. I'm supposed to take it out to a natural spring, when the sun is shining, and leave it for several hours. Then I'm supposed to take it with me to Japan and place it in a sacred place over there and leave it for awhile, then take it back home with me. It's for some sort of energy exchange.

"There are three Grandfathers over there now who are working and preparing the way for me. When I get there, they will work through me, use me as a tool to accomplish what is needed.

"There will be something special going on when we arrive. Like a sacred time of year. It's got something to do with honoring the dead ancestors. It also has something to do with World War II and some bombs, atomic bombs dropped on them. The spirits of those who died are in "pain," and they need praying for to be released to go on. There's still a lot of anger toward the U.S. that needs to be healed. I'm supposed to be doing something for them, somehow. I will know when my work is done, because it will rain all over Japan, like a symbol of cleansing."

The following day, Dennison went out in the afternoon to "charge" his crystal in a spring, as he was instructed, and to pray. When he returned that evening, he said, "They told me I'm going to be involved with a Buddhist high priest or someone like that, a spiritual elder. I'll be involved in doing some ceremonies with him.

"We think we're going to Japan for one reason, to do the seminar, but it's for something completely different."

God Consciousness Is Coming In
AUGUST 1994

A FEW DAYS LATER, ON THE 10TH, Dennison came home with another teaching: "The way I understand it, humankind is born during different cycles. Different groups are born together during different cycles. Right now, humans have reached a critical point where they have lost their spiritual beliefs. They've lost their connection with the God Source.

"In times past, there have come great teachers at these critical points, such as Christ and Buddha. This time there won't be a great teacher; instead, the God Consciousness is going to come in. If humans don't pay attention and open up to it, it will pass. The energy will disperse, and the opportunity will pass until the next cycle comes around. There will be those who will hold and radiate out the God Consciousness energy for the rest, but it's up to the individual to listen and open up.

"By the first of next year, a division between factions will begin to be strongly felt. There is a new 'religion' being born. Organized religion will come to strongly oppose it. The God Consciousness is being brought in this time through the Native or aboriginal peoples all over the world. Many spiritual elders will unite, and the people will follow. They will be for the Earth and our connectedness to all things. Many of the white peoples will oppose them. There will be two people who will stand out— be the leaders of this 'religion.'

"It's like two roads coming to a meeting point and two energies that can either join and blend together into one, or oppose each other. If they don't blend together, a lot of conflict and upheaval will follow. The opportunity of God Consciousness coming in will pass.

"Mankind has lost his awareness of his Spirit, his soul, his connection to the Creator, his awareness of his God-self. He doesn't know he is more than flesh and blood and part of something greater. Unless he allows this greater awareness to come in, the energy will disperse, and he will be left with all the negative consequences. Greed and corruption will overweigh the energies of the earth and set it off balance. This will be happening over the next three years."

Trip to Japan
AUGUST 1994

UPON OUR ARRIVAL IN JAPAN, we found the country was celebrating a time called Obon—a holiday time where everyone honors the spirits of the dead. Many ceremonies were going on, especially for those killed in the bombing of Hiroshima and Nagasaki. I immediately remembered how Dennison had been told a couple of weeks ago that this would be the case. Still, I marveled at the validation of it.

Early the morning after our arrival in Osaka, we were introduced to Toku-san, a highly respected Buddhist Priest. He was to be our host for the next few days and escort our small group to the Kinpusen-Ji Temple, high in the mountains in Yoshunoyama. Here at this ancient and beautiful Temple, we spent the night and part of the next day.

Within minutes after our arrival, we were given tea and a snack and shown our quarters. A short time later, we were slipping our street shoes back on and walking in the hot, humid afternoon, through the small temple village, about a quarter mile to the main Temple. The tiny shops lining the street beckoned me into their cool, dim interiors. There was no time to linger, so I hurried to catch up to the rest of the group. As I approached the Temple, the power and beauty of this 1600-year-old building left me speechless. Massive cedar pillars supported the structure. We were told there were no nails to hold it together; each part was interlocked into the next, like a puzzle—an art which has for the most part been lost.

A ceremony and prayer was about to begin. In front, we purchased sticks of incense, which we lit and placed in a huge pot; then we climbed the stairs to the dim interior, which seemed to offer respite from the oppressive heat. I was disappointed to find no difference in the temperature as we entered into the Temple. Toku-san gave each of us a generous pinch of pungent incense powder and showed us how to rub it into our palms and over our bodies in a sort of purification, much like the smudging with sage and cedar as done by Native Americans. Soon, several monks entered an area behind a large metal grate. Incense was burned and a chant began, along with the beat of huge drums, bells, and prayer wheels. The intense humid heat, pungent incense smoke, and rhythmic beat and chant soon had me struggling to keep conscious.

About an hour later, it was over, and we got up to leave, when a priest came out from behind the "screen" and spoke briefly to Toku-san. Toku-san turned to our little group and asked, "Would you care to go in back?"

As we stumbled along the ancient wooden floor, our circulation slowly returning to our legs, and our interpreter, Maya, whispered, "This is a very rare privilege. I've never even heard of it happening before." In single file, we walked past elaborate carved statues, ornate with paint and gold leaf. At each one, we folded our hands and bowed in respect.

As we walked back through the village, evening had fallen, and most of the shops were closed. In front of several, people were burning little paper boats in honor of Obon. When we got back to our quarters, sleeping futons had been laid out on the floor. We were told that if we wished, we could bathe, and that dinner would be served in thirty minutes.

A cold shower sounded heavenly, but I soon found it was a communal bath where the women all bathed together, and the men went to their own bath.

When we finished, dinner was already being served. The meal began with hot sake, then strong beer, gallons of hot strong green tea, as well as a milder wheat tea served at room temperature. There were mounds of sticky rice, and beautiful fish and meats and sauces. Everything was exotic and wonderful.

After the tables were cleared, we all relaxed on our cushions on the tatami mats. Maya was kept busy interpreting everyone's conversations.

Later, Dennison offered to do a small Native ceremony, and we all gathered in a circle with only a candle for light. It was very moving, and we all went to bed feeling blessed.

Our friend, Bob, the man conducting the seminar we were to take part in, asked Dennison the next morning what he had experienced in the Temple the previous afternoon. Dennison was thoughtful for a minute, then he said, "I just closed my eyes and meditated. . . . I saw several men sitting in a circle drumming. They were sitting back to back, drumming on large drums. They were wearing white, wrap-around tunics. There was a large circle and rays coming out of it, like a sun, on the back of them. As they drummed, I saw a large white flower begin to appear in the center of the circle of drummers, and the petals began opening up. Then, the next thing I knew, I was inside the center of the flower." Bob was silent for a few moments, then said, "You went into the Lotus. Many spend a lifetime trying to achieve this." This meant very little to Dennison, and he later asked me what a Lotus was.

As we prepared to leave, the keeper of the Temple met with us, and we had tea. As we sat there, Dennison said to our whole group, "Before I left home, I was told by the Spirits that when I arrived here in Japan, it would be during a sacred time when you honor the spirits of the dead. I was told a lot of healing needs to take place between my country and yours. My own father fought the Japanese during the war. There are many spirits of the dead who are still in pain here after the bombs, and they can't go on." Toku-san nodded in agreement. Dennison continued, "I don't know how, but somehow I'm sent here to help with this healing. They told me I'd know when my job here was finished, because it will rain."

Toku-san said, "I just returned from Hiroshima only yesterday, right before I joined with you to bring you here. There we did a powerful ceremony and a prayer for those who were killed. My prayer is for peace, always for peace. I watched your ceremony, and I understand it. We too honor the four directions, the sun, and the Mother Earth. We too honor all the things of the earth and know we are all one. We burn sage, much more in the past, though. We honor the fire, the water, the earth, and the air, as you do.

"I feel there is something powerful taking place here. I feel it on that other plane, that higher plane. We are in a drought here in Japan. There is a waterfall at one of my temples, and now it is only a trickle. We pray for rain."

The following day, Toku-san invited us to attend a ceremony at one of his temples. Upon arriving, we were given slats of wood, on which we wrote our prayers and wishes. These were added to a large bundle of prayers written by others who had visited the temple during the week. Toku-san was dressed in a fine silk robe and had several priests, including his mother, there to assist him.

Toku-san asked Dennison and Bob to sit upon the dais with him and the other priest—a real honor!

We sat on small cushions on the floor below. On an altar behind the dais were several figures. Candelabra adorned each end of the altar. Offerings of sake, fruits, and vegetables were laid below.

In the center of the raised platform was a large, brass bowl. In this bowl, a priest arranged some of the slats of wood. Toku-san began to light incense and chant prayers. The slats were then burned along with large amounts of incense, while prayers and chants were sung. This was accompanied by a huge drum and a prayer wheel. The oppressive heat and humidity and the cloying smoke and incense only added to the strange and exotic atmosphere, as great flames leaped to the ceiling and the room filled with the vibrations of the drums and chants.

When it was all over, Dennison asked Toku-san for permission to bless them all with corn pollen, which represents the essence of life and is most sacred to the Navajo. The priests all gathered on the floor in a semicircle, and one by one he blessed them, placing the pollen on their tongue, the crown of the head, and the heart. He then offered a prayer of thanksgiving.

After the ceremony, all of the men went into a room and changed into white cotton loincloths before climbing down into a grotto on the temple grounds, to the waterfall. It was indeed just a trickle, testimony to the need for rain.

First Toku-san stood under the fall preparing the energies. Next, he positioned Dennison under the fall. As Dennison prayed, sake from the altar was opened and poured on the rocks as an offering to the spirits. One by one, each of the men stood under the fall and prayed.

Later, a wonderful feast was prepared for us. We exchanged gifts and returned to our motel, tired, hot, and blessed.

The next morning, we headed to yet another temple in the mountains to meet with another priest—said to be the highest in Japan. We were told he sees only a few people a year, that is, grants audiences to them.

We were shown into a small room. There were no pillows for our unaccustomed American bottoms, but we were told we were allowed to put our legs out in front if we tired of sitting cross-legged (the height of rudeness had we been Japanese!). Behind a low table sat an elderly priest in casual clothes. A woman entered the room carrying a tray with a tea pot and tiny cups. She bowed low, as she sat the tray down. Our interpreter, Maya, whispered to me, "That's disgusting; I hate old Japanese customs."

I wished Toku-san could have been there with us, with his easy gentle manner and his casual, noncritical ways. Here I feared I might say or do some horrible thing to offend this holy man. I took small comfort in supposing that he knew how rude and offensive Americans can be and would overlook any mistake that I might make.

Quietly, he prepared tea and poured it into the tiny cups. He looked up smiling and bowed slightly to me as he offered me the first cup. I suspected that he knew my fears of making a blunder and challenged me with my fear. I got up and went to accept the cup, bowing slightly as I accepted it. He looked deep into my soul and smiled and nodded. We all drank the tea, thick and bitter as bile. I was very grateful that it was in such a small cup!

He began to speak. "I am always surprised when people want to see me. I am no one special. I am just like you. Yes, I have done some very exceptional things, but so has everyone, each in his own way. I wasn't always like I am now. I was once a very low man. I was bad and did things that were not good. I was past my fortieth birthday before I decided to become a priest. You see, my wife died. . . . So, I decided to join this sect, because they have a thing where one walks in the wilderness for one thousand days. It takes seven years to do. The first year, you have only your tunic and a bowl. You live off the land and avoid people as much as possible. You walk, pray, and meditate. The second year, you are given a pair of rope sandals. The third year, a hat, but you wear it on your back. The fourth year, you put it on your head. The fifth year, you get a walking staff, but you cannot touch it to the ground." He went on to tell of some of the ordeals he endured, such as being attacked by a wild boar.

At the end of the seven years, he realized he had done this for his wife, so he immediately repeated the seven-year journey, this time for himself. He went on to tell us of a Hindu practice he had heard of, where the priest walks for ninety days—continually, without stopping to sleep! Eating and drinking only once a day, as he is walking, and then only a bowl of rice with a spot hollowed out of the center and filled with tea. This practice was later outlawed. He decided to try doing this for himself and finally obtained permission to do it. It was an amazing ordeal. He is the only man alive who has accomplished it. The first time he tried it, he had to give up, because his legs became so swollen. But he tried it again, and again his legs became swollen after the second day, but this time he felt a cry and an exhalation of breath rising inside him. He began a sort of breathing exercise with this cry on the exhalation. Slowly he found he could continue while he did this breathing. He would walk around a temple compound all day and night. His only respite from the monotony was at a certain time each day, when he would descend the steps into a well, dip water, and bless the gods there. His body would crave the water, but he would leave it and climb back up and resume his rounds. He again protested his fame and proclaimed his humility.

Then he was silent as he looked at each one of us; then he said, "You wonder why I tell you this. You think it is the bragging of an old man. But when you do these things, you learn to go inward. You can go into other realities. There you learn many things. You see this reality for the illusion it is. Now I am here to tell you of some of the things I know."

Looking at Dennison, he said, "I knew already you would be coming. That is why I agreed to see you. A couple of years ago I met with some Hopi Elders. They came for the same reason as you. You are concerned about what is happening to the earth. No one respects her anymore. No one honors her anymore. Even here in Japan, no one really believes anymore. Their spirituality is gone. They pay lip service to the Buddha. Technology and greed are their God. What happens here is what is happening all over the world. They are destroying the rain forests. They have wars over oil. Greed. No one honors the earth. No one honors the spirits. The Buddha grows angry. The earth will reclaim what is hers.

Man is not necessary. Yes, I hear your message, I feel your pain, and I join with you in your prayers."

He went on talking about today's youth and how they are brought up in Japan, where education is paramount. They have forgotten how to feel and how to love.

At last it was time to leave. We shook out our numb legs and stretched our aching backs. We left feeling in awe of his wisdom.

The following week we worked with forty "students," who came to our seminar to learn to look within themselves and to reconnect with their spiritual selves.

On the first day of the seminar, it began to rain, and the rain continued for the next three days, flooding many areas of southern Japan with the much-needed moisture.

The last night of the seminar was a full moon, and we had decided to gather after dinner and go outside on a hillside near the hotel, in downtown Kyoto, to do a pipe ceremony.

As we were eating dinner, Toku-san came in. We were delighted to have the opportunity to see him once again before we left Japan. It seemed more than a coincidence that he should arrive just in time to join us in our pipe ceremony. He sat down beside Dennison and ate dinner with us. Afterward, he quietly said to Dennison, "Your work here is finished. . . ." He then looked up at the ceiling and said, "It rained. After you left, it rained."

There was another surprise in store for us before we left for our pipe ceremony. After dinner, the women were asked to return to the conference room. Awaiting us were brightly-colored cotton Ukatas (kimonos) and wooden sandals. Soon we all looked like Geishas. There were a lot of hoots and whistles as we joined the men. Together we traipsed out into the humid night and the full moonlight. Feeling awkward in our tight kimonos and shoes, we helped each other climb the small hill. We all sat on the damp grass in a sacred circle, East and West meeting and sharing in a ceremony conducted by a Navajo Medicine Man and a Buddhist Priest, witnessed by Grandmother Moon.

After our ceremony, we returned to our seminar room, where we all participated in a "give-away." Later, each person shared what was in their hearts. Toku-san took his turn and said, "I have only one prayer that

I pray. I pray for peace. Not for the end of war, but for peace in men's hearts, for if their hearts are at peace, then war will end. Something very great has taken place here. A lot has been happening on another level. Time will show us just what. Perhaps the beginnings of a spiritual awakening, where we are all one with each other and one with the earth."

As we said our good-byes, Toku-san hugged Dennison and said, "My brother, my brother."

We spent a couple more days doing our tourist duties, shopping, going to a tea ceremony, and visiting Mt. Fuji. While at Mt. Fuji, Dennison found a quiet spot and prayed and left a medicine bundle and sat his crystal there for a time to soak up the energies, as he had been instructed.

The last day, we took a train to Tokyo, where we caught our flight for home. It was a wonderful trip, but we were very, very glad to be going home.

More on the Japan Trip
AUGUST 1994

THE EVENING OF AUGUST 31, Dennison went out to meditate, the first time since we returned from Japan. He gave thanks for the successful trip and for the contacts we made. When he got home, he said, "We're not through with Japan yet. We'll be going back there some more. Some of them will be inviting us back there on our own.

"When we went over there some *very, very* powerful things took place, mainly on the spirit level. The greatest work was done while we were at that first temple. It seemed like a small thing to us, but there were thousands and thousands of spirits there, and all the Grandfathers—a lot of healing was done. We were just there, but the Grandfathers were working through us.

"Toku-san was at least partly aware of what was happening, because he works on the higher levels. When the priests did that fire ceremony and they saw a teepee in the fire, they also took that as a sign that they were on the right path. I think he's going to be getting some other priests together and maybe or maybe not involve me in doing some more work on the higher levels.

"Mt. Fuji was also powerfully affected—it also exists in the spirit world, and much healing needed to be done on this sacred spot. The medicine bundle I left there made some sort of a special connection.

"I guess I was once a priest or something there, and that's why I'm the one to be making this connection now.

"Somehow, this all has to begin in Japan, because that's where the first atomic bomb was dropped, and on the etheric level, so very much damage was done there. The universe is made of atomic and subatomic particles. Atomic power is the power that drives the universe, so the bomb affected the entire universe. That was the beginning of all the so-called earth changes. On a physical, spiritual, and emotional level, the earth and mankind began to change. In order to truly effect a change in the energies now, you have to begin there.

"There's still a lot going on over there. Several of the Grandfathers are still over there working."

Peacemakers Will Come; Many Tongues, One Voice
SEPTEMBER 1994

ON SEPTEMBER 10, Dennison said, "They were telling me there are a lot of energy changes taking place in the universe right now that will soon be affecting us.

"Mankind is at a point now where they have to change in a more spiritual direction or they will destroy themselves.

"The Watchers, or the cosmic energies, have the capability to make themselves known to everyone on earth, and they are going to do so soon. They haven't decided yet exactly how. They thought of doing it if a major war breaks out—making peace with both sides, and they thought of contacting receptive world leaders, but they want to not be seen in anything but a spiritual way—as messengers of a more spiritual way of living and thinking.

"They have been trying to make contact and give messages in much less dramatic ways, like with the crop circles, but most of the messages aren't being understood. The wrong people are involved in trying to figure them out. Time is short now, so they are going to take more direct steps to get the message out.

"They also told me that at this time there's a group of people who are being put in touch with each other who will become known as peacemakers. They will be of many tongues but of one voice. They will speak for the people, and they will speak for peace. They will be accepted everywhere and respected everywhere, because they don't represent any nation or any religion—only the people of the earth. They will be spiritual teachers of many races and many religions. I don't know, but I think I may be one of them.

"I'm also supposed to take that crystal I took to Japan and cleanse it in a spring again.

"There's supposed to be some powerful energy coming in within the next week, and when it comes, I'll feel it strongly. I need to be out there praying when it comes in."

More Predictions
SEPTEMBER 1994

ON SEPTEMBER 13, Dennison again got a warning about floods and hurricanes. "They were telling me there's going to be a lot of hurricanes, floods, and severe weather coming soon. On one hand, there will be droughts in places that normally have no problems, while on the other hand there will be floods, winds, etc., in places that haven't ever had them.

"They're still saying there's going to be a lot of people moving to all of the towns around here. A lot of the rural areas will have the same thing. The violence in the cities is getting really bad. Since we don't really see it, it's hard to understand how bad it really is, but in cities like L.A., Phoenix, New York, and cities in Florida, it's *really* bad. Then there's the natural disasters and refugees from political upheavals. These things will be getting worse. So people will leave the cities.

"There's going to be some things happening to California soon. Sometime between the middle part of October and the first of next year. Floods and maybe a big earthquake. Not *the* big one, but a big one.

"There's a volcano that I still sense happening too. There will be a major quake in Mexico, near Mexico City, too. I see it happening this year or next.

"There's so much crime in the cities and racial tensions building, gang wars and violence, that they will use the military to help keep them under control. When some of these disasters happen, the military will be used for the refugees, too. They already have a bunch of these guys trained and more in training. This is the new direction of the military. People will *want* their presence in the cities, and within a few of years, we'll all be kept under 'control' by them.

"They were telling me we'll be offered a new direction to go in pretty soon, if we want to take it."

UFO Dreams
OCTOBER 1994

DENNISON HAD BEEN HAVING SEVERAL "UFO" DREAMS—most only vaguely remembered. However, there were two he did remember. In one dream, he was on a UFO and was in some sort of a chamber with a fine mist spraying all over him. He was using what looked like a sponge to wipe his arms with, and it left something like a gel, as he rubbed himself with it. He noticed his "skin" felt different, sort of like plastic.

In another dream there was a large UFO that had landed near Mexico City. People from all over Mexico, Central and South America saw it as a sign of great changes, much the same way the Native Americans see the White Buffalo calf that was just born. The people came to leave offerings and religious items, and to pray. Like the White Buffalo, it was seen as the fulfillment of ancient prophecy.

Some More Predictions
OCTOBER 1994

ON OCTOBER 30, in meditation Dennison received: "Soon we will be hearing from people coming to us seeking direction. They felt guided to leave jobs and homes, and sometimes families, to move to certain areas and now don't know what to do. Nothing they thought would happen has happened, and now they are at the end of their resources. All I can tell them is, nothing is happening yet. They have to do whatever they can to survive financially until something happens.

"There's going to be a division, a split in Russia among the people. We'll be hearing about this soon. I think it is like a split in the government or people rebelling against the government.

"Is there a place called Choco-Vokia or something?"

"You mean Czechoslovakia?"

"Yeah, that's it, I think. Anyway, there's going to be a major UFO sighting there. Like maybe lots of UFO sightings or a landing or something. The people will see it as a sort of religious sign. They are looking at it like a savior. Everyone seems to be looking for saviors now. There will be a lot of people who will take advantage of this.

"They said, 'Remember what happened to President Kennedy?' Something like that is going to happen again real soon. An assassination or an assassination attempt on Clinton.

"There's going to be a lot of strong weather this winter; freezing snow followed by warm weather. Severe cold, even snow, in places where it is very unusual. Devastating floods and odd weather patterns all over the world."

Vision of a Plane Crash
NOVEMBER 1994

DENNISON WENT OUT TO MEDITATE THE AFTERNOON OF NOVEMBER 15. That evening, after he returned, we decided to go over to the cafe for dinner. As we were eating, Dennison said to us, (my son Eric was visiting), "While I was meditating, I saw this plane crash. I saw it just flying real low against a ridge, and then I saw it crash. Part of it was hanging in a tree." I asked, "Was it a small plane?" He replied, "Yes, it was blue and white. There were three people in it, and they looked like they were dead. I also saw something else; it looked like one of those Forest Service lookout towers." I asked, "Where do you think it was?" Did you get some sort of feeling for where?" He said, "No, not really, but I kind of sense somewhere around here."

We don't get good radio reception and no local station at all, so we don't listen to the radio much. I kind of listened to the evening news on TV, but there was nothing about a lost plane or plane crash.

On the 17th, we took our jeep into a nearby town for some repairs. As we were waiting for the mechanic to write up a repair order, he said, "I guess you heard that they found the plane." I said, "No, we never heard anything about it." He said, "Yeah, they found it just awhile ago, not too far from the airport. It crashed on a ridge. All three were dead. They're up there now, trying to get them." My son Eric looked at me, amazed; then he said to the mechanic, "What happened? I never heard anything about it." The mechanic explained, "Last Tuesday, (November 15), two Fish and Game guys and a guy from the Forest Service went out to spot elk before hunting season opens. They left the airport and never filed a flight plan. When they didn't come back when expected, everyone started looking for them. They just found them this morning. They must have crashed right after take off, just two or three minutes after they got off the ground."

The three men were local, and it deeply affected everyone around here. They were flying a small blue and white plane.

I guess the Forest Service lookout tower in Dennison's vision was to signify that it was indeed connected with the Forest Service.

Prediction of an Earthquake in Japan
DECEMBER 1994

ON DECEMBER 3, Dennison returned from his meditating and said, "I saw that red star again that I've been seeing off and on.

"I also sense something is about to happen in Japan, something catastrophic, like a war or an earthquake or something. I couldn't really get anything really clearly, a big earthquake or something."

Again on December 12, Dennison said, "I saw that Red Star again. Something is getting ready to happen that it is connected to. This time, I also saw a huge explosion. Maybe it is in China. I don't really know.

"There's going to be some more trouble in the Middle East again. This time it will be devastating, like WW III. The U.S. will be heavily involved. Our military will be going over again. There will be a lot of chemical and germ warfare used this time; a great loss of life.

"There's about to be a big shakeup in our government, and in the process a lot of 'secrets' will be revealed—things exposed. Big changes are coming up. This could end up affecting the economy.

"There's going to be some serious trouble in a large city. Chicago, I think. I sense it's racial based. The military will be called in.

"Something is going to happen in Hawaii soon. A big earthquake or something like that. Japan, too, will be having a large earthquake. It will be devastating. Remember that big earthquake that hit L.A. last year? There's about to be another one about the same time, only much bigger and more devastating.

"There's going to be a large gathering of Native Americans, a couple of large tribes uniting, and they will be making a statement for the earth and for peace and brotherhood. They will be gathering peacefully to send a message to the government. We will be involved in some small way.

"Our economy is going to have some problems, big problems."

Economy to Get Worse by End of Year
JANUARY 1995

ON JANUARY 4, 1995, Dennison went out to meditate. He returned saying, "I didn't get too much when I was meditating, except that we need to decide where we really want to be and what we want to do, because the economy is going to be getting bad pretty soon. Canada and Mexico are already having problems, and Japan will have its own financial crisis. It's going to start getting bad late this year, and we'd better start trying to get ourselves ready for it."

A devastating earthquake of 7.2 magnitude hit Kobe, Japan on the 17th of January, taking the lives of more than 5000 people. This same day, one year ago, a large earthquake hit LA. This is just as Dennison predicted in December.

Severe Weather, Floods to Come Soon
JANUARY 1995

ON JANUARY 29, Dennison received more information about severe weather, "There's going to be more really major rain storms coming—people ain't seen nothin' yet. Next month they'll really hit. There's something I don't understand, but somehow, out in the ocean, the currents are changing and getting warmer where they are normally cold, and this affects the tides and the weather patterns. (I think it maybe he's speaking of "El Nino"). They showed me swirling patterns traveling in circles around the earth. Europe, especially Germany and France, will have great storms, floods—so will the U.S.

"There was something about hidden effects of a comet, and there's a planet that's causing the currents to change. Jupiter comes to my mind." (I reminded him of the comet that hit Jupiter last July, and he had said there would be a backwash of energy that would hit earth in five or six months, and I asked if this could be it?) "It could be. . . .

"The weather is going to be a real problem over the next several months. There will be terrible storms. 1996 will be the worst. From now through 1997 we'll all be affected. All of mankind will feel the effects.

"There will be problems with electricity, power outages, severe dry electrical storms. Severe droughts, tornadoes, hurricanes, floods, winds, cold, heat, all in places where it's never happened before. It's already begun, and it will continue to get worse toward the end of the year. Then, the first part of 1996, the weather will be really, really bad nearly everywhere.

"There's also going to be serious problems with new diseases, strange illnesses that they have no cure for. Our current medicines won't be effective."

Dream of Riots in a City
FEBRUARY 1995

DENNISON WOKE ME UP AROUND 2:00 a.m. the morning of February 12 to say, "Lovie, I was just dreaming of a city in a riot. It was a lot of blacks rioting—burning houses and stores, breaking windows, looting, demolishing and burning cars. A lot of yelling and fighting. I saw two buses full of white people who were being held hostage by these blacks, and then they just burned up the buses with the people inside. It was horrible to see."

I asked him if he felt it was in the U.S. or in another country. He replied, "I couldn't really tell, but I felt in the dream it was in the U.S. Then I was also dreaming about Germany. I was like watching a newscast, and they said the German money had fallen or was devalued like Mexico's, and our government was going to try to help them with a loan, because if we didn't, the whole world economy would be in serious trouble. Then they were saying because Japan had another major earthquake, their yen was losing strength and their financial system was in serious trouble too, and the U.S. was in serious trouble because we were already stressed to our limit economically."

An Invitation to Go to Ecuador
FEBRUARY 1995

ON FEBRUARY 20, we were invited to go on a trip to Ecuador in March! This came about after a good friend of ours in Canada decided to go down there with an Eco-tour group. The proceeds from the trip go toward buying up land in the Rain Forest. The group was to meet with several of the Shamans of the Quechua Indians, who are descendants of the Inca, as part of the tour package.

Our friend told the leaders of the tour about Dennison, and they all felt it would be a neat thing to make a connection between the Shamans there and him. . . . All our expenses and air fare would be donated!

It sounded like a wonderful opportunity and I was very excited about going. For some strange reason though, Dennison felt very reluctant to go. He even went so far as to say, "Why don't you go and leave me here?" He couldn't tell me why he felt such a reluctance; he didn't even know himself. He did know, though, that when such a thing comes to you out of the blue, all expenses paid, it's time to pay attention. Spirit has a reason, and even in his reluctance he would go and wait to be guided. One day, he went out and prayed, to ask why this had come to us and what he needed to do while we were there. The only thing he was told was to bring a green stone with him and leave it as an offering at a sacred mountain. He was also told that the main purpose of his going, for now, was to build an energy bridge. He has gone East to Japan and North to Canada; now it is time to go South.

For some reason this reminded me of a vision he had after fasting on May 15, 1993, which I wrote about in the 1993 section.

Exodus from Cities to Rural Areas and Other Visions
FEBRUARY 1995

ON FEBRUARY 21, the weather was very warm, with the promise of spring. Dennison spent the afternoon walking in the forest, praying, and meditating. When he returned, he said, "I saw a lot of people leaving California and moving over here, especially to Tucson and Phoenix.

There's like a tension building over there, and a lot of people are quitting their jobs and moving. Some even move before they have a job or house over here. This is going on right now. Then they were telling me there's going to be another quake, soon, not 'The Big One,' but it will be the last straw for a lot of people. After fires, riots, floods, earthquakes, economic problems, street gangs, and all, they'll decide they've had enough and leave. Phoenix and Tucson will have a housing shortage, and the streets will be jammed with traffic. The worst part is, those cities will become rampant with street violence.

"Then I saw a bunch of stuff like watching a news program on TV with the sound off. I don't really know what it all was, or where, or when.

"First, I again saw a city burning. Miles of burned rubble and the rest of it still in flames. My first thought was Mexico City, but I don't really know if that was it for sure.

"I saw a huge wall of mud, like a wide river of mud, moving slowly. It was thick and as high as a house. It could have been lava, but I didn't see any fire in it.

"I saw a large cruise ship sinking; people floating in the water. Part of the ship was still sticking out of the water and on fire. There was oil on the water, burning, too.

"There was an explosion in space. I saw a long object break in half and tumble in opposite directions. I think it was the space shuttle or a Russian space craft.

"Next were long lines of people, just standing and waiting. They had bags and bundles of belongings with them.

"Last, I saw large numbers of whales lying on a beach, with palm trees bent in the wind. There were birds and fish on the shore."

Curiously, he has seen many of the above scenes several times before and even has received more elaborate visions of some of them, such as the one with the large numbers of whales on the beach and the one with the long lines of people standing and waiting.

What We Need to Do in Ecuador
FEBRUARY 1995

OUR BEAUTIFUL, SPRING-LIKE WEATHER didn't last long. By the 23rd of February, we were having rain. In spite of it, Dennison went out in the evening to pray. Four hours passed before he returned. I had grown a little worried that he might have gotten stuck in the mud. When he came in, I immediately noticed he had the special glow about him that I've noticed a few times before. He began by saying, "I need to take my pipe with me to Ecuador. Here I thought I could just kick back and enjoy this trip as a tourist, but they said I have a lot of work to do. They told me, 'There is a space being provided for you to do a pipe ceremony when you arrive. You will be guided. The reason you are going at this time is to help build a strong connection between the Natives there and the Buddhists. There will be special ceremonies going on while you're there. You need to bring the pipe into these ceremonies; this is very important. That is why you are going. You may be asked to stay a couple of days longer, because they want some others to come for this. If this doesn't happen, then you will be personally asked to return later.'

"The reason the energy connection is being made between these people and the Buddhists is because both are working for Mother Earth through Spirit.

"I asked them to help me meet my bills that will be coming up while I'm gone. You know what they told me? *'Are you hungry? Are your bills unpaid? Is your rent unpaid? Is there another tool you need? Something else to make your life easier?'* " (This hurt, because we had just received a gift of silversmith equipment and tools, as well as the use of a computer for a year, in just the past two days!) Dennison said, "That really made me feel like an ungrateful turd, and I was ashamed. Then they took pity on me and said, *'You will be traveling a lot this year, so you need to remain mobile. We cannot give you more than is needed, but your needs will be taken care of. You have a lot of work to do.'*

"Mankind must heal before the earth can heal. As you know, the earth changes come to force people to work together, but before this can really change people, there must be an energy connection between all races. Racial and cultural barriers must be overcome and a coming together, a uniting of all people, must happen. If this doesn't happen, the rest will be for nothing. All you will have is groups of people here and there struggling together to survive. Sooner or later they will feel their group is better, smarter, finer than another group, and the world will remain the same.

"They showed me a beautiful rainbow, except it made a full circle. They said, *'If you blend all of these colors, you will have white light. If you blend all of the races, you have one color—white light, God's Light.*

"'You have a great destiny, much greater than you can imagine. You've prepared many lifetimes for this. You are just barely beginning to climb this rainbow, to join all the colors together. Before you are finished, you will complete its circle and complete the joining. The energy has been set in motion. Things will move quickly now. You will have little control of the events soon to come.

"'You are one of twelve who are here to help bring mankind back together, to complete the circle. There are five who will stand in front; they represent the four races of man and the Creator. They also represent the four directions and the Creator. One of these five, the one who represents the Creator, will be the spokesman; he will speak for the Creator. Then there are the other seven. They are the seven colors of the rainbow and will be made up of many different peoples; they are the backup.'

"They told me Toku-san is a part of this. So are some of the people I will meet on this trip. I will soon be meeting an African, and there is a Polynesian, too. Someone from Canada is part of this, too, maybe Rocky, (a good friend of ours)."

Ecuador
MARCH 1995

HAVE YOU EVER HAD AN EXPERIENCE SO POWERFUL, that to speak of it was nearly impossible? So powerful that to encapsulate it into a box of words was to diminish the power? Such was our experience in Ecuador.

As we flew from Miami to Quito, the sky turned from twilight into night. I looked out our window and noticed a strange, reddish glow in the clouds below. As I watched the horizon, a full moon broke through, red as blood, bathing the sea of clouds with a beautiful and eerie glow. I wondered aloud if it could mean anything.

We landed in Quito, gathered with the rest of our group, retrieved our luggage, and got on the tour bus that was to be our home for much of the week.

Quietly, we sped through the misty, tropical night, up a winding road, into the Andes. Muted conversations, punctuated by silences, lulled us to sleep. An hour or so later, we arrived at a beautiful, colonial hacienda, dating back to the 1500s, which had been converted into a quaint hotel. As we climbed out of the bus, several remarked about the full moon, which had a magnificent rainbow or moon bow around it.

The next morning, we did our tourist duties and visited Otovalo, which has one of the largest markets of native goods in the world. Our wallets were much lighter when we finished.

Evening found us driving the dusty back streets of a town nestled between two sacred mountains, where many Quechua Indian Shamans (relatives of the Inca) live and work. At last we reached our destination. Juan, our guide and interpreter, led us up a dark, narrow street to a small house. He knocked at the door and spoke briefly to someone inside. There was a little commotion as things were prepared to receive our group. Soon the Shaman, a handsome Indian named Jose, greeted us and led us inside. I noticed a flicker of surprise, or maybe acknowledgment, in Jose's eyes, as Dennison stepped inside.

We were led up a narrow staircase, through a bedroom, and into a healing room, which held a couple of benches and an altar containing the tools Jose worked with.

After we all found a place to sit, Jose began his preparations by pouring a strong alcoholic beverage, similar to moonshine, into a small cup. He took a mouthful and sprayed it in a fine mist over his sacred tools. This was followed by lighting a cigarette and blowing smoke over everything. He repeated this procedure several times, then poured another small cup of the drink and offered it to Juan as a greeting. After welcoming our group, Jose poured another small cup of alcohol, walked over to Dennison, and offered it to him. Dennison drank it and gave the cup back to him. Jose remained standing in front of Dennison and began speaking to him. Juan translated, "He says you are a Shaman like him. He knows because he sees it in your eyes, and he can see it in the center of your forehead (Jose touched Dennison's third eye), and he has met you up here (Jose waved a hand in the air above his head), in the other reality." Jose paused a few moments before he continued. "He says you are very courageous to come here." It seemed an odd and rather cryptic remark to make.

Jose finished his preparations and then asked if anyone wanted healing. Several in the group were studying shamanism and wanted to observe and experience shamanic healing or cleansing of the energy fields around them. A volunteer came forward, and Jose began. It was very interesting to watch him work, spraying the patient with the alcohol, brushing the body with bundled herbs, whistling and smoking. Stones were selected to help balance the energies. Later, a woman came forward for healing. She had degenerative spine disease, and after an accident, she had had part of her spine fused together. The surgery had left her in constant pain and with a pronounced limp.

Jose began by having her rub an unused candle over her entire body. He took the candle and lit it to study the flame. After a short time, he vividly and accurately described her problem and her pain. He told her, "You will have to trust me completely." She bravely replied, "My heart is yours." After spraying, smoking, burning herbs, and manipulating the energies surrounding her, he asked her to lie down on a bench. He began deeply massaging up her legs. She winced in obvious pain as he worked his way up toward her hips and spine. Unable to withstand more pain, she cried out. Jose continued the deep massage as he firmly said, "You have to be strong." Moments later, she surrendered, all resistance gone. He continued to work the muscles in her hips and lower back for some time. At last, flushed with exhaustion, he finished her healing by balancing her energies. He then asked her to stand up and try walking.

We all held our breath in anticipation. Fearfully, she stood and took a few steps. A look of amazement and joy lit her face as she walked some more. Then she was laughing and crying with relief and wonder, her pain completely gone. It didn't return the remainder of our trip. As we ended our visit, Dennison offered to bless Jose with corn pollen, and in turn Jose blessed him. Afterward, they embraced; it was a beautiful and moving exchange.

Early the next morning, we boarded our bus and climbed another very narrow, winding road, into the misty, magical world of the Cloud

Forest. At one point, we got off the bus and walked down the road, as the bus followed slowly behind. The clouds swallowed us up, as if we had entered another world.

At last we arrived at our destination. Pack horses waited to take our luggage, as we walked behind, some three miles back into the mountains into the Intag Forest Reserve. Here, we entered Paradise.

We were met by Carlos, who was to be our host for the next two days and nights. Carlos and his family oversee this 500-acre area, set aside largely in its natural state, to allow individuals a chance to experience the rainforest. These people live in complete harmony with nature, growing most of their own food. They even grow the trees for lumber to build with, as opposed to robbing it from the forest.

We spent two days of peace and tranquillity in modest and simple accommodations. With no electricity, we had to use outdoor solar showers and outdoor toilets. We ate our meals under a bougainvillea-covered patio. The food was simple and pure. Fresh garden vegetables and fruits, even homemade breads and cheeses. I didn't want to leave.

While we were in this powerful place, another wondrous thing happened. I suppose it may have begun when we gathered together in the gentle rain and participated in a pipe ceremony with Dennison. The energy was strong as we joined our minds and hearts.

Later in the evening, we had all gathered under the bougainvillea for dinner. Dennison suggested that we all stand and join hands in a blessing to give thanks, each in our own way. First, he had us take several deep breaths. Then, as if he had forgotten about praying, Dennison sat down. He turned to me and softly said, "I love you. I appreciate each and everything you do for me."

He continued by profusely thanking everyone who was responsible for bringing us on this trip. At this point, I began to grow concerned, because he was acting a little weird, not at all himself. I whispered, "Lovey, what's going on? Why are you acting like this?"

He looked at me as if I had insulted or hurt him, and continued speaking. Soon he began to single out various individuals, questioning them on personal issues that they were involved in. It was obviously painful for some of them, and it concerned me greatly that he was doing this publicly. I tried to stop him, or at least tone him down, but he brushed me aside and continued. It was obvious to me that Spirit was speaking through him. It would have Its way. At one time, he tried to stand up, but his body was not its own, and he fell backward. Several people helped him stand up, but he fell forward onto the table. He attempted once more to stand. This time, he was held upright until he was able to regain some control of his body. His questions became less personal, and the message became one for all present.

Over and over, he spoke of the importance of LOVE, the need to love ourselves, to realize we are beings of light. The need to know we are a part of the Source, or that which we call God. That the divine spark which is in all life is also in each of us. We are all divine. He spoke of love being the force that heals. Not mumbo jumbo. Not mystical procedures. Only LOVE, LOVE, LOVE. He talked about loving the Earth, the Mother of us all.

Dennison encouraged commitments to working for Her and stopping the greed, rape, and plundering of Her resources. This, he said, must begin within ourselves and then radiate outward. Our efforts must remain pure, never to be motivated by greed or lust for power or self gain.

The telling of this incident greatly diminishes the impact it had on everyone present. Many were in tears; all were deeply moved. The end result united us all into a strong spiritual family unit who had experienced something powerful. We were all ordinary people, each with their own problems, recognizing each other's weaknesses and pain. We began forgiving, supporting, and loving each other. Each day this bond grew stronger and stronger, throughout the remainder of the trip.

The next morning, Dennison and I woke up with the sun. Quietly we slipped out and walked to the side of a gorge to greet the sun with a prayer and the pipe. Later that day, the group gathered together to hike into the exotic rain forest with Carlos. As our guide, he showed us trees covered with orchids, ferns thirty feet high, magical waterfalls, and thousands of other wonders. Later, we sat in the twilight on Carlos' patio, while he played his guitar and sang for us. The rest of the world and its problems seemed far away and unreal. For that moment in time, life was simple and pure, as it should always be.

The next morning we reluctantly said our good-byes, hiked out to our bus, and soon we were heading back to Otovalo. Later that same evening, we again drove through the dusty back streets of a town, to another Quechua Shaman, this time, a woman named Maria.

Upon arriving, we were invited into the house. As I walked into the door, I was surprised to find myself in a courtyard-type of area that housed a cow, a pig, and some chickens. The living quarters opened off of this. We were led into a small room where the healing was done.

Maria was a tiny, beautiful, and loving woman. She did her healings with the assistance of her husband, an equally loving man. Like Jose, she used a candle to do her diagnosis. She also used raw eggs, still in the shell, to rub the patient with, to absorb the negative energies of the illness.

As the healings began, some of those being healed wanted privacy, so the rest of us left to wait just outside the healing room. A young man in his early twenties was lying in a bed in this room, obviously ill. Several children were playing nearby. After a few minutes, one of the kids began playing some lively Native music on a tape player. Someone in our group began clapping her hands in time with the music and making some dancing moves The little girl suddenly grabbed the woman's hands and they began dancing. The other children were delighted. Soon, everyone had joined in. There was a lot of laughter, and the young man in the bed weakly raised himself up on one elbow and smiled at the crazy people in his home.

After Maria had finished with the healings, Dennison asked if he could bless her and her husband with corn pollen, as he had done Jose. After he had finished, Maria asked him to please bless her son, the sick young man in the bed.

As Dennison worked on him, he sensed the boy was near death. The family knew, but prayed it wouldn't have to be so. With this was also the understanding that death is a part of life. I thought about this as we left, for I too have a son about the same age. My heart ached for Maria. The scene of the dancing kept replaying itself in my mind, and I began to realize; here was a teaching for all of us who are from a culture where death is hidden away from the living, and feared. Here, in humble little houses, all of life is fully lived and shared—shared with cows and chickens, and with strangers, who are welcome to come and laugh, even to dance, in a room where a young man lays dying. Life and death. Two sides of the same coin. This is what life and death should be; a dance of joy and sorrow, shared by all.

The next morning, we boarded our bus and headed for the sacred mountain of Cotopaxi, the largest active volcano in the world. It last erupted in 1877, and is long overdue for its next eruption. We drove up a narrow road, past the treeline to where the earth was covered with beautiful lichens. The snow-covered mountain loomed just ahead. The bus continued up the mountain, until it reached a point where a part of the road had washed away. Everyone scrambled out of the bus to explore.

The air was crisp and thin, here at 14,000 feet. After a cold lunch of cheese and tomato sandwiches, hard-boiled eggs, and fresh pineapple, several decided to hike a little way up the mountainside.

Dennison felt this was where he needed to leave his stone and offering. Quietly, he drifted away from the group to find a place to offer his prayers and leave his offering bundle. As he finished, there was a rumble of thunder, and a rainbow appeared. Very rapidly, clouds began moving in, as if our purpose was served and we were no longer welcome in this sacred place. Soon, everyone was engulfed in a foggy mist. A gentle rain began falling as we drove down the mountainside.

We rode for another two hours on the way to meet with the final Shaman of our trip. The rain stayed with us all the way, letting up only as we neared our destination.

It was dusk as the bus crept up a narrow, cobblestone street, up a lane to a farm. We got out, stretched, and stood in a huddle, waiting. After a few minutes, a man came out and spoke to Juan, "They are just finishing a ceremony. Alberto will be out in a moment."

Soon, a man resembling the popular image of Jesus came out to greet us. Unlike the traditional Indian here, he was bearded, and he wore his hair loose. He wore white pants and a rough-woven, natural white serape. His feet were bare. The man's eyes were his most outstanding feature. They were kind and gentle, yet powerful. With his hand over his heart, Alberto greeted us, as Juan translated, "Welcome. You have come at a good time. A very auspicious time, because it is raining. It is good fortune to come with the rain. We have been in a drought. . . . it has been *seven months* since it last rained."

At this point, Juan said to Alberto, "There is someone I want you to meet. Where's Dennison? Dennison, come up here a minute. Alberto, this is Dennison Tsosie, he is a Navajo from Arizona."

Alberto studied Dennison for a moment as Dennison offered his hand. The handshake soon became a quick embrace and, smiling, Alberto said, "Now I know why the rain has come."

He continued speaking to the group for a while, and then he paused and again looked at Dennison. After taking a deep breath, he said, "So, at last the Condor and the Eagle meet." Juan and the others who were in charge of the tour whispered to each other, "I knew it, I just knew this was it." Tears were shed, and they embraced each other. I was a little confused at what was going on. Someone said something about the fulfillment of a prophecy, and then Alberto was speaking again. "We were just finishing a fire ceremony. As soon as we get cleaned up, you can go into that building; that's where you'll be sleeping."

We gathered our things from the bus, and soon we were led into a circular building with a conical thatched roof and a huge firepit in the center. Three logs propped against each other in a tripod shape were burning in the center. Surrounding the logs was a circle of stones and pineapples. The overall effect looked very similar to a medicine wheel.

We found a stack of woven mats, which we spread out on the floor to lay our sleeping bags on. As we were getting settled, a dinner of fresh garden vegetable soup, bread, and cheese was brought in. We all sat around the fire and ate and talked.

A little later, Alberto sat down and explained to us, "You have arrived during our equinox celebration; we have been doing ceremonies since Monday and will continue the rest of the week. Yesterday, today, and tomorrow are the most important days. We have just finished a fire ceremony. This fire arrangement represents the same thing as an egg. The center is Inti, life, the promise of the future. The stones and the fruit are the nourishment and the protection, the white and the shell. The equinox is the celebration of Inti, the return of the Sun. The promise of new life, and new hope. Tomorrow, if you wish to join us, we will get up at 5:00 a.m. and greet the sun and then walk to a sacred spring. You may bathe in it, if you wish, and then we will fill containers with water. Later in the day, we will go plant some trees and water them with this water. After that time, I will be available for healings, if you wish."

After Alberto had finished speaking, Dennison felt moved to offer to do a pipe ceremony in honor of the equinox and asked Alberto if it would be okay. Alberto replied, "We would be honored. Is there anything I can get you for your ceremony?" Dennison requested a feather for his smudge (since we were reluctant to bring ours through customs), and a wooden bowl of water.

Our group, along with several other people who had been involved with Alberto's ceremonies earlier, gathered around the firepit.

Dennison laid out a piece of buckskin on the earth and placed his tools onto it. Alberto withdrew a folded cloth from his poncho and opened it. Inside were several large, black feathers, some of them touched with white. "These are condor feathers. Someone in our group found them a few days ago. We wondered why they came to us at this time. Now I know." Dennison selected one for his ceremony, the longest, the guiding feather from the very tip of the wing. Suddenly he remembered that he had a small eagle feather in his hat, and he removed it, placing it beside the condor feather.

All lights were extinguished, and by the light of the fire, we began the ceremony. Dennison lit a mixture of sage and cedar. Then, using the condor feather, he walked around the circle, smudging everyone. The water in the wooden bowl was ceremonially blessed and shared with Alberto. Then the group was blessed with it. Dennison later told me that as the ceremony proceeded, he had felt that his very moves and even his words were guided by some other force working through him. As he prepared his pipe, he asked Alberto to take a bit of the tobacco and pray with it. He then added this to his pipe. As he prayed with the pipe, his voice became husky and choked with emotion. Everyone felt the power of the prayers. He passed the pipe to Alberto and joined prayers with the sacred smoke. Dennison took the two feathers, the Eagle and the Condor, and prayed over them. He then sprinkled them with corn pollen, which represents the essence of life to the Navajo. Finally, he joined the two feathers together, offering them to the Four Directions and to the Creator with his prayers. He turned to Alberto and gave the feathers to him. The two embraced, and as they did, the smoldering fire suddenly popped and burst into flames, as if Inti approved of the joining.

The group was now vibrating with incredible energy. Alberto spoke, "We have an ancient prophecy, which says at this time of the equinox, when we celebrate the renewal of life, a Native will come from the North, bringing the energy of the Eagle, to join with the energy of the Condor. This will bring a renewal of Spirit to all Native peoples. It will also bring a renewal of Native spirituality and the honoring of the Earth Mother to all mankind. So, at last we have embraced, and the vibrations of that embrace will be felt throughout the four corners of the earth. Already the trembling is being felt. Already the changes have begun. Already the old structures have begun to fall. This is the beginning of the healing. It is the dawn of a new age and a new direction for all people. This very night is the start of a new dawn. I hope to one day visit the Eagle in the North, and the circle will be complete."

When it was over, we all embraced; many shed tears. It was such an overwhelming experience that it was difficult to take it all in, and even more difficult to talk about.

Five a.m. found us sleepily doing exercises and walking to the sacred spring. On the way, we passed people going about their everyday chores. One woman was doing her laundry in the irrigation ditch in front of her tiny home, using a stone to scrub it on. Remarkably, she was singing. I thought about how easy my life is by comparison. I likely had brought more clothing for this short trip than her whole family owned! My compared wealth suddenly seemed ludicrous. Yet in many ways these people have so much more than most of us, for they are rich in Spirit. They find happiness in simple things, and they are still close to Mother Earth.

Later, we climbed a denuded hill behind Alberto's home. In the 1970s, the Peace Corps, in its well-intentioned efforts, had clear-cut the hillside and planted it with non-indigenous crops, which failed. The rains came and washed away the topsoil, cutting deep scars into its sides. Little by little, Alberto is replanting it with indigenous plants, in a valiant effort to restore it to wholeness. We each planted a seedling, our child, as he called it, leaving it with our prayers and our hopes for the renewal of life and love for our Mother Earth. Of course, we also left behind a part of ourselves.

It has since occurred to me, that the embrace of the Eagle and the Condor are again the dance of life and death; the two sides of the same coin. Death of the old way of thinking, of greed and disregard for the sacredness of all life. The birth of a new consciousness, a new spirituality and regard for the Earth.

It happened during the Equinox, symbolizing the death of one season and the birth of another.

The meeting of the Eagle of the North and the Condor of the South took place on the Equator, where the Northern and Southern hemispheres meet.

As it is in the fulfillment of all prophecy, it happened unexpectedly, and was unplanned. We had never heard of the prophecy, nor had we heard of Alberto. He had never heard of Dennison, and didn't know he was coming. Two humble, beautiful Natives, in one of the poorest, most exploited countries on earth, in a humble hut. They meet, embrace, and open the energies for changes that will shake the very structures of the world.

I think I now understand Dennison's initial reluctance to take this trip. On some level, he must have known the part he was to play, the awesome responsibility he carried. I think also of the cryptic comment made by the first Shaman, Jose, "You are very courageous to come here." Could he too, on some level, have understood what was taking place?

After telling a friend about the ceremony, she commented, "To me the Eagle symbolizes Spirit and life. The Condor is a relative of the buzzard, and I associate it with endings and death. If indeed this is the beginning of the earth changes, I think it's very significant that the Condor feather was so much larger than the Eagle feather."

Upon reflection, throughout the trip we were given repeated teachings about endings and beginnings, the dance of life and death.

Prediction of Meeting an Indonesian Yogi
APRIL 1995

ON APRIL 3, Dennison returned from his evening meditation and prayers, saying, "I felt like someone was trying to make contact with me in the Spirit plane. Like something trying to probe my mind. . . .

"What is a yogi? They were telling me I'm going to be meeting and working with an Indonesian Yogi. Does that mean anything to you? He will be like a spiritual teacher to me. They said Indonesians were an ancient culture and this an ancient teaching. Funny, I felt like he was here with me already, in a way. He knows something about how to put stones together to create certain energies. It is an ancient teaching that not very many people know. It's something I'm supposed to be shown, and we will be working together in some way.

"Then I was shown a stone. It was a large slab, cut out like a door. It had a hole in the center and some symbols or writing around it. It also had

Dragon Design Seen on Doorway

a dragon carved into it, holding a long pot or vase, or else sitting beside a vase. I think it might be a doorway or a door covering something special. Not very many people know about it. The Yogi will be taking me there and showing me something.

"Then I clearly, clearly saw and heard Toku-san doing his fire ceremony and praying. I heard a voice saying, 'You'll pray together again soon.'

"I also saw like an albino Condor, a white Condor, except the tips of the wings and tail were black. It was carrying a scroll or a rolled-up piece of white cloth, with one end hanging down, kind of like a flag . . . it had red threads or fringe hanging from it. I felt it was a message of some sort, kind of like what the appearance of the white buffalo symbolizes.

"I also saw an elephant and a donkey or mule running side by side. Neck and neck in a race, with clouds of dust boiling behind them. Then suddenly they both stumbled and rolled head over heels."

Most of the meditation was interesting, but a little puzzling. However, the last vision seemed pretty clear, if you saw it as the U.S. political parties and the upcoming presidential race.

A Few Brief Glimpses of the Future
APRIL 1995

Dennison came in this evening saying he had received very little in his meditation. "I strongly feel something is going to happen soon near Mexico City. I think a strong earthquake. There are going to be some strong storms, like hurricanes going up through the Gulf of Mexico, strongly affecting some of those islands there and also our Gulf Coast and Florida. Another area is in the Atlantic, off the coastline of the Carolinas and Florida. They will be hit with some hurricanes.

"There are going to be some earthquakes going up the coastline from the Baja and up the West Coast of the U.S., all the way to Alaska and the Aleutian Islands.

"I again feel like there is going to be a major upheaval happening soon in the White House. People will need to stand up for what they believe inside. Not let Government take away their rights because they are afraid to assume responsibility for themselves. . . .

"A Prime Minister will be assassinated. . . .

"There will be some more large earthquakes in Japan and a volcano erupting. I also sense we'll be hearing from someone there by July."

We Are Nearing the End of a Cycle
APRIL 1995

THE 29TH OF APRIL, Dennison's meditations brought the following: "They were telling me you really need to concentrate on getting your book out now, while the energies are high for it. Also, you will have a second book finished by the end of next year. You should have your current book finished by the end of this year if possible, and then you will know what to do for the next book." I acknowledged the necessity to concentrate on getting my book into the computer and working on getting it ready to submit to a publisher. It just seems there are so many other pressing needs going on in our lives right now. The thought of writing *another* book is almost too much to consider. I really am not a writer, and though I enjoy the creative process, our life has so many distractions that I find it nearly impossible to make the time to write.

After my protest, he continued, "They are still saying we're going to be doing a lot of traveling, this year and next year.

"Also, there will be more and things happening in the world. More devastation and turmoil will be happening more often now. Like every other month at first, then every month, then every couple of weeks, etc. We are nearing the end of a cycle, and as it nears, the energies for change speed up. The new cycle will begin with a complete change of values. Things that are important now will no longer be important. Our focus will be on other things.

"As this cycle ends and the energies speed up, people will become increasingly restless and agitated. Conflicts and wars will be sparked by nothing. There will be lots more suicides, as some people are unable to cope with the increased energies and what they bring. There will also be a lot of little wars or conflicts springing up in cities all over the world.

"People should begin watching the skies, especially in the West. There will be strange lights. These will be given as signs."

Gatherings of Native Peoples
MAY 1995

ON MAY 25, Dennison came home and told me, "It looks like we will be getting involved in some Native gatherings in the future. They were telling me that Native Peoples who are environmentally-minded will soon begin to reach out to all people to help them work for the Earth.

"For awhile, there will be a conflict within many of the more traditionally-minded, a conflict between their spiritual traditions and their need for outside help. They will end up reaching out to like-minded people for help to save the Earth.

"There are many highly-evolved Natives in many cultures who have been 'contacted' as I have been, who are receiving information from The Source. Until now, they have kept this to themselves. They have teachings and prophecies and things that will help the Earth and the fight to turn things around to a more spiritual way of living. They are now being told to come forward with their information. Our book will help bring some of these people together.

"There are going to be gatherings of these Natives and like-minded peoples to share this information. We are supposed to keep ourselves free and uncommitted, because we'll be asked to be involved in some of these gatherings. Once we get going, there will be plenty of backers financially. Money will not be a problem.

"Several Natives will gain a following, a support group. Like us, we already have ourselves a group started. They will help us a lot, as things get going."

Problems in Our Government
JUNE 1995

THE EVENING OF JUNE 4, Dennison came home and said, "Tonight I was told something is going on within our government; it will be brought to the attention of the people soon. There are some who say we are wasting a lot of money with government programs and people need to take responsibility for themselves. They are saying the President needs to say we can't go any farther like this.

"There are other people in the government who are trying to fight this, trying to find other alternatives. They point out how much we are wasting in the military and will try over the next couple of years to create something more beneficial than spending large amounts of money for Star Wars types of projects. Our economy is still geared for war and the military.

"This will cause a split in our government and some real problems can come up.

"People need to be aware that in the next year or so, if something doesn't change in the media and the producers of movies, we will have no real control over the kids. The kids, through movies, video games, and toys, are being brainwashed to be violent. Parents need to regain control of what's out there for their children to see.

"The school systems will fail, because these kids are too violent to be controlled in a classroom atmosphere, and teachers aren't wanting to teach any more."

Unexplained Visions

JULY 1995

DENNISON WENT OUT TO MEDITATE AS USUAL, the afternoon of July 9. He didn't return for more than five hours. When he got home, he said he had no idea he had been gone so long. "When I began meditating, I felt like I was inside of an invisible bubble or dome that sealed me off from all outside noises. Like there was nothing else in the world but me. It must have had its own light source, because I didn't even know when it got dark. Somehow I felt it was still daylight.

"I was shown a review of our trips to Japan and to Ecuador. The scenes were of the most spiritual moments. Of our temple ceremonies in Japan and our meeting with the old priest there, as well as the pipe ceremony we did during the full moon with those guys in the seminar. Then I saw scenes from our trip to the rainforest, when you and I got up and prayed with the pipe as the sun came up. When we went up to the sacred mountain and I prayed and left that medicine bundle, and then finally that ceremony I did during the equinox, with don Alberto.

"I had a strong feeling I was being shown this review because I am being prepared for something yet to come. Something really big, and each of these things is a significant part of the preparation.

"I was told I need to return and spend a lot of time meditating for the next five days. I told them I need to get ready for the art show, and I am under a lot of pressure because of it. Also, it seems like everyone in the country is in need of spiritual work at the same time, and there just isn't enough of me to go around. They asked me what is more important, my spiritual work or my art? I told them to cut me some slack; my spiritual work is the most important, but I have to eat too. They just told me I must give them the next five days, and that I should know by now I will be taken care of.

"After this, I was shown a bunch of different scenes that I didn't really understand the meaning of, but they didn't explain them to me.

"First, I saw a large, gold-colored Buddha rise upward until it disappeared. In its place was a large, open book. Around this book was a circle of Buddhist monks holding large, lighted candles. One monk came forward into the center of the circle and sat in front of the open book. Using a long, wooden pointer, he began to trace the words in the book and read them out loud. Then four more monks entered the center of the circle and sat across from the first monk, the large book between them. All heads were shaved, except these four had a circular area on top of their heads where the hair was long and pulled back into a ponytail. Each was holding a white flower against his third eye, as the first monk continued to read.

"As they meditated, the white flowers became long, slender, white sticks, looking something like long white sticks of incense. These sticks ignited, and sparks radiated out from them, forming an arch or a dome. From this arch of sparks came lots and lots of tiny people. They were of every race and color.

"That scene faded, and I saw huge sheets of paper forming stacks and stacks. It kind of reminded me of how the paper comes off the rollers at the paper mill. Sheet after sheet coming off and stacking up. Only this paper was gray, and it was about a quarter of an inch thick and about the size of a sheet of plywood. The stack of paper dissolved and turned into a large shallow bowl on a pedestal.

"Then I saw twenty-four large metal balls, maybe three inches in diameter. They were all lined up and lit from behind. They had some kind of strange writing on them. Each one represented an animal. One I remember was an elephant, and one was a rhino, and one was an exotic and colorful bird. The rest I can't remember.

"There were some waterfalls of different colors, blue, green, yellow, and blackish-silver. After watching them awhile, they all began to blend together and it became one waterfall of clear pure water.

"I saw straight rows upon rows of trees of every variety.

"I saw a multilevel freeway with a large arch-looking thing above it.

"Then I saw lots and lots of tiny, makeshift houses, temporary shelters. But I didn't see any people with them.

"I saw large fields of crops, going on for miles and miles.

"Then I saw a bunch of people gathered in one place, sitting in rows, like they were watching something.

"Then everything became hazy, and soon it faded away. It was like the bubble lifted, and I was surprised to see the stars and hear the night sounds. I felt like there was a lot more, but I can't remember, or it is on another level of my awareness.

"I really feel like I'm being programmed for something."

More Unexplained Visions

JULY 1995

DENNISON AGAIN SPENT SEVERAL HOURS MEDITATING, as he was instructed. When he returned, he said he had again been shown a series of scenes, but no explanation. I recognized many as being visions he has seen before, some more than once.

"The first thing I saw was two stars colliding, then I saw lots of meteors falling. I don't know if they were from the stars colliding or not.

"Next, I saw a ruin or the rubble of a city. There was a large bright light behind it, so it stood out. The light faded until only a blue glow remained.

"I saw a city on fire. Lots of buildings burning, fire and smoke everywhere.

"I saw lots of people gathered together like they were waiting. Most were sitting, some were standing. I felt like they were on an island and maybe refugees.

"I saw dolphins swimming round and round in a circle, churning up the water. The center became a waterspout, or like a tornado with dolphins in it. The sea goes out in huge waves in every direction, and it is foamy.

"There is an island with palm trees blowing, bending down to the ground. Ocean waves and wind level the area, and everything is washed away.

"Next I saw huge, huge flocks of many different species of birds flying without direction, and some crashing into others, some flying into buildings, and some falling out of the sky.

"I saw the Phoenix bird rise up out of the sea and fan its wings. It rocks back and forth, stirring up the sea into great waves as it rises up. Then it turns into a huge flame and burns itself up and disappears. After this, the sea is calm again, like glass.

"I saw a long straight stretch of road going on forever. There were fires lit on each side of it. It kind of reminded me of an airport runway and bonfires lit all along it, so something can land at night. In the distance are small lights, like something trying to land, but it doesn't ever quite come down all the way. Over and over again the lights come and take off, but they never land.

"I saw piles and piles of stones piled six or seven feet high. Stacks and stacks of stones, most are really round. There's a greenish stone on top of one of the piles, and there are these lights going in and out and all around these piles.

"There was a pyramid that opened up in half, and a purple light shone out, and then it closed back up.

"I saw a large bridge across the water. It begins to swing back and forth, and then it begins to break. I see cables snapping and cars sliding off and sections of the bridge falling; then the whole thing collapses.

"I saw plants begin to grow real fast, becoming vines that entangle each other and everything else. Lush and green everywhere.

"Then everything begins all over, and I see it all again real fast, then everything shuts off."

Dennison went out for the next four days, but was told only to pray and send energy to the Earth.

We May Be Traveling Again Soon
JULY 1995

ON JULY 16, Dennison came home saying, "They told me we will be traveling again soon. Maybe in August." I asked, "Do you have any idea where?" "I don't know for sure, maybe Japan. I feel strongly we'll be hearing from Japan soon. I feel like someone will be contacting me soon to go over there on our own.

"Remember the Buddha I saw rising up when I meditated a couple of weeks ago? I feel like that means there's a crisis in the Buddhist faith. It's in need of a change, like the other world religions. They are all on their way out, to be replaced by a religion without dogma.

"I also strongly, strongly feel we'll be going back to South America, this time in deeper, more for the people there."

Americans Will Be Forced to Examine Their Values
JULY 1995

ON JULY 19, Dennison received the following: "Something is about to happen that will force the people to examine their values, examine what we as Americans really stand for. American values and beliefs will be strongly tested.

"This is a time of testing. We're being pushed into a corner in order to change something in our lives, in our relationships to our fellowman, to our friends and our families.

"Next year, people who vote will have to examine what they are really trying to accomplish. Examine their political background and their political stand. Examine their moral and spiritual values. The democratic process will be in question. Many people will pull away from politics and not vote at all.

"The Government is trying to eventually create one political system and one religion.

"Mankind as a society will have to examine what they are going toward, what are they are gaining, and what they are losing.

"There will be many corporate layoffs, cutbacks, etc. Manufacturers who produce things that make man's life easier, things that simplify our lives, like computers, will be tested.

Family values will be strongly tested now. Money will be a critical issue. Lower income people will really be tested. Money exchange will be strongly affected. Money may completely disappear. Hard times are coming."

An Invitation to Return to Japan
AUGUST 1995

ON AUGUST 9, we received a phone call from Maya, the woman who acted as our interpreter during our trip to Japan last year. She was calling on behalf of some of the people who had participated in the seminar the previous year. They wanted very much to have us come back and share more Native teachings and spirituality with them and some others. They would be willing to pay all expenses.

Without much hesitation, we accepted and agreed on October 24 as the time most convenient to all concerned. We asked if it would be possible to see Toku-san while we were there, and she said they would try to arrange it if he was available.

We looked forward to going and knew it was right, because Dennison was told some time back we would receive an invitation to go.

An Unusual Dream
SEPTEMBER 1995

THE MORNING OF SEPTEMBER 3, I got up and found Dennison sitting outside, enjoying the sweet cool air as he watched the sun rise over the mountains. The coffee maker was making its final sputters, so I poured us each a cup and joined him. After a few moments of silence he said, "I was dreaming about when I was just a kid on the reservation; I must have been about eight or ten. I was out herding sheep, and it was late in the afternoon, sort of getting on toward evening. I was getting ready to take the sheep in. I was all alone. Nothing and no one around. All of a sudden, I saw this huge thing in the sky, right over me. I'm amazed and fascinated and a little afraid, because I don't know what it is. I'd never heard of UFOs, so I didn't think about that.

"As I stood looking up at this thing, there was a burst of bright, almost blinding light, that seemed to travel toward me in slow motion. This was followed by several pulses or bursts of light, each a different color, and each one seemed to come at me in slow motion and go over my body and penetrate into me.

"Then I saw this rope ladder come out of the bottom of the object and I felt like I wanted to reach up and grab hold of it, so I could climb up. I tried to get hold, but I couldn't quite reach it, and the object started slowly moving away. So I began running after it, trying to grab hold of the ladder. I was running through brush, getting scratched, jumping over rocks and shallow ditches, trying to catch hold of it.

"I felt like I was being left behind. Sad, like if your family is leaving without you. I woke up feeling a lump in my throat and an ache in my heart. Lonely and abandoned."

Keep Our Hearts and Minds Open
SEPTEMBER 1995

ON SEPTEMBER 8, Dennison came home saying, "Tonight they were telling me that we, the American people, need to keep our minds and our hearts open. Within a month or so, something is going to happen in our government. This will shake things up pretty much, and there will be a lot of changes that come out of it."

I was later to wonder if this was in reference to the President's inability to reach a budget agreement with Congress, leading to a partial Government shut down.

Teachings
OCTOBER 1995

THE AFTERNOON OF OCTOBER 2, Dennison gathered all of his stones and took them out to a spring to cleanse them and to meditate and pray. It was evening when he returned. Somewhat chidingly, I said, "You were gone a long time. Did you get anything in your meditation?" He gave me a quick glance, and replied, "Yeah, I received some teachings." He paused a few moments then continued, "They were giving me what they called a teaching of the hand.

"There are the five fingers, which represents the four races of man and the Creator. We are all connected and all related.

"The palm of the hand is crossed with lines. These are the paths each group of people took when we separated in the beginning. They end up at the wrist, showing that each group went separate ways. Now we have come back together as one and travel the path (up the arm) to the heart.

"Long ago, in the past, each race separated to their own land, so we could develop our own way and live in peace. Then the white race crossed the seas and changed everything. They interbred and changed the energies. It shouldn't have happened. Each race should have remained pure and separate. Now they have mixed, they must eventually become one. A new energy was born. This set everything off balance.

"Then the women lost their power. Masculine energy came in, with the concept that God was male (Father in Heaven). With this came technology, aggression, etc., and the energies were even more off balance.

"Now the new millennium will be bringing back the feminine energy, because the time of male dominance is at an end. Men have grown weak, and women don't know their position anymore, either. They don't know their power anymore. They are searching everywhere to find their power, but most have yet to realize it is inside themselves.

"There are five people who are being brought together. We represent the four races and the Creator.

"The energies are supposed to come in from the far country. Whatever that is . . . the Far East. I'm supposed to take a crystal to Japan and leave it with someone there. Toku-san, I think, or someone I will meet. Anyway, I will be making contact with someone there, and I will leave the stone with them. We will be making a few more trips over there, and they or he will come over here. We'll also be making at least one more trip to South America, and I'll be working with someone there. I already have a crystal there that is my energy connection.

"There are five of us who are being brought together through these connections and meetings we are making now. We're already working together on a higher level, and we will all be looking for each other.

"We aren't supposed to worry about what we are doing in the seminar, just stay open and come from the heart. Spirit will have its way. We can't control it. We're just there to plant seeds, live the example how we all should be. We don't have to do anything special, just be there, and Spirit will do the rest. That's what we're doing everywhere we go. Planting seeds of love.

"This is the end of the millennium, and things are speeding up. Soon we'll be entering a 'moment' where time will stop. It's like when the pendulum of a clock goes to one side and pauses before it goes back to the other side. When this happens, it will be like everything reverses itself. There are two worlds coming together at two vibrations. The physical and spiritual. The more spiritual the physical world is, the easier it will be. If we aren't spiritual enough, we will miss this chance.

"They were saying that if the earth's balance is affected and there is a pole shift, it will only be a few degrees; it won't completely change poles."

The Navajo Basket
OCTOBER 1995

THE EVENING OF OCTOBER 16, we were sitting in the living room, a cozy fire in the stove to take the chill off the room. Our conversation turned to some of the symbolism of the Navajo Basket. As we talked, Dennison began to hear a voice in his mind, which said, "The Navajo basket is also like a medicine wheel, and it carries some of the same teachings. If a line were drawn from top to bottom and from side to side, you would represent the four directions and the four races of man, as well as the gift each race has. For instance, the Yellow Race has the gift of vision, looking ahead; the Red race has the gift of the heart, feeling. The Black

Race has the gift of looking within the soul, introspection. The White Race has the gift of movement, doing. (They are explorers, inventors, and technologically-minded.) Now, if one side of the basket is too heavy, the basket will tip. The same is true if one gift is too strong; you will be out of balance. If you have technology without far vision or feeling, or say introspection without movement, doing something about your thoughts, you are out of balance, and so is the earth.

"As mankind reaches the end of the millennium, it will be like two baskets coming together, forming a bowl or a globe. There are two worlds coming together of different vibrations. One is negative, the other positive. . . .

"After this happens, we'll speak another language, the Mother Tongue. We all know it inside ourselves. It's all about certain sounds, certain vibrations. Our tongue's roots reach to our heart center. These sounds will speak to our hearts. Now our words can mean anything we want; they speak our minds. This language is of the heart to the heart. It will contain only truth. Each word contains certain vibrations, which carry its meaning. Movement will also be very important with the new language."

Our Trip to Japan
NOVEMBER 1995

OUR FIRST FOUR DAYS IN JAPAN were spent at a retreat in the mountains of Kobe. Here in this beautiful spot, we shared Native spiritual teachings around a campfire, soaked in steaming hot mineral baths, ate exotic food, and relaxed. Next, we went to Kyoto, the holy city of temples, and visited numerous temples that we had missed on our last visit. At one Zen temple, we stopped to see a famous rock garden where there is a placement of fifteen rocks, but a person is said to only be able to see fourteen rocks at one time. As we walked along a wooden porch at the edge of the garden, Dennison said, "I thought you couldn't see fifteen rocks." Maya asked, "Can you see fifteen rocks?" He laughed and pulled her in front of him. Sure enough, you could see all fifteen rocks from that particular spot.

Later, we visited another Zen garden where a lecture was in progress. The Zen master was chiding the people to keep their spines straight when they sat or walked. "Soon enough you will be old and stiff and won't be able to stand straight. Honor your gift now, and do not slump. Sit up and take a deep breath; see how much better you feel." He continued his discourse by saying, "As children you wear the faces of your parents, acting and dressing as they would have you do. As you grow older, you attempt to express yourselves in your own way, but most forget to find your Spirit within. You put on another mask of your own making, using makeup and clothing to create an illusion of who you are. Your time and efforts would be better spent searching for your Spirit within, for when you wear the face of the Spirit, you are radiant in its beauty. . . ." When the lecture was over, we were invited into a small room and joined one of the priests in tea. We spent a very pleasant hour asking about the discipline of Zen and hearing several koans and wisdoms. Learning how to quiet the mind to find the spirit, the true Self.

The last three days of our trip, we spent at Lake Syco, a small lake at the foot of Mt. Fuji. Again we shared Native spiritual teachings around a campfire at the edge of the lake. The highlight of the experience was when we were joined by Toku-san and two other priests. That evening under a nearly full moon, at the edge of the lake, with Mt. Fuji looming in the moonlight, Toku-san and Dennison joined in ceremonies and prayers for peace in men's hearts and peace on earth. It was very powerful and very moving. The damp autumn night was quite chill, and it was a relief when at last we went back to the lodge where we were staying.

We arranged to meet Toku-san and his group in the lobby for coffee and conversation. Later, Dennison gave him the crystal, as he had been instructed earlier, with a brief explanation of what it was for. He also gave him a medicine wheel pendant and explained some of the teachings of the wheel. Toku-san quickly understood and explained that the Tibetan Buddhists had a mandala that had the same meanings.

Toku-san then presented Dennison with a beautiful silk bag that is used by priests to carry their sacred tools in. He also gave him a crystal which he had picked up at a sacred place he had just visited in the Himalayas. Then he gave both of us prayer beads from a Bodhi Tree at the place where Buddha received enlightenment. We were both honored by his generosity.

Talk continued into the night. At last Dennison asked Toku-san if he had ever received any messages, while meditating, regarding the gathering together of twelve people of different cultures for the purpose of working together.

Toku-san was thoughtful before he replied. "I have started an organization for peace. We pray for peace and understanding in men's hearts, for it is there that peace on earth begins. Last year, while doing a ceremony down in Southern Japan, I was also praying for backing in this effort. Clearly it came to me that there would be eleven who would come forth to help. I never, until this moment, considered there would be twelve all together, because I didn't think to count myself. I was simply looking for eleven people to come forward to help. Then I never dreamed they would be of all races; I thought they would be Japanese and Buddhist."

The talk continued, and Dennison told of some of his visions and teachings. Toku-san listened attentively. Later he commented, "I too believe in these Earth Changes, and I have had guidance come to me much the same as you. I also believe these things can be changed or decreased through prayer and by making people aware and opening their hearts. I know time grows short, and I am willing to do whatever I can to help achieve this end."

Some ideas on how to proceed were exchanged, and the subject was left to develop as Spirit should choose to move it.

In the end, Toku-san invited Dennison to return to Japan in August and go with him to Hiroshima for the ceremonies and prayers honoring those lost in the bombing. To join him in prayers for world peace.

As we prepared to leave Japan, we heard the tragic news of the assassination of Israel's Prime Minister. This brought to mind what Dennison had been told during a meditation last April: ". . . a Prime Minister will be assassinated. . . ."

How desperately needed are all our prayers for Peace.

A Look Forward into 1996

DECEMBER 1995

ON DECEMBER 28, Dennison came in from his prayers and meditations. He said, "The Government shutdown is going to cause a lot of changes to take place this next year. There are tough times ahead. Even after everyone goes back to work, there will be a lot of changes in how things are done. There will be a lot of restructuring done and the loss of a lot of jobs, both within the government and in other businesses.

"Women are going to be having a lot of emotional and physical problems this next year. They are strongly connected to the Earth Mother's energies, and as she changes, so they will reflect these changes. Men will be affected too, with their feminine side becoming stronger, and many will struggle to come to terms with these feelings.

"The earth changes will continue to worsen, with severe storms happening in places where they have never been so severe. I sense a big snowstorm or blizzard hitting the whole East Coast in January or February of this next year. It will be the biggest they have ever had. We will be having some more volcanoes. I think Japan can expect another major quake. I still feel a large quake and a volcano in Mexico. California is also going to have its share. Some parts of the world will be in drought where none has been before, while others will experience severe weather and cold temperatures. The weather will continue to be crazy everywhere.

"Our social and economic structure will be changing a lot, and it will be very hard for many, especially the poor.

"People are getting tired of governmental bullshit, and this election year will bring a lot of changes.

"The migrating and breeding habits of many animals, birds, and insects will be changing, and the change will be noticed. There will be fewer young born in some species, and some species won't migrate when they should, and some will go to different places. This will be a reflection of the changes taking place in the earth.

"There will be more wars, and violence breaking out all over the world. As the cycle speeds up, tension is felt everywhere."

Epilogue

ABOUT A YEAR AGO, a friend loaned me her computer so I could put everything Dennison had received over the past several years into one book, hoping then to find a publisher. It was a daunting task, but it would afford me an opportunity to go back through the boxes of notes I'd kept from the beginning and re-evaluate some I'd previously left out of my original manuscript, and possibly include them. As I was putting everything into the computer, I began to notice a recurring theme that I hadn't noticed before. It began on February 29, 1990, when Dennison was told of four "spiritual brothers" who would be coming into our lives in the future. Again and again I found tucked neatly into other messages similar references to his meeting and working with others like himself: "a Japanese person coming into our lives," of a meeting with "your brother the Inca," or "meeting with other spiritual leaders for healing the Earth." And "You will be of many tongues, but one voice."

A picture was forming. As 1995 progressed and he received more information, it became clear that these spiritual people were presently being brought together to help bring in a new spirituality, a true teaching, a new religion without dogma, the teaching of LOVE. Dennison would be a part of this.

It was an astonishing feeling to me, because even as I was putting it into the computer, this was beginning to happen. Things had simply been concepts up until now, visions and dreams, somehow real and unreal. Now we were meeting and interacting with these people that we had been told about years ago.

For some reason, perhaps because it came in segments sometimes years apart, I had been viewing most of the information as complete unto itself. Little capsules of separate teachings and predictions. There was, of course, the theme of the Holy Grail and the theme of Earth Changes, but even they seemed to be capsules of information not relating to anything else. I was more caught up in the possible accuracy of the predictions than in seeing everything as a whole teaching.

Now I started to look for other themes, and as I did this, I began to see everything as a whole. *Dennison was being prepared for a greater purpose,* receiving an education of sorts. He was shown glimpses of other times and other places, of sacred information hidden away. Hints of alien contact and of earth's unknown past. Almost as if to trigger a remembrance of some sort.

There were teachings of various metaphysical concepts he would have never looked into himself. Teachings of philosophy, healing techniques and environmental issues. Even politics. Things he had little knowledge of and little interest in. What was strange was, these little tidbits of information he shared with me seemed also to be greatly expanded upon somewhere deep in his mind, so that later he knew much more about the various subjects. These things would often prompt me to read and research to gain a better understanding. He would always be way ahead of me.

I know our future holds many surprises. I am learning to surrender, to allow Spirit to lead. Our lives have taken on a magical quality, seemingly always slightly beyond our complete control.

As example of how Spirit works, on March 17, 1996, Dennison had an odd dream. As we ate breakfast the next morning, he related, "I dreamed about a dolphin last night. It came up out of a sort of well or pool of water. It just raised up in the water and told me to squeeze its nose and make a wish. So I squeezed its nose, and I think I wished for money or something like that, because it said, 'No, you can't wish for that. It should be for something that would benefit others as well as yourself.' So I wished again, but now I can't remember what I wished for."

I laughed a little and replied, "I think I could have made a case for how I'd use the money to help others as well as myself."

Dennison remained thoughtful, "I wonder what it means? It seems like something that means something."

The only thing I could come up with was the pool of water might represent Spirit or something spiritual. Someone had once given us a deck of animal medicine cards, and I thought I remembered them saying the dolphin was a messenger . . . so maybe this was a messenger from Spirit? A wish being granted? I made a note of it in case it should mean something later.

The following week we received a packet of information and a letter from Blue Dolphin Publishing, Inc. The letter said, "I was going through boxes and found your manuscript . . . what has happened since 1992? Please give us a call. . . ."

I was astounded! It had been four years since I had mailed out manuscripts to a few publishers. A lot had happened since then.

Later, as I prepared to call them, I noticed their letterhead had a dolphin leaping up. Only then did I make the connection to the dolphin dream. So, I looked at the postmark . . . March 17th. Sure enough, Dennison had the dream that same night!

I stand in awe of this whole process.

The Struggle for Mother Earth

EARLY IN MAY, 1995, we received a very poignant letter from the man who was our host last March, when we visited the Intag Forest Reserve in Ecuador.

The Reserve covers five hundred acres of some of the most beautiful land on earth. More than half of this acreage is kept in a natural state, so that the wildlife can have a chance to make a comeback. Many rare and very endangered species are doing just that. The problem with this is it attracts poachers and the dollars such rare animals can bring.

The past seven years have been spent in court fighting to save his forests and the animals who have only him for protection. He grows weary.

In his letter he expresses the deep loss he feels inside, and he struggles with, "Is it worth it all?" He wonders if the rainforests are more precious than his peace of mind, if it wouldn't be better to have inner clarity before he tries to save the forests, or teach others about loving Mother Earth. As he puts it, "If it's true only still water can reflect with precision and clarity the realness of things, the worldly life can at times muddle things up."

There is another question that nags in the back of his mind. Is peace of mind and clarity worth it, if in the process of non-involvement, we lose our Mother Earth?

He has lived in this Reserve for sixteen years, and his heart and soul are very much a part of the land. The pain and anguish he would suffer, should he leave it all behind, for a quieter, more "normal" life, is at least as great as the turmoil he feels by staying with the fight. He seeks advice and comfort.

The following is Dennison's reply, and I feel it speaks to all who are out there fighting for our Mother Earth.

MAY 16, 1995

DEAR CARLOS,

I received your letter of April 25th with mixed emotions, for I too wrestle from time to time with similar thoughts. I feel your pain.

No one could blame you, should you give up the fight for now and seek peace of mind. Only you know how much you've given of yourself and how much is left to give. It is okay to leave the battle to others who are not yet jaded. You have made a difference; perhaps it's time to nourish self and family. It is a question only you can know the answer to.

We Natives believe everything has a spirit. The water, the air, the earth, and every rock, insect, bird, fish, and animal. When some of us were being born into this world, we agreed we would work with these spirits, to help protect the earth in a way so it will always be there for man and all the species on it. (Sometimes I think the spirits neglected to tell us we were coming into a funny farm, full of greed, selfishness, and fear.)

I feel with you very strongly, but I am told by the "grandfathers" that you and I and others like us made a commitment long ago to be the tip of the spear. To sacrifice SELF for the sake of Mother Earth and her Children. Our Mother hurts and her children are lost. It is up to us to somehow uphold the earth and lead the people to a more loving and spiritual understanding. If man's heart can be opened enough to feel his connectedness to all things, we can begin to heal what is left of our Mother Earth.

At some level we all know what is needed, but we are few who are working and standing for what we believe is right. Our Spirits grow weary. I went out this evening to pray for you and people like you to be strong.

Sitting there looking out over the forest and feeling one with the trees, they seemed to speak to me, to my spirit and heart. Being there alone with nature reinforced the truth that the world is truly in need of people like us. People like you, who work to preserve the earth and her resources, while people like me work to open up people's hearts and heal their minds and reconnect them with their Mother. Without us there is no hope. Time grows short.

I feel that the land chose you to be the caretaker of what's left of the Cloud Forest. You didn't choose what you're doing; it's more like the spirits there voted you in. (You retain the right to resign at any time.)

So, my friend, the struggle must continue for people such as ourselves. Mankind must be reeducated, not with books, but with love for the earth and a spiritual connectedness with his surroundings. Yes, there is a hardness, an impenetrable armor around so many, but there is a vulnerable spot and a heart that has feeling beneath it.

The Navajo creation myth tells of monsters which once walked the earth, destroying the land and the people. Their bodies were covered with a heavy, impenetrable armor. The people were defenseless and unable to stop them.

There were two young warriors, twins, who were the sons of Changing Woman, the Mother of Creation (Mother Earth). The twins set out on a journey to find their Father, the Sun (the Creator), to ask him to destroy the monsters before everything was destroyed. On their journey they met with many obstacles and trials. At last they reached their father and made their plea. Their father at first said, "Go on back home; this is no place for you. Here are some fine clothes and lots of good food to take with you. Here is a new bow and arrows too." The boys refused the fine gifts and again stated their plea. Their father offered them great wealth in addition to the other gifts. Again the boys refused. Their father was silent for awhile, then said, "I see you are very courageous and have withstood many adversities. You have a pure heart, and greed and selfishness have not corrupted you. But you see, my children, the monsters are too my children; I cannot destroy them." The boys then replied, "Then let us do it for you. Just show us how." Their father agreed, saying, "I will strike first and crack the monsters' armor, so you can follow behind and pierce it, reaching their hearts and destroy them. Through your prayers I will guide you where to strike."

We too are warriors fighting monsters. We must trust Creator to show us where to send our arrows. When we are tired, hopefully we will have reached others who will come to take our place.

Thank you for sharing yourself with me and for the work you've done and are doing to preserve that sacred place where you live. A part of my heart remains there.

Walk always in beauty, my brother.

We welcome any comments or insights the reader might wish to share. Please send a self-addressed stamped envelope to:

Dennison & Teddi Tsosie
c/o Blue Dolphin Publishing, Inc.
P.O. Box 8
Nevada City, CA 95959-0008

About the Authors

Dennison Tsosie, a traditional Navajo silversmith and artist, did not ask to be a prophet. Neither did he think he would be a Healer or Shaman—yet that is where his life path has led him. With a humble and pure heart, Dennison's prayers and presence are like balm to those who are sick or in need. He prays in his native tongue and lets the healing energy and words from the ancient ones flow through him. Dennison says, "It's not me; I'm just a tool for Creator."

Dennison and his wife, Teddi, live a normal life in a small town in the White Mountains of Arizona where there is firewood to chop and chores to do. They make their living by selling their artwork—well-known, beautifully crafted jewelry and visionary paintings.

The book—*Spirit Visions: The Old Ones Speak*—at first photocopied and given out to friends and family—has a life of its own which has taken Dennison and Teddi to meet and pray with spiritual leaders in Ecuador, Canada, and Japan.

Index